Preparing Teachers
for
Cultural Diversity

Preparing Teachers
for
Cultural Diversity

Edited by
JOYCE E. KING
ETTA R. HOLLINS
WARREN C. HAYMAN

Foreword by Linda Darling-Hammond

Teachers College
Columbia University
New York and London

Published by Teachers College Press, 1234 Amsterdam Avenue, New York, NY 10027

Library of Congress Cataloging-in-Publication Data

Preparing teachers for cultural diversity / edited by Joyce Elaine
   King, Etta Ruth Hollins, Warren C. Hayman ; foreword by Linda
   Darling-Hammond.
        p.   cm.
     Includes bibliographical references and index.
     ISBN 0-8077-3606-6 (cloth : alk. paper). — ISBN 0-8077-3605-8
   (pbk. : alk. paper)
     1. Teachers—Training of—United States.   2. Multicultural
   education—United States.   3. Multiculturalism—Study and teaching—
   United States.   4. Educational change—United States.   I. King,
   Joyce Elaine, 1947–   .   II. Hollins, Etta R., 1942–   .
   III. Hayman, Warren C., 1932–   .
   LB1715.P734   1997
   370'.71—dc21   96-37523

ISBN 0-8077-3605-8 (paper)
ISBN 0-8077-3606-6 (cloth)

Printed on acid-free paper
Manufactured in the United States of America

04 03 02 01 00 99 98 97   8 7 6 5 4 3 2 1

Contents

Foreword

This collection of powerful essays assembled by Joyce E. King, Etta R. Hollins, and Warren C. Hayman could not arrive at a better time. Meeting the challenge of cultural diversity is an agenda that is central to today's quest to develop schools that can educate all students for the challenging world they face—a world that is both more technologically and more multiculturally rich and complex than ever before in our history. The work of educating educators is, at root, the work that will enable us to sustain a productive and pluralistic democracy, for it is the capacities of teachers that make democratic education possible—that is, an education that enables all people to find and act on who they are; what their passions, gifts, and talents may be; and how they want to make a contribution to each other and the world.

Such education is profoundly social. As John Dewey (1916) suggested, it enables a person not just to be good, but "to be good for something," and that something is "the capacity to live as a social member so that what he gets from living with others balances with what he contributes . . . not external possessions, but a widening and deepening of conscious life—a more intense, disciplined, and expanding realization of meaning" (pp. 359–360). This volume provides one of the most comprehensive current accounts of how teachers can be prepared to create the productive social opportunities and deepened cognitive experiences that will enable such futures for an increasingly diverse community of students.

The collection provides a vision of teacher preparation for diversity grounded in principles of social justice and possibilities for social imagination. It describes how the education of teachers can enable them to truly see the students they teach so as to support the students in confronting and challenging ideas as well as in building more inclusive social communities. Many of the chapters reflect the goals articulated by James Baldwin (1985) in his "Talk to Teachers," recognizing that the capacity for independent thought is essential to democracy, even when it is threatening to the contemporary status quo.

> The purpose of education, finally, is to create in a person the ability to look at the world for himself or herself, to make his own decisions, to say to himself

this is black or this is white, to decide for himself whether there is a God in heaven or not. To ask questions of the universe, and then to live with those questions, is the way he achieves his identity. But no society is really anxious to have that kind of person around. What society really, ideally, wants is a citizenry that will simply obey the rules of society. If a society succeeds in this, that society is about to perish. (p. 326)

These are especially critical times for democratic education. In important respects, our future rests on the ability of schools of education to prepare teachers to find pathways that help all of their students learn in much more powerful ways and to create community among cultures where there is now dissension. As the 21st century nears, most nations around the world are seeking to transform their education systems to respond to changing economic, demographic, political, and social imperatives. Nearly all countries are engaged in school reform aimed at much higher levels of education for much greater numbers of citizens—a demand created by a new information age, major economic shifts, and a resurgence of democracy around the globe. In the United States as elsewhere, efforts to rethink schooling have been stimulated by the need to prepare a much more diverse and inclusive group of future citizens and workers to manage complexity, find and use new resources and technologies, and work cooperatively to frame and solve novel problems.

We enter an era in which all people must learn flexibly and effectively to survive and succeed in a fast-changing world. If we cannot accomplish this task at this moment in history, a deeply stratified society—one divided by access to knowledge and the opportunity to learn—will undo any future chance for democratic life and government. These changes define a new mission for education and for teaching: one that requires schools not merely to "deliver instructional services" but to ensure that all students actually learn, and that requires teachers not merely to "cover the curriculum" but to enable diverse learners to construct their own knowledge and develop their talents in effective and powerful ways.

This rich volume describes how teachers can be prepared so that they, in turn, can prepare their students to be successful participants in a highly demanding, pluralistic democracy. It illustrates how teachers' success in engendering both academic and social learning rests on developing their own levels of social/cultural awareness and competence, as well as providing them with tools for engendering such awareness and competence in their students. These abilities are the building blocks for surmounting what Gordon, Miller, and Rollock (1990) call "communicentric bias: the tendency to make one's own community the center of the universe and the conceptual frame that constrains thought" (p. 19). The ability to appreciate and incorporate multiple perspectives in one's thought and action is an important aspect of both cognitive and social functioning; it is one of Piaget's indicators of higher stages of cognitive development as well as a goal of socially responsive education.

This is a radically different undertaking than what we have been engaged in for most of this century. It demands that teachers understand learners and their learning as deeply as they comprehend their subjects and teaching strategies. It also requires that schools structure themselves to support more productive forms of student and teacher learning than they currently permit—learning that is more intensive and more collaborative and better supported by extended human relationships. In contrast to the rote learning expected of yesterday's schools and the high levels of educational failure they permitted, tomorrow's schools must find a way to connect with students wherever they begin and to take them to the common high standards they need to succeed in a more demanding world.

It is ever more clear that current reforms are establishing new expectations for teachers that many have not been prepared to meet. Teaching for understanding and teaching for diversity require a much more complex set of knowledge, skills, and dispositions than has ever been required of teachers before. In order to succeed with today's students and today's demands, schools are finding that they need to create communities in which students are well known—academically as well as personally—so that teachers can understand and address their individual learning needs. Teachers are finding that they need to involve parents as partners, and they need to use new approaches that build on their students' knowledge, interests, and experiences to create bridges between the students' diverse starting points and common, challenging learning goals. The wide range of languages, cultures, and learning styles demands an equally rich and varied repertoire of teaching strategies.

In addition, teaching for universal learning demands a highly developed ability to discover what children know and can do, how they think and how they learn, and to match learning opportunities to the needs of individual children. Skillful teachers function as "child developers," as James Comer (1980) puts it, continually evaluating children's progress in order to nurture their academic, social, and psychological growth. The new demands on teachers suggest a view of teaching as contingent on students' needs and instructional goals and continually shaped and reshaped by students' responses to learning events. This view contrasts with that of the recent "technicist" era of teacher training and evaluation, in which students were regarded as homogeneous and teaching was seen as the implementation of set routines and formulas for behavior, which were standardized and disconnected from the diverse needs and responses of students. What we now know about effective teaching defies the single, formulaic approach to delivering lessons that has characterized much regulation of teaching, many teacher education and staff development programs, and most teacher testing and evaluation instruments during this century.

The good news is that reforms have stimulated major changes across the country. As this volume so vividly documents, teacher preparation programs are reinventing themselves; new opportunities for teacher learning are emerging from a variety of school/university partnerships; and standards for accreditation and licensing are being strengthened to take account of the kinds of teacher learning that will support culturally responsive teaching. The new standards take into explicit account the multicultural, multilingual nature of a student body that also possesses multiple intelligences and approaches to learning. In so doing, these efforts seek to encourage initial and continuing professional development that will address teachers' needs for deeper and more varied understanding of learners and learning, so that they can be more effective in their work.

The bad news is that these efforts are currently layered on a schooling system that generally does not support the acquisition of teacher knowledge and skill and that permits extraordinary levels of inequality in all aspects of education. Disparities in salaries along with irresponsible hiring procedures have led to the widespread hiring of unqualified teachers in central cities and poor rural areas. Rather than develop incentives that will attract and retain well-prepared teachers, districts hire more than 50,000 untrained individuals annually and assign most of them to schools serving low-income children and children of color.

Thus, while some children are gaining access to teachers who are more qualified and better prepared than in years past, a growing number of poor and minority children are being taught by teachers who are sorely unprepared for the demands of their jobs. This creates even greater inequality in opportunities to learn and in the outcomes of schooling—with all the social dangers that implies—at the very time we most need to prepare all students more effectively for the greater challenges they face. A major social challenge before us is to ensure that the kind of teacher education described in this volume is made available to those who will serve *all* students in *all* communities.

Linda Darling-Hammond
William F. Russell Professor in the Foundations
of Education, Columbia University
and President, the American Educational Research Association
New York City, 1996

Acknowledgments

The publication of this book completes the work we began with our first volume, *Teaching Diverse Populations: Formulating a Knowledge Base* (Hollins, King, & Hayman, 1994), which was supported with a grant from the Ford Foundation. Several chapters in this volume initially were prepared for the teleconference on "The Challenge of Cultural Diversity in Teacher Preparation and Assessment," which was a part of that project.

We are greatly indebted to the authors of this volume for their sustained commitment to this project and their excellent work. We especially appreciate their patience and diligence in helping us to prepare a manuscript that reflects not only their dedication to teacher preparation for diversity but their high standards of professionalism and service. The preparation of the chapters for this book has involved many people, including colleagues, practitioners in the schools and community, as well as our students and graduates. Many of them read portions of the manuscript in the early stages of this project and graciously gave permission for their experiences and voices to be included. We are grateful to all of them for their contributions and for the success of this collaborative process.

We deeply appreciate the encouragement and support of Linda Darling-Hammond, who took time from her busy schedule to review the entire manuscript and to write a Foreword that is both inspiring and profound.

We are thankful to Executive Vice Chancellor and Provost Louis V. Paradise at the University of New Orleans for his support of the senior editor, Joyce E. King; to Bernard Oliver, Dean of the College of Education at Washington University at Pullman, for his enthusiastic support of Etta R. Hollins; as well as to Johns Hopkins University for Warren C. Hayman's involvement in this work.

We also wish to acknowledge the excellent editorial assistance of Kimberly Hollins, without whose contributions this volume would not have been completed on schedule. Finally, we thank Brian Ellerbeck, our editor at Teachers College Press, for his earnest support throughout the completion of this project.

Preface

Accrediting agencies, professional associations, scholars, and practitioners are continuing to call for "multiculturalism" in teacher preparation. Although the inclusion of "multicultural education" in teacher education programs has been a requirement of the National Council for Accreditation of Teacher Education (NCATE) since 1978 (Gollnick, 1995), significant progress in this area of teacher preparation practice, research, and policy has been slow. For example, recent publications such as David Dill's *What Teachers Need to Know: The Knowledge, Skills, and Values Essential to Good Teaching* (1987) fail to address the challenge of preparing teachers to teach diverse populations. Or, as in the case of Joseph Larkin and Christine Sleeter's edited volume, *Developing Multicultural Teacher Education Curricula* (1995), teacher preparation for diverse populations is addressed more narrowly in terms of curriculum matters. James Banks's *Handbook of Research on Multicultural Education* (Banks & Banks, 1995) addresses the state-of the-art multicultural education scholarship and research, and several chapters focus on the literature on teacher preparation. However, one contributing author, Gloria Ladson-Billings (1995), concludes that "the failure of major reform efforts to acknowledge the multicultural needs of tomorrow's teachers is illustrative of the marginal status that issues of multicultural education and multicultural teacher education typically receive" (p. 747). It is also worth noting that there is little consensus in the field about what it means to prepare teachers for a multicultural society. Thus, the faculties of teacher education programs often lack the knowledge and expertise to educate teachers to teach students of diverse backgrounds.

Some teacher education program developers are meeting the challenge of cultural diversity in teacher preparation, as the title of this volume suggests. These programs and the professional knowledge and practice their teacher candidates develop go beyond fragmented approaches that involve simply appending special courses onto existing structures. These program approaches are solidly grounded in the literature on teacher preparation and teaching and learning.

The complexities of the changing demographics of U.S. schools warrant urgent and deep transformations in teacher preparation (AACTE, 1990;

Center for Education Statistics, 1987). These conditions have generated an urgent need for this book. Demographic shifts in the nation's population have resulted in increased ethnic, cultural, and linguistic diversity in public schools, but the teaching force remains predominantly white and female, and the faculties in U.S. colleges and universities remain predominantly white, older, and male. Of the whites who responded to the 1990 AACTE/ Metropolitan Life Survey of Teacher Education Students, 95% reported that when they attended high school their neighborhoods were "more white than minority." Some research suggests that, as a result of their social origins and previous educational experiences, many teachers often resist the racial, cultural, and social awareness they need to become effective teachers of diverse students. This crisis in education is exacerbated by the fact that the percentage of teachers and teacher preparation candidates from culturally diverse backgrounds continues to decline. The concern of this present volume is to address what is being done to prepare tomorrow's teachers to meet the challenge of diversity.

Several publications focus on relevant issues but fall short of providing what teacher educators and policy makers need to know to respond effectively to the crisis. For example, Mary Dilworth's edited volume, *Diversity in Teacher Education: New Expectations* (1992), addresses important issues related to teacher education, school reform, and diversity. However, it does not provide specific information to guide efforts to restructure teacher education programs in order to educate teachers for diversity. Moreover, notable publications on teacher education such as *Knowledge Base for the Beginning Teacher* (Reynolds, 1989); *Tomorrow's Schools: Principles for the Design of Professional Development Schools* (Holmes Group, 1990); *Teachers for Our Nation's Schools* (Goodlad, 1990b); and *Places Where Teachers Are Taught* (Goodlad, Soder, & Sirotnik, 1990b) represent benchmarks in describing the state of the art of the professional knowledge of teachers and their preparation. Yet, these publications do not build upon the emergent knowledge base about teaching diverse populations. Furthermore, Goodlad and his colleagues (1990b) make the troubling observation that "the urban problem" in teacher education involves a "diminishing commitment to urban education" (p. 66).

According to Goodlad's research, teacher education is characterized by:

1. a reluctance to place student teachers in urban classrooms;
2. a lack of minority students in teacher preparation programs;
3. unsuccessful recruitment efforts in predominantly white and black institutions; and
4. racism in education that affects both white and black teachers (and diverse others, of course).

There are also the following confounding factors: "Multicultural" change in teacher education often has been limited to adding on a special course, following the "additive" model predominant in schools; there is a limited presence of teacher educators of diverse backgrounds in the 1,300 colleges and universities where teachers are taught; the need to respond to issues of diversity often is perceived as the responsibility of concerned individuals rather than as an institutional commitment; and higher education institutions reflect societal structures of exclusion.

This book addresses both the theoretical parameters and practical dimensions of transforming teacher education programs to educate teachers for diversity. We have used the knowledge base for teaching diverse populations that we presented in our earlier volume, *Teaching Diverse Populations: Formulating a Knowledge Base* (Hollins, King, & Hayman, 1994), as a point of departure to organize this one. This volume extends the existing literature on preparing teachers for diverse student populations. The chapters put teacher preparation for diversity in an historical context and identify a number of critical dimensions of teacher development. Program developers describe processes of teacher preparation that address culturally sensitive teaching strategies; instructional strategies for exceptionalities; the centrality of culture in human experience and ways that culture and cultural difference influence learning and teaching; teacher assessment and licensing policies and procedures; and community-based and culturally diverse field experiences for teacher candidates and, in some cases, teachers with credentials. In other words, the programs described in this book build on what is known about effective instruction for all students and for students of diverse cultural and linguistic backgrounds in particular. Thus, we present concrete models for teacher preparation that meet the challenge of diversity.

The authors include scholars who have studied diversity issues and leading program developers who describe a variety of ways their programs are meeting the challenge of cultural diversity in teacher preparation and assessment. In addition to presenting exemplars of transformed teacher preparation programs, this work focuses on research that is needed and model policy initiatives in teacher credentialing and assessment at the state level. Such policies can have a direct impact on the structure and content of professional preparation programs and the recruitment of a more diverse teaching force.

The book is organized to focus attention on pragmatic models for transforming teacher education in three general areas.

1. delineating the historical dimensions of, contemporary perspectives on, and guiding rationales for the transformation of teacher preparation;

2. explicating the theoretical underpinnings of program processes for preparing teachers for diversity; and
3. presenting model programs that incorporate curriculum and pedagogy, field-based professional development, and assessment strategies to prepare teachers who are effective in culturally diverse settings "in their practice and in their perspective." This includes an exemplary state department of education initiative for the preparation of teachers of linguistically and culturally diverse students.

The programs in this volume address the necessity of providing credential candidates with learning experiences that go beyond adding on special courses to develop the "self-awareness" of teacher candidates. Rather, the emphasis in these programs and approaches is on developing an integrated process for teacher development that supports preservice teachers in acquiring the competence necessary for facilitating learning in a culturally diverse school setting and for pupils from diverse backgrounds taught in isolation. In other words, these program descriptions identify the competence, skills, knowledge, and attitudes candidates need to teach ethnically, linguistically, and culturally diverse populations effectively and equitably.

Common features of the programs and practices profiled in this volume include methods and experiences that enable preservice teacher candidates to expand their understanding of diversity, racism, social justice, and culturally responsive instruction. Thus, meeting the challenge of diversity is conceived not as enabling teachers to learn *about* exotic and diverse "others," but rather in terms of teaching that is democratic, multicultural, and consistent with social justice values and purposes. This places needed emphasis on the capacities of teacher educators, on teacher preparation *processes*, and on *society*—and these are recurring concerns throughout the volume. As Gollnick (1995) has pointed out, "competencies not included by most states were attention to equity, effective practices and second-language acquisition" (p. 56).

The approach of this book toward meeting these challenges of diversity in teacher preparation and assessment is to include information that is comprehensive and multifaceted; both theoretical and practical; and both generalizable and more specifically relevant to particular populations (e.g., linguistically diverse students). These chapters illustrate *how* teacher preparation programs are changing course content, pedagogy, field experiences, and assessment methods. The authors link such changes to effectiveness in teaching and learning for all students and to the knowledge base for teaching diverse populations that all teachers and teacher educators need.

Delineating the Challenge: Historical and Contemporary Perspectives

The four chapters in Part I provide empirical data and first-person observations that begin to delineate the intellectual and professional development needs of preservice teachers *and* teacher educators. If preservice teachers need specific preparation to overcome their own parochialism and lack of knowledge about diverse others, which impede their effectiveness, then understandably teacher preparation for diversity assumes that teacher educators will be prepared to assist teachers in developing the knowledge, attitudes, and skills required. The need for such a comprehensive approach to teacher preparation is supported by the literature reviewed in Part I and the authors' critical assessments of historical and current trends and practice.

In Chapter 1, entitled "Historical and Contemporary Perspectives on Multicultural Teacher Education: Past Lessons, New Directions," A. Lin Goodwin reviews the historical and ideological context out of which multicultural education and teacher preparation for diversity have evolved. The chapter points out a theoretical lacuna in the underpinnings of and a lack of coherence regarding the intended outcomes of teacher education and teacher preparation for diverse student populations. Goodwin emphasizes that teacher preparation for diversity must begin with teacher self-awareness that enables preservice teachers to confront their own cultural values, identities, and commitments to social justice and equity. Two studies are presented regarding preservice teachers' beliefs about multicultural education and their concerns when teaching in culturally diverse environments; the chapter concludes with a discussion of a field-tested model for multicultural teacher education that attends to preservice teachers' beliefs and the kind of instruction they need.

In Chapter 2, "Enhancing the Capacity of Teacher Education Institutions to Address Diversity Issues," Susan L. Melnick and Kenneth M. Zeichner present a conceptual framework for teacher education for diversity based on their ongoing study sponsored by the National Center for Research on Teacher Learning (NCRTL). This framework encompasses the problems of student selection and socialization as well as institutional change. The overview of teacher preparation for diversity in this chapter focuses on the extent to which programs (1) integrate diversity issues in all program components; (2) emphasize culture-general or culture-specific preparation; and (3) engage teacher candidates in interacting with as opposed to studying about cultures. The authors also emphasize the role and effectiveness of using community experts and community-based learning in descriptions of three model programs that "employ different organizational arrangements and instructional strategies"—Teachers for Alaska, the Native American Cultural Immersion Project at Indiana University, and the Urban Education Program of the Associated Colleges of the Midwest.

Rosalinda Quintanar-Sarellana is the author of Chapter 3, "Culturally Relevant Teacher Preparation and Teachers' Perceptions of the Language and Culture of Linguistic Minority Students." This chapter reports the outcomes of a study that reveals a significant correlation between teachers' characteristics and their attitudes toward linguistic minority students and bilingual education. For example, teachers who share the language and culture of their linguistic minority students view these factors as more significant, assume more responsibility for incorporating such factors into instruction, and have higher expectations for the academic performance of their students. Teachers who are themselves bilingual, although they may not share their students' culture, also tend to value language and culture as important factors to incorporate into instruction and tend to view their linguistic minority students more favorably. These results correspond to three stages of teachers' cultural awareness in the research literature: (1) culturally unaware teachers; (2) transition stage teachers; and (3) culturally aware teachers who not only understand the relationship between the students' culture and language and school learning, but have the knowledge and skills to incorporate these student background factors in instruction.

The title of Chapter 4 is "Removing the Mask of Academia:

Institutions Collaborating in the Struggle for Equity," In this chapter, Valerie Ooka Pang, Mary Gresham Anderson, and Victor Martuza present "insider" reports on an intensive faculty development program sponsored by San Diego State University's Multicultural Education Infusion Center. In this intensive 2-week seminar for faculty from a 15-college and university consortium the focus was on changing teacher preparation at the participating institutions by infusing multicultural and bilingual education content and teaching strategies into teacher education curricula and practices. The "mask of academia" refers to various aspects of the culture of power in academia, which during the seminar prevented professors and colleagues of higher "rank" (i.e., deans and department chairs) from relating honestly and candidly with each other about diversity, societal racism, or the changes needed in higher education to support "the struggle for equity." This chapter describes what amounts to a crisis of leadership in higher education with regard to preparing teachers for diversity. The authors conclude that the hierarchical nature of higher education is an enormous obstacle to real change.

1

Historical and Contemporary Perspectives on Multicultural Teacher Education

Past Lessons, New Directions

A. LIN GOODWIN

Beginning in January 1979, colleges and universities applying for accreditation of their professional education programs by NCATE have been required to show evidence of planning for multicultural education in their curricula (Gollnick, 1992a). While multicultural education has been, in many forms, part of the American fabric from the turn of the century, the idea of multicultural teacher education is relatively new. In 1973, the American Association of Colleges of Teacher Education's (AACTE) first Commission on Multicultural Education issued the following policy statement:

> Multicultural education programs for teachers are more than special courses or special learning experiences grafted onto the standard program. The commitment to cultural pluralism must permeate all areas of the educational experience provided for prospective teachers. (p. 264)

This statement signaled to the AACTE membership that teachers needed specific preparation to teach a culturally and racially diverse citizenry. The Commission's work triggered subsequent changes in NCATE standards by 1979, heralding an era of greater accountability whereby rhetorical commitments to the notion of multicultural teacher education were required to be bolstered by substantive actions in order to meet professional requirements of practice.

Today, at national conferences, in the popular media, and in academic literature, teachers' ability to instruct an ethnically and culturally diverse school population appropriately is a common theme. Yet, a closer examination of the literature and dialogue surrounding this issue reveals that we have not made noticeable progress. As an illustration, in a 1978 survey of institutions seeking NCATE approval, 80% indicated they were equipped to provide multicultural education; 75% placed their student teachers in settings serving culturally diverse students. In contrast, a recent comparable assessment of 59 institutions disclosed that "only 56 percent were found to address adequately cultural diversity and/or exceptionalities in the professional education curriculum" (Gollnick, 1992a, p. 236), while only 68% had teacher certification candidates working with culturally diverse children. This is indicative of an approaching crisis.

This chapter examines the notion of multicultural teacher education from both historical and contemporary perspectives in order to gain insight into the lack of progress in this area. The chapter will help pinpoint what has been missing in teacher preparation and discuss several difficulties that confront teacher educators, including limited research and models for practice (Goodwin, 1994; Grant & Secada, 1990). Why does teacher education continue to suffer from the "additive" approach (Banks, 1991c), whereby multicultural content merely is stirred into the existing mainstream curriculum? How can the profession change this phenomenon? One response may lie in the understanding that meaningful multicultural education must begin with teacher self-awareness, which then becomes the genesis for transformed thought and action (Ramsey, 1987). Teachers must "come to grips with their own personal and cultural values and identities in order for them to help students from diverse racial, ethnic, and cultural groups" (Banks, 1991c, p. 139). Therefore, this chapter also (1) presents the findings of two studies, one on preservice teachers' beliefs about multicultural education (Goodwin, 1994) and the other on the concerns preservice teachers identify when they teach in culturally diverse environments (Goodwin, 1993); (2) describes a model for multicultural teacher education that responds to the questions raised by the studies; and (3) discusses the preliminary results of field tests of the model.

RACE, EDUCATION, AND TEACHER EDUCATION

Baptiste (1979) identifies three distinct educational approaches to the schooling of a culturally diverse population—dual, plural, and multicultural. Baptiste's typology of educational approaches parallels three social scientific paradigms that have defined social interactions and educational policies vis à vis visible racial/ethnic group people[1] in this country: the inferiority, cultural deprivation, and cultural difference paradigms (Carter & Goodwin, 1994; Sims, 1981). The inferiority paradigm is grounded in the assumption that visible racial/ethnic people are genetically inferior in comparison to whites, an assumption that condoned slavery and resulted in visible racial/ethnic group people, particularly African Americans and Native Americans, being considered uneducable and barred from formal or adequate schooling. Segregated schooling based on race was written into law (*Plessy* v. *Ferguson*, 1896) as the doctrine of "separate but equal" (Baptiste, 1979). In practice, when schooling for visible racial/ethnic group people was permissible, it was characterized by neglect, segregation, and intolerance for racial differences (Cremin, 1976; Estrada & Vasquez, 1981; Hiatt, 1981). Under the dual system of education, the concept of multicultural teacher education[2] was moot. Culture was defined in white, Anglo Saxon, middle-class terms, and the aim of education was cultural indoctrination or annihilation. Two major events disturbed the status quo—the end of World War II in 1945, and the 1954 court ruling in *Brown* v. *Board of Education* that separate schooling was not equal schooling.

After defending democracy during World War II in Europe, African American soldiers returned "home" to a country that denied them basic freedoms and rights; they, in turn, began to agitate for change. Schools were called upon to respond to this heightening turmoil, a response that took the form of the Intergroup Movement (Ramsey, Vold, & Williams, 1989).

The Intergroup Movement focused on interracial harmony and understanding as well as conflict reduction and resolution. It targeted elementary and secondary schools through a variety of activities, units, and intergroup gatherings. The movement, however, experienced limited success because it was based on the faulty premise that the acquisition of cultural information would result in racial acceptance and respect (Banks, 1981), thus sidestepping issues of educational and racial inequities and "connections between ethnic group conflict and cultural differences" (Olneck, 1990, p. 153).

In the mid-1950s, the Intergroup Movement faded in the wake of court-ordered school desegregation resulting from the *Brown* decision and the dawn of the Civil Rights Movement. The dual approach to education was replaced by a plural approach that was more inclusive and, ostensibly, more equal. "Federal legislation established desegregation centers to prepare inservice teachers to teach effectively in cross cultural settings" (Baptiste & Baptiste, 1980, p. 45). This preparation usually consisted of isolated, self-contained workshops that focused on helping educators develop intercultural awareness. In addition, a number of colleges developed programs to prepare teachers and other education professionals for multiracial classrooms. Much of this training was confined to human relations, conflict resolution, and understanding students of color.

In the ideological shift in American education from dual to plural during the late 1950s and early 1960s, concern about social class disparities and the caste structure of the United States captured the interest of scholars (Ornstein, 1982). Ornstein (1982) notes that

> since then educators have become increasingly concerned with the need to study the problems of the poor, especially the black poor, in order to remedy their plight. The term "disadvantaged" and its derivative terms "deprived" and "underprivileged" began to appear with reference to the children and youth of lower-class and minority groups. (p. 197)

The cultural deprivation paradigm added the sociological meaning of race to the biological to create a criterion whereby visible racial/ethnic group members were compared with a white standard in order to demonstrate the various ways in which they were deprived or deviant (Carter & Goodwin, 1994). This paradigm gave rise to a variety of compensatory education programs, such as Headstart, designed to help children labeled as having "cultural gaps" or deficiencies acquire the experiences and skills deemed necessary for success in school (Allington, 1991; Boyd, 1991; Passow, 1991) according to a white middle-class standard (Helms, 1992). The delivery of educational services was plural in the sense that children of color had been factored into the educational equation. However, in its infancy, the plural approach was intersected by an undercurrent of dualism whereby children of color were still considered an anomaly. The emphasis of "multicultural teacher education" was on integrating children of color into predominantly white schools.

The plural approach to education was fueled during the mid-1960s by the agitation of African Americans and others for curriculum reform and community control of their schools (Banks, 1988b; Gay, 1983). Inspired and bolstered by the struggle of African Americans, other cultural groups— Asians, Latinos, Native Americans, and women—joined the press for greater representation and political clout. During this period, says Banks (1993), "there was little demand for the infusion of ethnic content into the core or mainstream curriculum—that demand would not emerge until the 1980s and 1990s" (p. 18).

The mid-1960s through the mid-1970s was a time of excitement and turmoil when Americans, particularly American youth, began to question traditional mainstream values. This period saw the passing of the Bilingual Education Act, the Ethnic Heritage Act, and the Special Education Act, legislation that provided funds for a plethora of teacher training offerings, special programs, conferences, and materials development.

When teacher education in America is examined holistically in relation to racial and cultural diversity from the turn of the 20th century through the 1960s, it can be characterized as reactive in nature. The goal of multicultural teacher education was the remediation of visible racial/ethnic children who were perceived as deprived and disadvantaged. The coupling of a reactive posture and an ameliorative ideology resulted in educational reforms that were hastily conceived and, therefore, conceptually weak. These changes, layered over the existing curriculum, became curricular appendages designed specifically for visible racial/ethnic audiences. The core of American education with its attendant white, middle-class values and perspectives remained intact. Multiethnic or multicultural education was synonymous with "minority" education. Thus, teachers, despite cultural "training," continued to function within a Eurocentric framework.

The general understandings about multicultural teacher education discussed thus far explain the philosophical tenets undergirding the preparation of teachers for culturally diverse populations. Teacher education practices grounded in these philosophical tenets were inadequate to transform schooling for children of color. Teacher training activities for cultural diversity were often fragmented, one-shot offerings with little follow-up or long-range planning (Banks, 1988b; Baptiste, Baptiste, & Gollnick, 1980; Ramsey et al., 1989). Multicultural teacher education also was deemed more appropriate for inservice rather than preservice teachers. Thus, teachers entered the profession having little background in or understanding of cultural diversity in classrooms.

CULTURAL DIVERSITY AND MULTICULTURAL TEACHER EDUCATION

The idea of including cultural diversity training in preservice teacher education programs began gaining currency in the early 1970s. The belief that teachers, rather than students, needed "fixing" also gained currency within the academic community, which began to re-examine previously held convictions about the disadvantaged nature of visible racial/ethnic children. Ryan articulated this sentiment in *Blaming the Victim* (1971).

> We are dealing, it would seem, not so much with culturally deprived children as with culturally depriving schools. And the task to be accomplished is not to revise, and amend, and repair deficient children but to alter and transform the atmosphere and operations of the schools to which we commit these children. . . . To continue to define the difficulty as inherent in the raw materials—the children—is plainly to blame the victim and to acquiesce in the continuation of educational inequity in America. (cited in Gay, 1983, p. 561)

Arguments that cultural difference was not synonymous with deviance or deprivation formed the basis for the cultural difference paradigm (Baratz &

Baratz, 1970; Billingsley, 1968), and the field shifted to a multicultural approach to education (Banks, 1991b).

The difference between a plural approach and a multicultural approach is that pluralist ideology "suggests, at least in its extreme form, that the nation is made up of various ethnic subsocieties, each of which has a set of largely independent norms, institutions, values, and beliefs" (Banks, 1988b, pp. 77–78). A multicultural approach to education acknowledges that people in America

> are multicultural, not only by racial and cultural mix but by identification with common needs, interests, and concerns. It is to this sense of identification that education must be developed. It must function within a changing social scene that is aware of and sensitive to cultural diversity and, at the same time, it must realize that all cultures interact with and may have implicit commonalities with all others. (Baptiste, 1979, p. 11)

Multicultural Teacher Education Curricula and Programs

The idea that teachers needed to receive specific preparation in order to work effectively with a diverse population began to take hold as the education profession began to define goals and curricula for multicultural teacher education. For example, Gay (1977) outlined three components for multicultural teacher education—*knowledge*, whereby "teachers become literate about ethnic group experiences" (p. 34); *attitudes* "to help teachers examine their existing attitudes and feelings towards ethnic, racial, and cultural differences" (p. 43); and *skills* "to translate their knowledge and sensitivities into school programs, curricular designs, and classroom instructional practices" (p. 48). The National Council for the Social Studies Ethnic Heritage Task Force on Ethnic Studies also developed specific guidelines for the education of preservice teachers. While this period saw a proliferation of models (Baker, 1974; Banks, Carlos, Garcia, Gay, & Ochoa, 1976), most of the multicultural teacher education programs included some of the components of Gay's model (Gollnick, 1977) and tended to emphasize instructional skill, knowledge acquisition—including historical knowledge and sociological knowledge about ethnic groups in America—and attitude development.

This period saw the implementation of a variety of teacher education programs designed to meet reforms sparked by the new NCATE requirements (Ramsey et al., 1989). Programs such as Cooperative Urban Teacher Education (CUTE) (Houston, 1973; Klassen & Gollnick, 1977) and Community, Home, Cultural Awareness and Language Training (CHCALT) (Mazon, 1977) represented attempts to provide students with authentic, field-based experiences with a variety of cultural groups. (See Chapter 2, this volume, for a fuller discussion.) Educators began to make concerted efforts to integrate multiculturalism throughout teacher education programs by attending to governance, faculty, students, curricula, and evaluation (Gollnick, Osayande, & Levy, 1980; Klassen, Gollnick, & Osayande, 1980).

The late 1970s saw the development of Performance and Competency-Based Teacher Education (P/CBTE), which came "in response to professional and lay dissatisfaction with existing teacher education programs in the late 1950's and 1960's" (Grant, 1977). Although Grant and others expressed concern about the relationship between P/CBTE and multicultural teacher education, teacher education programs began to reflect the P/CBTE movement as educators started to define the specific competencies teachers needed to teach a variety of cultural and ethnic groups (Baptiste & Baptiste, 1980).

Thus, by the late 1970s, while the multicultural movement had affected legislation (Gollnick, 1977) and multicultural teacher education appeared well positioned, its hold in the education field was tenuous and, as a result, was easily dislodged by the political and economic climate of the country. As teacher education enrollments plummeted and universities experienced budget cutbacks, the attention of schools and colleges of education shifted to the sustenance of anemic and rapidly weakening teacher education programs. Multicultural teacher education seemed to be gasping for life. Discussion about multicultural teacher education changed in tone from positive to negative, as more and more criticisms were voiced about "the fragmented and superficial modifications that many teacher education programs employed to meet the NCATE standards" (Ramsey et al., 1989, p. 120).

The 1980s Through the 1990s: A Period of Educational Reform

The publication of *A Nation at Risk* (National Commission on Excellence in Education) in 1983 "helped to bring key educational issues to the forefront of public consciousness" (Brown, 1992, p. 2) and initiated a period of reform that continues today. The focus of this reform movement shifted from an initial emphasis on school curricula to a consideration of teacher quality and how teachers ought best to be prepared (Darling-Hammond & Goodwin, 1993). This shift in focus was accompanied by burgeoning racial and ethnic populations in the nation's schools at all grade levels (American Council on Education and the Education Commission of the States, 1988; Banks, 1991c; Commission on Minority Participation in Education and

American Life, 1988; Gonzalez, 1990; "Today's Numbers," 1986). Yet the population of teachers, teacher educators, and administrators continues to be predominantly white (AACTE, 1990; Dilworth, 1990; Fuller, 1992; Goodwin, 1991; Research About Teacher Education Project, 1990). Consequently, whites are teaching non-whites in increasing numbers (Goodwin, 1990; Grant & Secada, 1990; Pallas, Natriello, & McDill, 1989).

It has become clear to educators that the teaching profession cannot avoid the issue of working effectively with diverse school populations. In terms of educational practice, educators have begun to articulate the idea of pedagogy that is multicultural or culturally responsive (Estrada & Vasquez, 1981; Irvine, 1991; Nieto, 1992; Ramsey, 1987). According to Irvine (1990): "A culturally responsive/responsible pedagogy addresses students' cultural knowledge, history, personal style, language and dialect, cognition and learning styles, as well as their parents and community" (p. 17).

The emergence of the cultural difference paradigm also sparked investigations into the mediating influence of race and culture in educational processes to address visible racial/ethnic group children's ways of knowing, how they access information, and how they make sense of the world (Cummins, 1986; Irvine, 1990; Nieto, 1992). New understandings of the relationship between culture and learning, coupled with a multiracial school population that does not seem to be achieving at levels comparable to their white counterparts and a predominantly white teaching force, have injected both substance and urgency into multicultural teacher education. Although research into multicultural teacher education is weak and limited (Grant & Secada, 1990; Irvine, 1992), we now know that single courses, short-term interventions, and student teaching placements in culturally diverse settings are ineffective or produce mixed results (Grant, 1981; Grant & Koskela, 1986; Haberman, 1991a; Henington, 1981; McDiarmid & Price, 1990; Washington, 1981).

Ramsey (1987) articulately captures what multicultural teacher education should seek to accomplish.

> Multicultural education is not a set curriculum, but a perspective that is reflected in all decisions about every phase and aspect of teaching. It is a lens through which teachers can scrutinize their options and choices in order to clarify what social information they are conveying overtly and covertly to their students. In a sense, it is a series of questions to induce educators to challenge and expand the goals and values that underlie their curriculum designs, materials, and activities. This perspective infuses educational decisions and practices at all stages and is an expansive way of thinking that enables teachers to see new potential in both familiar and novel activities and events. (p. 6)

This idea of guiding preservice teachers to look inward to examine their own implicitly held beliefs about culture, their own and others', as a precursor to working responsibly and effectively with children of color is gaining support (Banks, 1991a; Carter & Goodwin, 1994). While this is not necessarily a new concept, the idea that self-knowledge ought to precede content and strategic approaches to multicultural teacher education is gaining prominence (Sleeter, 1992).

PRESERVICE TEACHERS' CONCEPTIONS OF MULTICULTURAL EDUCATION AND ISSUES

From investigations into teacher beliefs and teacher thinking, we know that teachers' conceptions of teaching and learning undergird and frame the decisions they make in the classroom (Clark & Peterson, 1986). The relationship between teacher expectations and student achievement and the correlation between low expectations and correspondingly low student achievement have been documented by a rich body of research (see, for example, Brophy & Good, 1986; Clair, 1992; Dusek & Gail, 1983; Good & Brophy, 1984; Irvine, 1990). Consequently, any efforts by teacher education programs to prepare multicultural educators should begin with an understanding of how preservice teachers define and conceptualize multicultural education.

In a study of preservice teachers' conceptions and definitions of multicultural education (Goodwin, 1994), preservice teachers were asked to share their thoughts about multicultural education. The study unearthed their misconceptions, tacit assumptions, or concerns surrounding this construct and revealed their lack of preparedness to deal with diverse classroom populations.

We asked 120 preservice teachers from a variety of institutions representing both public and private education, as well as undergraduate and graduate programs in different regions in the country, to complete, near the end of their teacher education programs, an open-ended questionnaire designed to capture their conceptions of multicultural education. Of 120 questionnaires, 80 (67%) were returned completed. The demographics of the respondent group were as follows: 23 African Americans, 8 Asian Americans, 47 European Americans, and 2 Latinos. Thus, the final sample from which data were obtained was 41% non-white and 59% white. The gender breakdown in the final sample was 10 (12.5%) male vs. 70 (87.5%) female. Data were analyzed in relation to three research questions.

1. What are preservice teachers' conceptions of the goals of multicultural education?
2. What do preservice teachers identify as multicultural practices?

3. What are preservice teachers' concerns about the implementation of multicultural practices?

In this study, respondents indicated that the goals of multicultural education should focus on: (1) knowing others; (2) developing affective attitudes; (3) the individual child; and (4) social change. The range of goals is misleading, however, since 41% of the responses emphasized coming to know others, while 30% indicated support of the "human relations" approach to multicultural education (Sleeter & Grant, 1987). Only 9% of the responses suggested that multicultural education should focus on achieving social change. Thus, student teachers seemed to perceive multicultural education primarily as a mechanism for delivering cultural content or for changing the way children behave with one another. This finding was echoed in the practices that student teachers identified as multicultural and in their questions about multicultural teaching. Fifty-four percent of the responses indicated that multicultural practices were defined by specific cultural content, the use of certain materials, or special celebrations such as Black History Month. Finally, the questions respondents expressed about multicultural education revealed that they defined it as primarily procedural or technical; it required knowing something and doing something. What they indicated they were prepared to do seemed dependent on how much control they would be given, the kinds of preservice teachers or communities they would work with, the models or materials available. While some preservice teachers expressed confusion with the concept itself and questioned their own abilities to be multicultural educators, this represented less than a quarter of the responses. The majority of the responses came from preservice teachers who seemed unconcerned with their own efficacy; for these respondents, multicultural education appeared to be reactive education—it depended on the circumstances one was in.

From this study, it would appear that the respondents seemed to define multicultural education as an externally driven concept; apparently one reached outside oneself for the answer to multicultural education. These teachers did not seem to include themselves in the multicultural equation. While the results from this study cannot be generalized given the modest sample size, the fact that it found few differences in thinking within such a diverse group of preservice teachers is troubling.

In another study of preservice teachers' concerns about multicultural education (Goodwin, 1993), 83 preservice teachers were asked to write critical incidents or "vignettes" (Miles & Huberman, 1984) based on instances when they were confronted with a multicultural issue or dilemma. Of the 83, 75—27% of whom were visible racial/ethnic group members (African

American and Asian American)—returned completed vignettes, which became data for this study. Each vignette asked respondents to indicate the players involved in the incident and to describe what occurred. Respondents also were asked to articulate the questions or concerns the incident raised for them and to recommend solutions to resolve the issue. Data were collected toward the end of the respondents' first term of student teaching. The three research questions addressed were

1. What kinds of multicultural/diversity issues are preservice teachers concerned with?
2. What kinds of questions do these issues raise for preservice teachers?
3. What solutions do preservice teachers recommend in terms of dealing with multicultural dilemmas?

The study found that preservice teachers' vignettes clustered around nine specific variables—race, language difference, sexuality, gender, religion, class (socioeconomic), curriculum, exceptionality, and equity. Of the nine variables, race surfaced as the key defining variable in 50% of the vignettes. All the rest of the variables were associated with between 9% and 2.5% of the vignettes. These figures clearly indicate that multicultural issues or dilemmas that feature race as a central construct are either most troubling to preservice teachers or surface most frequently in schools. It seems safe to say that race and racial issues are primary multicultural concerns; certainly in this study racial concerns almost overshadowed all the other issues combined.

When the different categories of vignettes were cross-referenced to tease out the modes of response teachers and children enact when interacting with racial or cultural difference or when confronting those labeled as racial minorities in this country, several response modes surfaced immediately: rejection, internalization, suspicion/attack, disregard, derision, ambivalence, and discomfort. The vignettes placed teachers and children in dysfunctional or oppositional postures that would exacerbate any possibility of equitable resolution of multicultural dilemmas. This finding delineates how teaching and learning, which are complicated processes to begin with, are further complicated by racial and cultural issues.

When preservice teachers articulated their questions and concerns about these incidents, four general responses emerged. First, preservice teachers were surprised to witness racist and inequitable behavior. Second, preservice teachers expressed indecisiveness about the issues themselves; they had questions about how incidents should be named, whether they were indeed, for example, racist or sexist incidents. Third, respondents raised questions or concerns about the individual who had been the target of negative responses. Their questions revealed their concern with how this child should fit into an unaccepting environment rather than how the unaccepting environment should be changed. In essence, preservice teachers engaged in some victim blaming. Finally, preservice teachers expressed concerns about what to do, how to proceed or respond. Some of this concern was couched in terms of their own feelings of inadequacy.

In terms of the solutions respondents recommended, three were mentioned most frequently. Over 50% felt that talking things out was the best solution. Twenty-six percent of the preservice teachers suggested curriculum changes—in the form of materials or activities—that would help expose children to cultural diversity. Nineteen percent suggested that special attention be given to the child on the receiving end of negative incidents. This special help ranged from highlighting the child in some way, providing special assistance, or treating the child equally. While the preservice teachers in this study described substantive and serious issues, they approached the incidents in an ahistorical and decontextualized manner. Thus, their questions and recommendations skated the surface of these critical concerns and appeared not to match the gravity of the situations they had witnessed. Preservice teachers' ideas seemed to suggest a reactive rather than a proactive stance whereby problems are dealt with as they occur. A sense of addressing multicultural concerns more broadly or more comprehensively was not apparent. Thus, preservice teachers seemed to define multiculturalism as a contingent endeavor, something to enact when the circumstances call for it, a finding mirrored by the study described earlier.

From these two studies, it appears that the majority of these preservice teachers hold superficial understandings about multicultural education irrespective of racial or cultural background. This suggests strongly that multicultural teacher education may need to concentrate on disturbing the beliefs or initial dispositions that student teachers bring with them to teacher preparation programs.

Much of the literature and research on how teacher beliefs and preconceptions influence and interfere with teacher education suggest that teacher preparation programs should help fledgling teachers reflect upon and analyze their perceptions of teaching, learning, schools, and children (see, for example, Feiman-Nemser & Buchmann, 1985). I believe this reflective analysis also should occur in the context of multicultural teacher education.

One could interpret the multiple conceptualizations of multicultural education as manifestations of different levels of multicultural development. Clarifying self-conceptions can be only one step in the long journey to developing into a culturally responsive pedagogue. Preservice teachers need opportunities to articulate their own beliefs about multicultural education, misconceptions, naive thinking, hidden assumptions, and prejudices. Otherwise, these feelings and implicit theories remain buried even while they guide and influence behavior and possibly deflect new understanding. Student teachers also need to understand the historical and sociopolitical context of education and race in this country. The school experiences of children of color in America cannot be divorced from this painful and inequitable legacy.

A MODEL FOR MULTICULTURAL TEACHER EDUCATION

Following is a six-phase model for teacher education that attends to prospective teachers' beliefs, their need for content and strategies, and their comprehension of the historical context of education in America (Figure 1.1).

Figure 1.1. A Theoretical Model for Multicultural Teacher Education

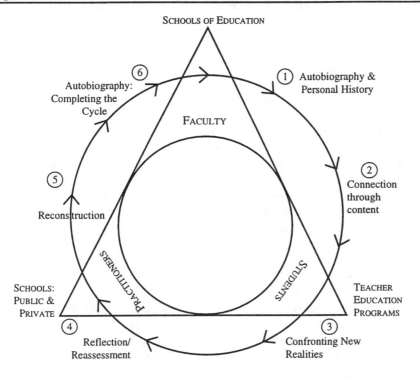

1. *Looking at Ourselves: Autobiography and Personal History.* In the first phase, the emphasis is on unearthing conceptions of multiculturalism, race, equity, diversity, class, and so on. The key here is to encourage preservice teachers to think deeply about their own development as cultural beings, to identify their values and the antecedents for their beliefs, to discuss questions/concerns they have about multicultural issues, to analyze biases. In essence, the goal is to enable preservice teachers to look inward.

2. *Connection Through Content: Intellectual Multiculturalism.* Phase two involves providing preservice teachers with content and information about multiculturalism and multicultural teaching. This content should respond to their questions and offer authentic data about, for example, the culture of different groups, multicultural teaching practices, and cultural learning styles. This phase is necessary not merely because preservice teachers need information, but because multiculturalism as an intellectual pursuit is familiar and can be comforting given the dilemmas the next phase will raise.

3. *Confronting New Realities: Learning Through Disequilibrium.* Phase three is designed to introduce preservice teachers to alternative realities that cause them to question the universality or validity of their own understandings. Conceptual and emotional disequilibrium can engender thoughtful reflection and questioning. This phase forces preservice teachers to re-examine what they thought they knew and to confront their vision of the world. Avenues for this self-analysis can include critical pieces by authors such as Helms (1990), Kozol (1991), Fine (1991), Ogbu (1987), or Gould (1981); simulations such as BaFaBaFa; interactions and community service within a variety of contexts different from those they are familiar with; presentations on controversial topics; and so on. It is also during this phase that preservice teachers should engage in the "study of the interaction of race and ethnicity, class and gender, within economic, political, and cultural spheres" (Gollnick, 1992b, p. 65) in order to acquire a broader sociopolitical framework for education. Preservice teachers also should be guided to use racial identity theory (Helms, 1990) as a mirror to their own behavior, experiences, and development. Simply put, the key during this phase is lighting fires under preservice teachers.

4. *Reflection and Reassessment.* A period of reflection and personal re-evaluation is a natural follow-up to a period of imbalance. This phase guides preservice teachers to reconstruct conceptual schemata given what they learned and experienced in phase three. Critical questions to ask might be: What do preservice teachers now think about educational

equity? What did they learn about themselves and their values? What were their assumptions before and after?

5. *Reconstruction: Thinking and Behaving Differently.* Phase five directs pre-service teachers to action driven by different or new ways of thinking. Most of the individuals who enter teaching are motivated by a desire to make a difference, to make a significant contribution. From experience, this desire often is only partially realized as intentions fall short of actions and new teachers easily slip into assumptions about "good" students, poor districts, predominantly minority schools, and so on. Preservice teachers are challenged to be change agents by bolstering their good intentions with real work. By helping them cultivate a proactive mindset, an internal safeguard against complacency, this phase demands that teachers assume responsibility for actively seeking whatever skills and information they might need to make sound pedagogical decisions that benefit children. Phase five places accountability for learning squarely on teachers' shoulders; teachers take it upon themselves to do or learn whatever is necessary to make a difference.

6. *Autobiography: Completing the Cycle.* The sixth phase is actually a return to the first. New understandings and actions necessarily change one's own story. Autobiographies are dynamic and fluid; new chapters in each person's book require further and continuous examination. The model recycles and begins again.

PRELIMINARY RESULTS OF MODEL FIELD TESTS

The model was piloted over the 1992–93 academic year with a group of 11 female and one male elementary preservice teachers—three Asian Americans, one African American, one Latina, and seven European Americans—all of whom volunteered for the experience. The pilot revealed that the first phase—autobiography—requires much more time than originally anticipated. Participants spent 4 months looking inward and exploring their own conceptions of culture. This exploration resulted in the white preservice teachers seeing the diversity that was inherent in each person and recognizing that, as whites, they had culture, too. Thus, the group came to define culture as a quality that all individuals possess, not just visible racial/ethnic group people.

In the second phase of the model, the multicultural models and strategies presented were couched in the sociopolitical and historical context so that what preservice teachers received in terms of multicultural practice also was grounded in an understanding of past practices. Students also read critical readings that provided information about multicultural education and immersed them in the depth and persistence of racism in contemporary American society (e.g., McIntosh, 1989; Tatum, 1992).

Thus, as the model unfolded, phase two naturally melted into phase three. This was a period of turmoil and pain for the group. This was also the first time that the group briefly splintered into a variety of configurations—some individuals seemed to withdraw from the group, while small groups of two or three met outside the common gathering times. Journal entries during phase three began to express fear, anger, and pain instead of the themes of community and safety expressed during phase one.

This was probably the one period during the year when the group was in danger of dissolving. However, the group gradually began to recement itself as members renewed their commitments to one another, a signal that they were moving into phase four. This rocky but delicate transition between phases three and four framed the single most important finding of the pilot— the extended amount of time phase one required actually helped the group build a foundation of intimacy, a level of personal obligation that enabled them to work through phase three. Without the feelings of safety, community, and commonality that group members were able to develop as a result of phase one, they would not have been able to transcend the distress, rawness, and even hostility of phase three.

During phase four, participants began to open up in deeper ways and began also to express different thoughts about race and racial issues. One white student wrote, "I'm beginning to see my responsibility for racism"; another student indicated, "I feel the need to express or unpack the racist baggage that I carry."

Three-fourths of the graduates from this experience have selected to teach in contexts that demand that they consider issues of race and culture on a daily basis. Phases five and six, interviewing and observing each student in their classroom, will reveal whether the effects of the model continue to influence their thinking and their pedagogy. Preliminary results reveal that the model holds much promise.

It would be inaccurate to perceive the model as a process that simply emphasizes individual difference. Rather, the model is deliberately structured to move participants beyond the simple exploration or celebration of individual differences to an examination of power, oppression, and domination through both sociohistorical and sociocontemporary lenses. While the model is initiated by a period of *personal reflection* that guides participants to examine themselves as racial and cultural entities, this period allows the group to establish an affective bond that will support the more difficult discussions that will follow. Ultimately, success of the model depends on social action, not cultural exchange.

Model Implementation

The model is designed for use with college faculty, school practitioners, administrators, and students. Applying the model at an organizational level ultimately should result in institutional change as individuals are guided to consider collective practices, programs, and norms. Indeed, the inherent flexibility of the model should allow for implementation in multiple ways. For example, the model could be layered over a teacher education program so that it becomes a screen for instruction, materials, and assignments. The phases could be separated so that the process fits more readily into traditional staff development or inservice training schedules in schools. Individual phases are apparently pliable and could, therefore, be extended or brief, depending on need. As a process-approach, the model is adaptable to diverse settings, which heightens the possibility of implementation and success.

CONCLUSION

The concept of multicultural teacher education has evolved through three distinct phases: exclusion, inclusion, and infusion. During the exclusion phase, pedagogy to address the needs of a culturally diverse school population was, to a major extent, absent from teacher education curricula. The idea of multicultural teacher education was excluded from common conceptions of what teachers needed to know in order to be effective. During the inclusion phase, an awareness that teachers needed to be prepared to work with students who were culturally and ethnically diverse was incorporated into teacher education norms. However, the responsibility for multicultural teacher education resided in special courses or workshops. These special offerings were not integrated into the "regular" teacher preparation program, and student participation in these courses was generally on a volunteer or self-selection basis. Thus, multicultural teacher education, while included in teacher education, remained on the periphery of professional preparation. The third phase is where the field's intentions seem to be now—infusion. This is apparent in AACTE's latest recommendations regarding revisions of the NCATE guidelines whereby the Commission on Multicultural Education and Committee on Accreditation have supported stronger multicultural language and goals woven throughout the standards that guide the accreditation process (AACTE Commission on Multicultural Education and Committee on Accreditation, 1992). The message seems clear—multicultural teacher education cannot satisfactorily happen if the concepts and content of multiculturalism remain on the margins of teacher preparation. Now, teacher educators are grappling with how multicultural teaching practices can be infused throughout the entire teacher education curriculum. Preparing teachers who are multicultural in their practice and their perspective is a challenge the teacher education field is beginning to undertake. The model presented represents one way in which we can move teachers beyond multicultural education that superficially tinkers around the edges of change. Rather than perpetuating the notion that multicultural education is something "done" to or for others, the model offers an avenue whereby we learn to accept others by understanding ourselves. In essence, making the transition from self to other starts not with knowing others but rather with knowing ourselves.

NOTES

1. A term used in place of "minorities," this term refers to Hispanic or Latino, Asian American or Pacific Islander, American Indian or Native American, and Black American or African American; see Cook and Helms, 1988.

2. For consistency, the term "multicultural teacher education" is used throughout the chapter to define teacher education that prepares teachers to work effectively with culturally diverse school populations. It is understood, however, that this term is not used universally and may be considered contemporary nomenclature. Also, the concept of preparing teachers for cultural diversity has been differently named in the evolution of the multicultural education field.

2

Enhancing the Capacity of Teacher Education Institutions to Address Diversity Issues

SUSAN L. MELNICK AND KENNETH M. ZEICHNER

Most teacher education programs acknowledge in principle the importance of pluralistic preparation of teachers, but in practice most actually represent what Goodlad (1990b) has called a monocultural approach (Grant, 1993). Such programs perpetuate traditional teaching practices that largely have failed to provide quality instruction for poor and ethnic and linguistic minority students. Although teacher candidates may come to teacher education with limited direct interracial and intercultural experience, with erroneous assumptions about diverse youngsters, and with limited expectations for the success of all learners (Zeichner, 1993, 1995), a related problem exists. Many teacher educators are themselves limited in cross-cultural experiences and understandings—they are overwhelmingly Caucasian, monolingual, and culturally encapsulated (Ducharme & Agne, 1989; Villegas et al., 1995). Thus, the ability of teacher education programs to promote an appreciation for diversity and equity among prospective teachers is questionable (Hixson, 1992). Although the vast inequities in U.S. society cannot be attributed entirely to the failure of schools, the failure to provide quality education for *all* students represents a crisis in education that is intolerable in a democratic society. The current review of NCATE's Professional Accreditation Standards clearly attests to this need.

NCATE's PROFESSIONAL ACCREDITATION STANDARDS: ASSESSING INSTITUTIONAL CAPACITY TO ADDRESS DIVERSITY

In response to the Constitutional provision for continuous review of the Professional Accreditation Standards (Article IX), the Standards Committee of the Unit Accreditation Board of NCATE undertook a review of the 1987 standards in early 1992. This review resulted in several refinements to the existing standards, and the results were circulated for reactions and recommendations during the latter part of 1993. As described in the memorandum on the draft of the "Proposed Refinement of NCATE's Professional Accreditation Standards" by President Arthur Wise (1993), the Standards Committee paid careful attention to two characteristics of the Standards and Indicators of Quality relevant to our concerns about preparing teachers to teach culturally diverse learners: the interweaving of "the place of conscience or moral dimensions of teaching" (p. 2) into some of the standards and indicators, and the "infusion of attention to multicultural and diversity issues across all standards" (p. 3).

The draft document entitled "Proposed Refinement of NCATE's Standards for the Accreditation of Professional Education Units" (NCATE, 1993) indicates that the Committee's goal was threefold: to reduce duplication across standards, clarify language, and reorganize the standards to emphasize importance (p. 1). In accomplishing these goals, the Committee rewrote existing indicators and generated new ones that clearly specify a template for addressing issues of diversity. These revisions or additions concern most of the standards, thereby making attention to diversity explicit where it was heretofore, at best, implicit. They include explicit references to the design and content of the teacher education curriculum, the quality of instruction for teacher candidates, collaborative relationships within the professional community, the composition of the faculty and teacher candidate body, faculty qualifications and governance, and accountability of the unit responsible for preparing teachers. The following list delineates some of these additions:

> *Design of the curriculum*: Courses and experiences in professional studies incorporate multicultural and global perspectives. The integrative studies enable candidates to develop meaningful learning experiences for students within the context of students' cultures, language backgrounds, socioeconomic status, communities, and families.

Quality of instruction: Instruction reflects knowledge about multicultural education, cultural context, exceptionalities, curriculum design, instruction, and evaluation.

Faculty qualifications: Faculty have developed multicultural competencies through formal study or experiences in culturally diverse settings.

Faculty composition: The unit ensures that the professional education faculty represent cultural diversity.

While we agree with the intent and thrust of the Standards Committee's efforts to make multicultural education a more central concern in all teacher education programs, our ongoing research on preparing teachers for diversity sponsored by the National Center for Research on Teacher Learning (NCRTL) suggests both possibilities and problems for institutional responses to the refined NCATE standards and indicators.

THE NCRTL STUDY

In this chapter, we report on portions of a study on "Teacher Education for Diversity," which we have been conducting since 1990. The overall study includes an ongoing analysis of relevant literature that has generated a conceptual framework describing the range of existing positions on teacher education for cultural diversity (e.g., see Zeichner & Hoeft, 1996). It also includes the development of three case studies of exemplary programs employing different organizational arrangements and instructional strategies that contravene or compensate for the cultural insularity of teacher education faculty (characteristic of most of the 1,300 institutions that prepare teachers in the United States). Although an adequate definition of "diversity" needs to be broad and inclusive, with attention to such other areas as gender, age, religion, exceptionalities, sexual orientation, etc., the use of the term "cultural diversity" in this study refers primarily to differences related to social class, race, ethnicity, and language.

The specific concern in our study has been to understand the variety of arrangements and strategies currently being used to prepare a largely white, monolingual student teaching force to teach poor students of color who historically have been unserved, ill served, or inappropriately served by traditional teaching practices.[1] Despite the rhetoric surrounding multicultural education and diversity in recent years and the attempts of bodies like NCATE to force teacher educators to pay more serious attention to the issues, there are, in actuality, few programs substantively addressing these concerns. Only eight of the first 59 institutions that sought national accreditation for their teacher education programs under the 1987 standards were in full compliance with the minimum multicultural education requirements for teacher education programs. Gollnick (1992a) reports that "although most institutions included references to multicultural education in the unit's objectives or mission statement, NCATE evaluators were often unable to detect where these were implemented in the curriculum" (p. 236).

Much of the literature on efforts to educate teachers for cultural diversity is fugitive, and some of the good work that is going on has received little public attention beyond program sites. Our purpose in the overall study is to make some of these exemplary practices more visible, to capture the voices of teacher educators who take matters of diversity seriously in their attempts to educate preservice teachers, and to encourage more thorough and widespread attention to issues of diversity in initial teacher education programs throughout the United States.

Over the course of our study, we have come to regard the problem of teacher education for diversity as one having three dimensions: (1) the problem of selection; (2) the problem of socialization through curriculum and instruction; and (3) the problem of changing the institutional environment of teacher education. We will summarize briefly our initial findings related to each of these three dimensions, with special attention to the problem of institutional change in relation to the proposed NCATE refinements.

The Problem of Selection

Much has been written in the United States about the growing disparity in backgrounds and life experiences between teachers and teacher educators, on the one hand, and public school students on the other. It is clear from our work as both researchers and teacher educators, as well as the work of others, that most prospective teachers come to teacher education with very little direct intercultural experience. In addition, they tend to view diversity as a problem rather than as a resource. They have little knowledge about different ethnic and racial groups in the United States—their cultures, achievements, histories, contributions to the making of the nation, and especially their records of discrimination, disenfranchisement, and suffering. Further, most teacher candidates want to teach students like themselves and are not even convinced that all students are capable of learning (Gomez, 1996; Goodlad, 1990b; Paine, 1989; Zimpher & Ashburn, 1992).

While it may be possible to remedy these factors to some extent, most teacher education programs as they are currently organized largely fail to do so. The literature on teacher learning overwhelmingly suggests that, even in the best of circumstances, teacher education is a weak intervention

(Zeichner & Gore, 1990). Some researchers, like Haberman at the University of Wisconsin–Milwaukee, have argued that typical teacher education students who are young and culturally encapsulated are not developmentally ready to make the kinds of adjustments needed for successful cross-cultural teaching. These researchers are pessimistic about the likelihood that preservice teacher education can become a powerful enough intervention to change the attitudes and dispositions developed over a lifetime (Haberman, 1991b).

We clearly need to modify programs to deal with teacher education students' shortcomings, as suggested by NCATE's proposed refinements related to curriculum design and content, student body composition, faculty composition and qualifications, and candidate progress issues. However, it is becoming progressively more clear that some selection screens—such as the interviews Haberman (1987) developed to screen candidates for teaching in urban schools—also must be used to determine potential abilities necessary for successful cross-cultural teachers. It is clear that instead of depending solely on grade point averages, test scores, and glowing testimony of young college students wanting to be teachers because they love children, we have to find ways, as Haberman says, to focus more on picking the right people than on changing the wrong ones.

In one of the programs we are studying, the American Indian Reservation Student Teaching Project, students are required to undergo a systematic year-long period of cultural study before entry to the program. During this time, students attend regular meetings where, under the guidance of program staff, they read and study about various American Indian groups, their histories and lifestyles; read American Indian literature; and interact with American Indian consultants. It is argued by teacher educators in this program that this kind of systematic preadmission orientation program screens out people who are not serious about the cultural diversity aspects of the program.

The Problem of Socialization Through Curriculum and Instruction

Most of our research has centered on the identification of curricular and instructional strategies teacher educators have used to attempt to prepare preservice teachers to teach diverse students. Our literature reviews suggest that these strategies generally are organized in two ways: through the *infusion* approach, which integrates attention to diversity throughout the program's various courses and field experiences, or through the *segregated* approach, which treats diversity as the focus of a single course or as a topic in a few courses, while other components of the program remain untouched.

While studies indicate a clear preference for the infusion approach, not surprisingly the segregated approach dominates (Gay, 1986).

Our analyses of the literature also have identified a tension in the field
between *culture-specific* approaches, which seek to prepare teachers to teach
specific cultural groups in particular contexts (e.g., urban Puerto Rican students), and *culture-general* approaches, which seek to prepare teachers to be
successful in any context that involves cross-cultural interactions. The latter
approach focuses on identifying and understanding general cognitive processes that mediate cross-cultural interactions and emphasizes experiences
that people are likely to have during cross-cultural encounters. According
to Kushner and Brislin (1986), teachers who experience a culture-general
emphasis in their preparation programs

> Would be expected to be more knowledgeable about factors that contribute to
> cross-cultural misunderstanding, be sensitive to such factors when interacting
> with students and parents and be able to approach potentially conflicting situ-
> ations with an awareness and ability to ask questions in such a way that takes
> culturally determined factors into account. (p. 54)

An example of the culture-specific approach that seeks to prepare teachers to be culturally sensitive and interculturally competent teachers with
regard to specific groups of students is the community-specific and com-
munity-controlled approach to teacher education advocated by a U.S. Office
of Education Commission on Teacher Education in 1976 (Study Commission, 1976). Here specific communities of people would develop teacher
education experiences designed specifically for their own schools and communities. While this kind of culture-specific preparation for teaching specific groups of students in particular contexts (e.g., Navajos) may help develop sensitivities and capabilities among teachers that are useful in other
cross-cultural contexts (see Willison, 1994), the emphasis is on the particular contexts into which they are being inducted. All teacher education for
diversity efforts can be analyzed in terms of the degree to which they emphasize culture-general and culture-specific approaches.

Another dimension along which teacher education for diversity efforts
vary is the degree to which they emphasize *interacting with cultures* as opposed to *studying about cultures*. While all programs that seek to prepare teachers to teach diverse students probably include at least some direct field experience in diverse schools and/or communities, programs vary as to how much
they emphasize these direct experiences and according to the degree to which
they put their students into contact with students and adults from different
cultural backgrounds.

Self-Knowledge. Our research suggests that a wide range of curricular and instructional strategies are used within these various dimensions to attempt to socialize prospective teachers to see themselves as members of a culturally diverse society and to value cultures other than their own. These include the use of autobiography, biography, and life history methods to help students understand their own cultural identities, and intellectually focused and socially supportive strategies of collaborative reflection such as "storytelling" to help them re-examine their attitudes, assumptions, expectations, and beliefs about ethnic, racial, and language groups different from their own (see Zeichner, 1993; Zeichner & Hoeft, 1996). This approach of helping teacher education students locate themselves within our culturally diverse society and examine their attitudes toward others is exemplified in the work of King and Ladson-Billings (1990) formerly at Santa Clara University, the work of Hollins (1990a, 1990b) formerly at California State University–Hayward, the work of Gomez and Tabachnick (1991) at the University of Wisconsin–Madison, the work of Banks (1991c) at the University of Washington, and the Teachers for Alaska program (Noordhoff & Kleinfeld, 1993).

Much of the data from our literature reviews and case studies suggest that in some circumstances, these strategies have a positive and immediate impact on prospective teachers' attitudes and dispositions. However, there is some evidence to suggest that students often resist teacher educators' efforts to change their views (Ahlquist, 1992) and, at times, teacher education practices designed to combat negative stereotypes actually reinforce teacher candidates' prejudices and misconceptions about diverse students (Haberman & Post, 1992).

Cultural Knowledge. Another set of strategies is designed to provide students with cultural and historical knowledge to overcome what Ellwood (1990) has called their cultural ignorance of groups different from their own. In one of the programs we are studying—the University of Indiana's American Indian Reservation Student Teaching Project that prepares students to student teach on the Navajo reservation in the southwestern United States—these strategies include helping prospective teachers gain knowledge about both the common elements and rich diversity within the history and culture of the Navajo people through literature, film, poetry, artwork, and discussions with Navajo people. During the cultural preparation preceding the student teaching semester various people from the Navajo reservation come to Indiana for brief periods to introduce prospective teachers to various aspects of contemporary Navajo life. During a recent orientation workshop these cultural experts included a Navajo poet who read and discussed her work with the student teachers and a dormitory aide who taught the students basic Navajo words and discussed issues related to culturally appropriate and inappropriate behavior on the reservation.

Cultural knowledge strategies also are used in our other two case study sites. At the University of Alaska–Fairbanks, the focus is on preparing students to work primarily with Native Alaskan students in remote villages and in urban multicultural schools; in the Urban Education Program of the Associated Colleges of the Midwest, the focus is on preparing students to work in urban schools serving the many different ethnocultural communities in the city of Chicago.

In all three programs, efforts are made, through carefully structured and monitored cultural immersion experiences in communities, to have students experience firsthand the cultures they are learning about and subsequently to analyze their experiences (e.g., Zeichner & Melnick, 1994). In two of our three case study sites (Teachers for Alaska and the American Indian Reservation Project), prospective teachers live for a semester in the communities in which they teach. Students in the Chicago program all live together in a multiracial and economically diverse northside community and participate in structured activities that take them into many of the city's ethnic neighborhoods. An important part of these immersion experiences is the use of community people as cultural experts (Mahan, 1982, 1993). In the American Indian Reservation Project, Navajo dormitory aides, with whom student teachers live, help the prospective teachers to make friends in the community and to participate in many community activities such as chapter house meetings, pow-wows, rodeos, and so forth. (Willison, 1994). The Chicago program hires many community members as consultants to introduce teachers to various community resources, such as the Mexican Fine Arts Center Museum, the People's Music School, and the Puerto Rican Cultural Center. These community members also introduce the teachers to various perspectives, such as what it is like to live on public assistance (Iazetto & Russell, 1994). In the Alaska program, elders in the village of Minto have been hired to introduce prospective teachers to traditional lifestyle patterns in remote Native Alaskan communities (Ongtooguk, 1994).

In other cases the involvement of prospective teachers with community members is more informal. For example, student teachers in the Alaska program are encouraged during a one-week "dunking" experience in an Athabascan community, which precedes student teaching, to

> Put themselves in roles outside of the classrooms (e.g., community basketball, skin sewing or beading groups, church attendance) and to spend time in such places as the store and post office where people are likely to congregate or share news. . . . Students [are advised] to seek out the expertise of teacher's aides who live in the community and to make home visits. (Noordhoff & Kleinfeld, 1993, p. 34)

While relatively brief community experiences are a common strategy in U.S. teacher education programs (e.g., day-long bus tours through inner-city areas), they risk being superficial experiences that create what has been referred to as "interested tolerance" at best and reinforcement of existing stereotypes at worst. The most effective ones are sustained efforts to help prospective teachers learn how to interact in more authentic ways with parents and other adults from different racial and ethnic backgrounds.

To avoid stereotypic responses to different cultural groups, some programs, including two of our case study sites (Teachers for Alaska and the American Indian Reservation Project), help prospective teachers learn how to learn about, and subsequently incorporate into their practice information about, their own students and their students' families and communities as a starting point for teaching and learning (e.g., Mahan, Fortney, & Garcia, 1983; Noordhoff & Kleinfeld, 1993). Both of these programs require a series of activities through which student teachers learn about the communities in which they are teaching (e.g., identifying cultural norms) and think about the implications of this cultural knowledge for teaching their pupils. In the American Indian Reservation Project, the community activities and analysis of community norms and their implications for the classroom continue throughout the student teaching experience and are closely monitored by program staff through journals that students send back to Indiana. In Alaska, while student teachers live in their school communities, the structured community activities mainly precede the student teaching semester. In the Urban Education Program, there is also very little emphasis on community experiences during student teaching. Here, as in the Teachers for Alaska Program, most of the structured community experiences precede student teaching.

Case-Based Instruction. Another instructional strategy that is used to prepare teachers for cultural diversity is case-based teaching. In one of our program sites, the University of Alaska–Fairbanks (Kleinfeld, 1989), as well as at the Far West Laboratory in San Francisco with the Case Methods in Multicultural Education Project (Gallagher, 1993; Shulman, 1992; Shulman & Mesa-Bains, 1990), teacher educators are using case studies, illustrating the challenges of teaching diverse students, to prepare more culturally sensitive and interculturally competent teachers.

Teacher educators have argued that cases are uniquely suited to the analysis of the complex and emotionally charged issues of teaching in culturally unfamiliar contexts. It is felt that cases can help prospective teachers develop a social map of a cultural terrain and to interpret the social meaning of unfamiliar cultural events (Kleinfeld, 1989). As Shulman and Mesa-Bains (1990) observe:

Cases allow teachers to discuss race and class issues openly, reflect on previously held views about different cultures, and confront their own potential prejudices and stereotypes. . . . The case approach can also provide a mechanism that enables both majority and minority teachers to talk together, through the distance of the case, about issues that might be too difficult to discuss openly. (p. 4)

Shulman (1992) points out, however, that cases, like other instructional strategies used to prepare teachers for cultural diversity, do not, by themselves, lead to greater cultural sensitivity and intercultural competence. The cultural sensitivity of the teacher educators using the strategies is critical. Shulman observes that

Cases, even with commentaries, do not teach themselves. Discussion leaders must not only be sensitive to the issues represented in the cases but also acutely aware of their own biases and intercultural blindness. They must understand the problems portrayed from multiple perspectives. And they must be able to anticipate in detail the variety of responses each case evokes, both emotionally and intellectually. (pp. 21–22)

Field Experiences. Perhaps the most common strategy used to prepare teachers for diversity is a field experience in schools serving ethnic and/or language minority students. Many programs and states like California now require all teacher education students to experience a variety of culturally different schools prior to certification (e.g., Ross, Johnson, & Smith, 1991). Other efforts combine both the school and community immersion experience and require student teachers to spend some time in communities during their practicums and student teaching (Zeichner & Melnick, 1994). However, merely requiring the school experience, the community experience, or both, does not necessarily ensure that students will develop the cultural sensitivity and intercultural competence needed for teaching diverse learners. Our work and that of others has shown that careful preparation for the field experiences as in the year-long cultural training in the American Indian project, careful monitoring of the experience while students are in the field, and opportunities to reflect about and analyze the experiences are important. It also has been argued that it is important for those who supervise these experiences to have had successful teaching experience in the kinds of communities in which student teachers are working (see Zeichner & Hoeft, 1996).

In general, the empirical evidence regarding the success of these various strategies in helping to prepare prospective teachers to teach diverse students is very weak. At best, some teacher educators, such as Hollins (1990b), King and Ladson-Billings (1990), and Beyer (1991), have been able to demonstrate some immediate influence of one or more of these strategies through the presentation of student teacher self-reports. These studies clearly show that under certain conditions, teacher education programs are able to help prospective teachers re-examine both themselves and their attitudes toward others and to gain knowledge about various cultural groups in the United States that had been excluded from their own education. For the most part, however, the literature is filled with assertions about the value of particular practices that are not substantiated by empirical evidence (Grant & Secada, 1990). In no case have we been able to find in the literature convincing evidence related to the long-term impact of these strategies on teachers and their teaching practices. Our case study design includes interviews with graduates of each of the programs we are studying. Through these interviews, we hope to be able to provide some insights into the question of the long-term impact of particular strategies to educate teachers for diversity. Ultimately, we need to better understand how to prepare teachers for diversity in ways that are connected to active and successful efforts by teachers to promote greater equity and social justice in schools.

The Problem of the Institutional Environment

While the foregoing examples of selection and socialization strategies show some promise, despite limited empirical evidence of long-term impact on teachers and their practices, the fundamental problem is that in using these potentially effective strategies teacher educators often define the task of teacher education for diversity only as one of socialization and have ignored the selection and institutional aspects of the problem. The institutional environment in which teacher education is embedded is critical in determining the success of curriculum and instructional strategies. Despite the rhetoric to the contrary, efforts to reform U.S. teacher education to address cultural diversity are severely hampered by the cultural insularity of the bulk of the education professorate and the lack of commitment to cultural diversity in teacher education institutions (Grant, 1993).

There is an old adage—teachers teach what they know—and so do teacher educators. The correlate is that we can't teach what we don't know. Teacher education for diversity involves much more than the transfer of information from teacher educators to their students. It involves the profound transformation of people and of the worldviews and assumptions that they have carried with them for their entire lives. As Nieto (1992) says, an important part of becoming a multicultural teacher is becoming a multicultural person. This kind of transformation is beyond the current capabilities of most faculties of teacher education in the United States, and NCATE's proposed refinements related to faculty composition and qualifications in particular further highlight the problems.

In addition to the limitations posed by the cultural insularity of teacher education faculty, there is also a general lack of a broad institutional commitment to diversity in the college and university environments that offer teacher education programs. The degree of institutional commitment to diversity is evidenced in such things as an institution's hiring practices, student recruitment and admission policies, and curricular programs. Making issues of diversity central to the intellectual life of a college or university community legitimizes efforts within programs to educate teachers for diversity. Villegas (1993) supports this conclusion and makes the point that

> The success of any teacher education program in restructuring for diversity is largely influenced by the norms and processes of the host institution. Teacher education programs found in institutions actively committed to the inclusion of people from diverse backgrounds are more likely to succeed in addressing issues of diversity than those located in institutions that are insensitive to or silent on matters of cultural inclusion. (p. 3)

In our research, we have uncovered four different approaches to dealing with the institutional aspects of teacher education for diversity and the current limitations of most teacher educators to prepare teacher candidates to work with diverse students. The first is the *active recruitment of faculty of color* through the establishment of new institutional policies and programs like the Madison Plan at the University of Wisconsin–Madison and MSU IDEA at Michigan State University. These programs provide special incentives to departments, like specially funded positions, to hire qualified faculty of color.

A second approach is the creation of a *consortium*, where a group of institutions combine their resources to hire staff with expertise in teacher education for diversity to provide part of the teacher education program, usually field experiences and a few courses and seminars related to teaching for cultural diversity. One of our case study sites, the Urban Education Program in Chicago (a part of the Urban Education Program of the Associated Colleges of the Midwest), employs several faculty, not directly associated with any of the member colleges, whose expertise is in teacher education for diversity. This program, which has existed since the fall of 1963, has provided courses in multicultural education and in instruction for limited-English-proficient students, and school and community experiences to hundreds of prospective teachers from small liberal arts colleges that were unable by themselves to offer these experiences.

Our research also has discovered two other consortia focusing on teacher education for diversity. One is the Cooperative Urban Teacher Education Program (CUTE), which involves approximately 20 colleges and universities in six states. This program, begun in 1967 and based on an earlier program at Central Missouri State College, has graduated over 2,000 teachers to date. At one point during the 1970s CUTE was adopted by institutions across the country (McCormick, 1990).

Another cooperative arrangement, involving eight colleges, is the Urban Education Semester of the Venture Consortium coordinated by Bank Street College. This urban educational experience in New York City, for college juniors who have not necessarily made a commitment to a career in teaching, involves interdisciplinary coursework at Bank Street and field experiences in East Harlem schools (Levine & Pignatelli, 1994).

All three of these consortia, the Urban Education Program of the Associated Colleges of the Midwest, the CUTE Program, and the Urban Semester of the Venture Consortium, have provided preparation for teaching in urban schools for students from colleges that do not have the faculty or schools to implement an intensive cross-cultural teacher education program themselves.

A third approach to the institutional aspects of the problem of teacher education for diversity involves the provision of systematic *staff development for teacher education faculty* to help them learn about various aspects of teacher education for diversity and how to incorporate it into their institutions and programs. For example, the Multicultural Education Infusion Center at San Diego State University in California, with funding from the U.S. Office of Bilingual Education and Minority Language Affairs, provided teams of faculty from 15 teacher education institutions, with a 2-week intensive institute in June 1993 and a follow-up network experience, that was designed to increase the capability of these institutions to prepare teachers for work with diverse students (V. O. Pang, personal communication, April 1993). (See Chapter 4 of this volume.)

Also, the Association of Teacher Educators (ATE) and George Mason University, with funding from the U.S. Office of Bilingual Education and Minority Language Affairs, has been offering a series of three-day institutes across the country for school and university teacher educators. These institutes are designed to encourage teacher educators to give more explicit attention to language-related issues in the preparation of all teachers.

A fourth approach to the institutional aspects of teacher education for diversity is *partnership* agreements between predominantly white teacher education institutions and other colleges or universities with significant numbers of faculty and students of color or schools and school districts in areas with large numbers of ethnic or linguistic minority students. This approach was exemplified in the 1970s by the partnership between Louisiana Tech, a formerly white segregated institution, and Grambling State University, an historically black institution, which shared a common geographical area (Mills, 1984). Another form of partnership to enhance the capacity of a teacher education program to prepare teachers to teach diverse students is one between a teacher education program located in a predominantly white area and K–12 schools and school districts that provide teacher education students with field placements in schools serving students of color. The American Indian and Latino Immersion Projects coordinated by Jim Mahan at Indiana University in Bloomington (Mahan, 1982) and the partnership between Moorhead University in Minnesota and the San Juan–Alamo School District in South Texas (Cooper, Beare, & Thorman, 1990) are examples of these school–university partnerships.

Promising Approaches: A Cautionary Note

Although these four approaches to the institutional dimension of the task of teacher education for diversity all have some promise in their own right and in specifically addressing the proposed NCATE refinements in standards related to multicultural education, they all have their particular problems. The recruitment and retention of faculty of color in largely white institutions is both a critical need and a moral responsibility, but opportunities for such practices clearly are limited. Despite specific institutional policies to recruit faculty of color, higher education in the United States is currently subject to severe financial restrictions, and recruitment of *any* new faculty is the subject of intense scrutiny.

In addition, white institutions with few faculty of color often offer little more than inhospitable environments for new faculty of color, especially those who come with expressed commitments to address issues of diversity. There is often the assumption that issues of diversity should be "their" concern and not the concern of the entire faculty. There is also the perception that faculty of color have few, if any, "mainstream" interests and they often are automatically relegated to limited roles and responsibilities in education schools, finding themselves marginalized at best. While seemingly well intended, many of these recruitment policies fail to provide opportunities for all faculty to learn from the variety of perspectives on a number of educational issues that faculty of color bring to white institutions.

Further, the practice of teacher education is not highly valued within academe generally, and most college and university norms and reward structures neither reward teaching nor provide the kind of incentives needed to sustain programmatic efforts of faculty to bring about the kind of personal and professional transformation of teacher education that students need (Liston & Zeichner, 1991). Promotion and tenure decisions still depend heavily on criteria related to research and scholarship, and faculty who devote large amounts of their time to teaching and teacher education program development have little time to spend on activities necessary for academic success. Some of these same problems point to shortcomings in the staff development approach that exports a small group of faculty to another location and then returns them to an unchanged environment in which they are expected to shoulder the burden for teacher education for diversity. Without a concerted effort to create a culturally diverse learning community and programmatic and personnel practices committed to the promotion of diversity and equity in all parts of the programs and the culture within the teacher education institution, there is little hope for widespread success of either of these two approaches.

The consortium approach also relegates concerns about diversity to "them" rather than to "us." For example, while the Chicago program, over its nearly 30-year history, has documented numerous successes with individual students and has provided teacher education expertise unavailable on the home campuses of students, it nonetheless largely segregates (with some exceptions) teacher education for diversity to experiences outside of students' home institutions. Although the 15-member colleges are geographically unable to provide field experiences in diverse settings for their students, and while we know of a few faculty in these colleges who care deeply about issues of diversity and equity, the fact remains that these concerns are not treated systematically in the students' liberal education. Yet, as Bok (1986) has noted, a liberal education should include

> . . . [the development of] an awareness of other cultures with their differing values, traditions, and institutions. By having the chance to explore many opportunities, they should acquire lasting intellectual and cultural interests, [and] gain in self-knowledge. . . . Through working and living with a wide variety of fellow students, they should achieve greater social maturity and acquire a tolerance of human diversity. (pp. 54–55)

Quite simply, teacher education for diversity is the responsibility of the total institution. While consortia can provide special opportunities for students that home institutions might be unable to provide, the home institutions should not abdicate their responsibilities for the full scope of a student's liberal education on the road to becoming a teacher.

The partnership approach also has limitations. Cooperative efforts between higher education institutions were more popular in the 1970s and 1980s than they are now, as a result of federal and state legislation and judicial decisions to desegregate racially separate colleges and universities and to restructure state systems in response to shrinking revenues. Although some such partnerships remain, the lessons learned from prior efforts indicate that governments and courts cannot automatically legislate cooperation between institutions, especially those that historically have been unequal. Success of these efforts demands a commonly desired goal in the education of teachers, a sense of shared responsibility, an acknowledgment of shared expertise, the "creation of a climate of mutual trust and cooperation, and a willingness to break with tradition by combining and reorganizing existing resources" (Mills, 1984, pp. 22–23).

CONCLUSION

In this chapter we report results of an ongoing study of program practices and components for preparing teachers for diversity that can be identified in the literature and in three exemplary case studies. Although we have pointed out both strengths and shortcomings from our preliminary findings, as we continue our research we hope to provide further, more detailed evidence of the success of efforts in which teacher educators are currently engaged. In particular, little actually is known about the lived reality of teacher educators in attempting to address diversity with their students or about how teacher candidates interpret and give meaning to attempts to influence them in particular ways. Although the faculty in our case study sites and some other teacher educators elsewhere can demonstrate immediate influence of their efforts through prospective teachers' self-reports, there is no convincing evidence in the literature related to the long-term impact of these strategies on teachers and their practices or on teacher education institutions and their faculties. We hope that our observations and interviews of faculty, students, and program graduates, and consideration of the positive aspects of institutional arrangements, will provide evidence pointing to directions for meaningful and effective program change to better prepare teachers to teach everyone's children. Without such change, we will continue to fail to keep our social contract to educate *all* children to high academic standards.

NOTES

This chapter, a revised version of a paper presented at the annual meeting of AACTE, is sponsored in part by the NCRTL, College of Education, Michigan State University, which is funded primarily by the Office of Educational Research and Improvement (OERI), U.S. Department of Education. The opinions expressed in this paper do not necessarily represent the position, policy, or endorsement of the Office or the Department.

1. While the focus in the literature is mainly on the preparation of white teachers to teach poor students of color, we are not assuming that teachers who are mem-

bers of a minority group can necessarily translate their cultural knowledge into culturally relevant pedagogy (Montecinos, 1996). We also are not saying that it is unimportant to continue to try to recruit more people of color into teaching. These efforts are extremely important, but even under the most optimistic scenario for their success, the problem of educating teachers for diversity in the United States will continue largely to be one of educating culturally encapsulated, monolingual white teachers to teach many poor students of color. Finally, we are not saying that multicultural education and culturally responsive teaching are important only for poor students of color. Multicultural education, culturally responsive pedagogy, and the intercultural competence of teachers are important issues in all schools and for all teachers. Our study focuses on a small aspect of a much larger issue.

3

Culturally Relevant Teacher Preparation and Teachers' Perceptions of the Language and Culture of Linguistic Minority Students

ROSALINDA QUINTANAR-SARELLANA

How should we prepare teachers who will be able to teach students from culturally diverse backgrounds? This question must be framed within a broader educational context if we want relevant answers. A more appropriate question would be: How can teacher training institutions and teacher candidates be better prepared to communicate and interact with a culturally diverse community of learners? The research described in this chapter recognizes the need to provide linguistic minority students with an education that is culturally relevant. Before presenting the results of this investigation, a discussion of culturally relevant education is needed. Culturally relevant education is defined as a pedagogy that incorporates the language and culture of linguistic minority students into the educational process. Recognition that the teacher is a key element in promoting educational improvement can be traced back to the early days of the educational system (Tyack, 1974).

CULTURAL CAPITAL AND LINGUISTIC MINORITY GROUPS: A THEORETICAL DISCUSSION

Within the theoretical framework of class conflict, Bourdieu and Passeron (1977) developed the concept of cultural capital, which they defined as the behavior patterns, set of values, and linguistic expressions that members of a certain socioeconomic or ethnic group transmit to other members of society. For example, in schools the linguistic patterns, social behavior, and mannerisms, or cultural capital, of the middle class are used as if all children have equal access to these standards. Schools favor children who have acquired the linguistic and social patterns of the middle and upper class, and promote these competencies as the "natural" patterns of behavior.

As such, the knowledge transmitted in schools is never questioned. Who will benefit from it? What are the ultimate objectives of transmitting it? Which groups will not be represented? Such questions are not addressed openly. The reason for this omission is rooted in the way any system of unequal power in society is maintained and partly recreated: by means of transmission of culture. Thus, Bourdieu and Passeron (1977) argue that dominant groups manage to impose knowledge as legitimate and conceal the power relations that are the basis of their force. This means that powerful and influential elites are the ones who select the "legitimate" knowledge that the school transmits.

Dominant groups impose certain cultural values by means of an arbitrary mode of inculcation (education). Educational institutions collaborate in reproducing a cultural capital that is conceived of as the jointly owned property of the whole society. In reality, because the institutional structures correspond to the material and symbolic interests of classes differently situated within societal power relations, the school system tends to reproduce the structure of the distribution of cultural capital, thereby contributing to the reproduction of the social structure.

The academic achievement model emphasizes the efficiency of the school, and thus sometimes the actual content of knowledge itself is overlooked. Linguistic and cultural minority children, for example, are expected to perform in school on an equal basis with other children whose language and culture are represented as natural in school. In applying this theory to linguistic minority groups, two elements of cultural imposition can be detected. The first refers to a language that may be unknown to the child; and the second is the set of cultural values of a dominant group, which also may be unknown to the linguistic minority child. In the study described in this chapter the term *cultural capital* refers to linguistic and cultural values of a certain social class that are imposed as a common and legitimate denominator on all groups attending school.

The Teacher's Role

This study asks: Do teachers assign any value to the cultural and linguistic background of the linguistic minority child? If teachers perceive the cultural discontinuity between the child's background and the school, do they perceive themselves as being able to use the curriculum as a bridge that may help to minimize this gap? Cultural discontinuity, a term used in anthropology, describes "a rupture, breaking point, an incongruity in rearing practices or cultural patterns" (Spindler, 1974, p. 279). In this study, cultural discontinuity refers to the abrupt change in language and culture that a linguistic minority child faces in school. If schools are ideological institutions that serve to transmit knowledge and socialization values that reinforce the interests of the dominant group (Apple, 1979; Bowles & Gintis, 1976; Sharp & Green, 1975), what is the teacher's role in this process? How is this role conditioned and constrained in society and teacher training institutions?

According to Freire (1970/1968), teachers most commonly teach skills but not how to think or to question. In the process of education for liberation, Freire focuses on the dialectical role of the teacher and the need to make the learning process relevant to the student by incorporating the child's language and culture into the educational process. Freire's pedagogical method emphasizes the need for learning material to be culturally specific. This means that students learn by using their immediate environment and by learning how to question the world around them. This idea is pertinent to the analysis of the role of the teacher in bilingual programs, since one important aim of bilingual programs is to make schooling relevant to the linguistic minority child. Freire emphasizes the need to incorporate the student's background in the educational process.

Freire's theory of education places great emphasis on the teacher's role and the restraints society places upon educators. Schools exist in time and space; thus, educational institutions are influenced by the structure of society and tend to transmit and reflect its values. That is, schools are affected by the socioeconomic and ideological structures of a given time. Within the structure of domination, they function largely as agencies to prepare individuals to perform within a specific social system. For Freire, the teacher acts as a mediator to initiate the student into the reflection on and interpretation of his or her reality (Freire, 1970/1968). Freire's philosophy transcends the educational realm by approaching educational concerns from many angles. Thus, he presents a global view of education as opposed to the atomistic view of knowledge presented by many educators who fail to perceive schooling in a wider context (Sharp & Green, 1975). Freire stresses that education is not a separate sphere; it is connected to a philosophical and sociopolitical system. Although this chapter concentrates on the role and perceptions of teachers, it is necessary to view this analysis in a wider context. Following is a brief summary of Freire's reflections on the nature of education and critical consciousness.

Teaching, Learning, and Critical Consciousness

Freire (1970/1968) believes in learning through dialogue. When teaching becomes entirely the activity of the one who instructs, and learning the "duty" of the student, the teacher is viewed as possessing knowledge, just as one might possess private property. Students are assumed to possess no knowledge and to be in need of receiving it. Freire calls these attitudes and methods "banking education," because teaching consists of depositing bits of information and skills into a presumably empty and passive student mind. Freire, like Bourdieu and Passeron (1977), believes that the dominant group's imposition of curricula, ideas, and values is a type of violence.

Other social scientists apply these concepts to the education of linguistic minority students. Cárdenas (1976) states in his theory of incompatibility that

> The educational failure of minority children is attributable to a lack of compatibility between their characteristics presupposed by typical instructional programs tailored for a white, Anglo-Saxon, English-speaking, middle-class school population. Rather than changing the child to fit the instructional program, the theory proposes changing the instructional program to fit the child. (cited in Teitelbaum & Hiller, 1977, p. 151)

Likewise, Chan and Rueda (1979) describe the "hidden curriculum" as certain skills that educators expect children to acquire in their home environment. These skills and predispositions are: (1) command of standard English; (2) motivation to attend and perform in school; (3) curiosity and willingness to explore their environment; and (4) proper school behavior (talking and responding to adults). These skills constitute a hidden curriculum that is mastered by middle- and upper-class children and in which minority and low-income students usually fall behind.

Freire (1970/1968) also emphasizes that humans relate to their world in a critical way: They reflect upon their reality. As people relate to the world by responding to the challenges of the environment, they begin to dynamize, to humanize reality. They add to it something of their own making by giving meaning to geographic space, by creating culture. It is this interplay of human relations with the world and other human beings that creates history. In order to allow men and women to act and not remain mere spectators, education must be humanized. Humanizing education starts with the resolution of the teacher–student contradiction. Any other approach denies the creative aspect of knowing and perpetuates oppression. The reflective nature of critical consciousness means that teachers and learners seek to know together in order to transform the world. When they perceive knowing as a social process, the teacher–student dichotomy gets resolved in a synthesis that emerges as "educators" become "educatees" (the persons being educated) and vice versa (Freire, 1970/1968).

The Teacher–Student Dichotomy and Dialogical Education

Freire's (1970/1968) opposition to banking education does not eliminate the role of teachers, nor does it deny the legitimacy or necessity of expert knowledge. Rather, Freire insists that if dialogical education is to occur, the role of educators as experts must change. Teachers can be students, that is, they can learn with their students. The teacher also must be aware that dialogue is not a technique, that it does not start in the classroom, and so must prepare a program that recognizes the role students play in the creation of knowledge. This role also involves students in the preparation of their own further education. A critically conscious teacher also knows the importance of involving the child's parents in the school's activities. A teacher in a multicultural classroom may help to resolve the teacher–student dichotomy by recognizing the child's linguistic and cultural background. The objective of bilingual/multicultural education is to incorporate the language and culture of linguistic minority students into the educational system. This objective presupposes that the teacher is aware of the discrepancies that might exist between the culture of the linguistic minority student and the culture of the school. The next section presents a brief review of the literature concerning teachers' attitudes toward linguistic minority students, bilingual programs, and parent participation. This literature and the findings of this study suggest a continuum of different stages of teachers' cultural awareness.

Stages of Teachers' Cultural Awareness

Three stages of cultural awareness can be identified in the literature and the study of teachers' perceptions that will be described here. The three stages are the cultural unawareness stage, the transition stage, and the cultural awareness stage.

Culturally Unaware Teachers. The *cultural unawareness* stage, as defined in this study, includes teachers who may or may not be aware of differences between the culture of the students and the school. Culturally unaware teachers actively reject students' language and culture, either overtly or covertly. Researchers have identified both types of teachers (Ahlquist, 1991; Delgado-Gaitan, 1987; Levin, 1986; Modiano, 1977; Quintanar-Sarellana, 1990; Sotomayor, 1974). Teachers in the "overt" category openly express their conviction that the students and their families need to change. These teachers assume that students have nothing to contribute; perceive students' language and culture as deficient; and view parents as not caring about education or as incapable of contributing to the educational process of their children (Baca, 1972; Parsons, 1965; Sotomayor, 1974). Teachers in the "covert" category complain about students' lack of academic achievement and their inability to conform to the culture of the school. These teachers take an academic and linguistic approach to the students' "problem" and do not think it is their responsibility to make the educational process relevant to linguistic minority students (Buriel, 1983; Campos, 1983; Elliot & Argulewicz, 1983; Kanowith, 1980; Laosa, 1977; Levin, 1986; Lopez, 1981; Phillips, 1983; U.S. Commission on Civil Rights, 1971–74).

Transition Stage Teachers. Teachers who share their students' language and cultural background and can enrich the curriculum are in the *transition stage*. In this stage teachers start to gain insight into the culture and language of linguistic minority students. These teachers are more open in their attempt to communicate with parents and to attend inservice training programs. This is a period of professional search and growth. This process of transformation sometimes begins with enrichment programs in which teachers receive inservice training and an abundance of curriculum materials and support staff. Anderson (1969), Kimball (1981), and Sotomayor (1974) identified teachers in the process of this kind of transformation. One teacher in Sotomayor's research expressed herself this way: "I was told that my first graders would be slow learners, but I've held them to high standards and they do excellent work" (p. 12). Sotomayor has illustrated through various examples how an understanding of the Chicano community helped many teachers change their beliefs and practices.

Culturally Aware Teachers. Teachers who share and understand the students' cultural capital are on the other end of the continuum at the stage of *cultural awareness*. These teachers can be characterized as being conscious of the differences between the cultural capital of the students and the school; able to incorporate the students' language and culture in the educational process; and able to try different teaching techniques and methods that are more appropriate for linguistic minority students. In addition, these teachers are able to communicate effectively with students and their parents. Finally, these culturally aware teachers are knowledgeable about different interpersonal strategies that allow them to relate to their students in a more effective and humane fashion (Baca de McNichols, 1977; Ellwood, 1991; Levin, 1986; Macías, 1984; Mathews, 1988; Modiano, 1977; Quintanar-Sarellana, 1990; Rodríguez, 1980).

THE STUDY AND THE RESULTS

We developed a questionnaire with six domains of teachers' perceptions toward education: (1) attitudes toward the role of education; (2) significance of the language and culture of linguistic minority students; (3) discrepancy between the language and culture of the school and the home; (4) role of bilingual programs; (5) role of bilingual teachers; and (6) parent participation. The questionnaire was administered to 71 teachers involved in bilingual programs and 56 teachers who worked in English-only programs. The research was conducted in a large city in northern California. A three-way analysis of variance permitted the examination of the effects of each independent variable (ethnicity, work experience, and Spanish proficiency), while holding the other variables constant. The analysis focused on the explanatory power of each of these main effects and their interactions.

The statistical analysis shows that certain characteristics of teachers are important factors in the attitudes they hold about linguistic minority students. The weakest association between teachers' characteristics and their perceptions was found on the first scale, the role of education. This scale consists of items taken from different theoretical frameworks concerning the role of education. (For example: "School rewards students who are willing to learn and work hard," "Education provides linguistic minority students with a vehicle for social mobility.") Ethnicity, work experience, and Spanish proficiency did not affect teachers' ratings on this scale. It seems apparent that teachers in this study were aware of the many functions being fulfilled by schooling.

The second scale, language and culture, measures how teachers perceive the cultural capital of linguistically minority students. Two main effects, ethnicity and work experience, as well as their interaction effect, were found to be statistically significant. That is, teachers working in bilingual programs perceive the language and culture of minority students more favorably and believe that the language and culture of students can be integrated in the classroom.

There are three possible explanations for why such teachers hold these positive attitudes: (1) teachers in bilingual programs are self-selected, because they like working with and/or understand the culture of minority students; (2) their awareness has been enhanced through their interaction with linguistic minority students; and (3) Hispanic teachers share and understand the cultural capital of linguistic minority students. In the open-ended portion of the questionnaire, Hispanic teachers addressed the fact that teaching in a bilingual program helped them discover the value of their own language and culture. Some teachers elaborated by writing about the thrill and satisfaction of transmitting knowledge using culture as a catalyst. These teachers act as mediators to initiate students into reflecting on reality. As a result of dialogue with their students, many teachers felt gratified that they had been able to reach students and enable them to learn. In the process, teachers also were engaged in the pursuit of re-evaluating their own cultural capital. Their sentiments support Freire's (1970/1968) belief that the best learning occurs through dialogue that recognizes the learner's culture.

These findings are also consistent with the research that indicates that ethnicity is an important factor in the way teachers view Mexican American students (Baca, 1972; Campos, 1983; Elliot & Argulewicz, 1983; Levin, 1986). Baca (1972) and Levin (1986) report that Hispanic teachers perceive Hispanic students in a more favorable light than European American teachers do. This research also reported that European American teachers were not convinced that "culturally different" children could learn (Baca, 1972; Campos, 1983). Campos (1983) found that European American teachers cited their students' lack of academic skills and lack of parental participation in the children's education, but did not know how to improve or change the situation. In other words, these teachers did not understand their students' cultural capital and how to use it to benefit the students.

The third scale measures teachers' perceptions of the discrepancy between the language and culture of the school and those of the home. Spanish proficiency was the only main variable for which we found a statistically significant effect. This finding supports the obvious; that is, a Spanish-speaking teacher is able to communicate with Spanish-speaking students and their parents. As a result, a Spanish-speaking teacher is also more likely to acknowledge the difficulties linguistic minority students face. Teachers related in their personal comments that language was a frequent barrier for linguistic minority students that needed to be overcome. This finding also is supported by Torres (1983) and Campos (1983), who found that European American monolingual teachers felt extremely frustrated and were unable to communicate with Hispanic students and their parents. Levin (1986) reported that students and their parents were more likely to participate in school if a migrant teacher was part of the staff.

The fourth scale measures the teachers' perceptions of bilingual programs. (For example: "There is a discrepancy between the linguistic minority child's culture and the culture transmitted at school," "School does not take advantage of the linguistic and cultural contributions that parents and children make.") Hispanic teachers with high Spanish language proficiency who were working in bilingual programs had the most favorable perceptions. The interaction effects between ethnicity and work experience, and ethnicity and Spanish proficiency, also proved to be statistically significant. Not surprisingly, teachers who lack knowledge of the students' language and culture find it difficult to understand the role of bilingual programs. When teachers were asked to list the contributions of bilingual programs, teachers in bilingual programs not only were more favorable but also were able to identify specific situations that clearly demonstrated their experience and expertise. These are some examples of teachers' responses.

- "Students identify with the educational process when they see their language and culture as part of the curriculum."
- "Bilingual programs make students feel that their language and culture is valuable; they feel pride instead of shame."
- "Students feel their experiences are worthwhile and are more willing to express themselves."

These comments support postulates that Freire (1985) has posed: (1) Students will learn if schooling is made relevant to them; and (2) Students must be able to relate the academic content that they learn in the classroom to their own life.

The fifth scale assesses teachers' perceptions of the role of bilingual teachers. (For example: "Teachers in bilingual programs help the student in overcoming differences between the home and the school environment," "Teachers have a lot of influence on students' academic achievement.") Ethnicity was the only statistically significant main effect to emerge from the analysis of this scale. Teachers in bilingual programs in this study saw themselves as having the ability to improve their students' experience in the classroom. These results support earlier findings of researchers like Rodríguez (1980) who identified and differentiated the competencies of exemplary bilingual teachers. A very important component is sociocultural knowledge, which teachers demonstrated by actively validating students' language and culture. Similarly, Macías (1984) describes the performance of Papago teachers who were trying to preserve their culture while helping Papago students make the transition into the educational system.

The sixth scale, parent participation, measures the efficacy teachers ascribe to parent participation and teachers' perceptions of linguistic minority parents. (For example: "Parent participation helps lessen the gap between home and school," "Parent participation is essential in the success of bilingual education," "Parents of students in this school don't care if their children obtain low grades.") The results on the parent participation scale clearly show that Hispanic teachers are more favorably inclined toward parent participation than are European American teachers.

The literature on participation indicates that individuals who believe that their involvement will have an impact, will participate more often. Moreover, if parents perceive that teachers value their participation, they will be encouraged to continue participating. Anthropological studies in education underscore the importance of establishing relations between the teacher and the community, especially for the benefit of the lower socioeconomic and minority students (Spindler, 1974). Research in bilingual settings indicates that parent participation seems to offer an effective way of integrating the child's culture in the school (Baca de McNichols, 1977; Quintanar-Sarellana, 1992; Torres, 1983). One of the objectives of bilingual education is to bridge the cultural gap between home and school. A teacher who acknowledges and promotes parent participation is supportive of the basic premises of bilingual education. Understanding the students' language and culture makes it possible for teachers to communicate more effectively with students and parents. Previous research (Baca de McNichols, 1977) has shown that Hispanic teachers are more favorably disposed than European-American teachers toward parent participation. This study corroborates these findings.

Teachers' Comments on Bilingual Programs

Interestingly, teachers in bilingual programs, regardless of their ethnicity, are overwhelmingly in favor of maintenance-type bilingual programs. This corroborates their positive perceptions of bilingualism and biculturalism as a valuable educational goal. Not surprisingly, teachers in English-only programs, on the other hand, support a transitional language approach. Teachers in bilingual programs also wrote comments regarding the disadvantages of bilingual programs. Their comments reflect their perception of a lack of support from the educational system. Their comments were not directed toward bilingual programs as such, but expressed frustration at the fact that little recognition was given to a child for being bilingual. Except for those few who are committed to bilingual education, teachers do not acknowledge the cultural capital of linguistic minority students. The fact that these students are potentially fluent in both English and Spanish is overlooked, and rather than being encouraged for their dual-language competence (Cummins, 1978), they are discouraged or punished for it.

Discussion and Recommendations

An important finding to emerge from this study is that ethnicity alone is not the crucial variable in understanding how teachers perceive and interact with Hispanic students and their parents. We saw from the data that European American respondents who also were high in Spanish language performance scored higher on several of the scales than did the Hispanic teachers with low Spanish proficiency. Specifically, European American teachers with high Spanish language proficiency had a higher mean score than Hispanics with low Spanish proficiency on all of the scales except parent participation and the role of education. This finding demonstrates that Spanish proficiency is a very important factor in the way teachers perceive linguistic minority students and bilingual education.

The same response pattern appeared when the interaction effects of ethnicity and bilingual classroom experience were examined for each scale. European American teachers with bilingual classroom experience expressed more favorable perceptions toward the language and culture of linguistic minority students, bilingual education, and the role of teachers in bilingual classrooms than Hispanics with no bilingual classroom experience. Parent participation and the role of education were the only two scales on which Hispanics with no bilingual classroom experience expressed more positive attitudes than European American teachers with bilingual classroom experience. This finding underscores the importance of two factors: (1) being trained as a bilingual teacher, and (2) daily contact with linguistic minority students, which results in understanding and sharing the students' cultural capital.

As alluded to earlier, the teachers who participated in this study can be placed along the continuum of cultural awareness discussed above. Hispanic teachers in bilingual programs can be categorized as the most culturally aware. These teachers have the highest mean scores on five of the scales. Additionally, the comments these teachers wrote show their understanding of the language and culture of minority students. European American teachers with low Spanish language proficiency and no bilingual classroom experience can be placed at the opposite end of the continuum and described as the most culturally unaware. Their responses to the various items on the questionnaire show that they are largely unaware of the educational value, or cultural capital, that the language and culture of minority students represent.

Implications for Culturally Relevant Teacher Preparation

This study suggests that sociocultural knowledge is a key element in the area of teacher preparation. Sociocultural knowledge includes the understanding teachers have of their own culture as well as appreciation of other cultures and cross-cultural knowledge. The findings in this study show that ethnicity and bilingual classroom experience are important characteristics that influence teachers' perceptions of the language and culture of linguistic minority students. Hispanic teachers and teachers in bilingual programs in this study, regardless of ethnicity, indicated their belief that the cultural capital of minority students should be part of the classroom learning process. These teachers also perceived themselves as mediators between the culture transmitted by the schools and that of linguistic minority students. Moreover, they felt that parent participation was essential in the educational process.

Teachers who either share the same culture as the students or who can speak Spanish can be viewed as linguistic and cultural brokers between linguistic minority children and the school, and thus constitute a valuable asset to the teaching profession. Sometimes minority teachers view their own culture from the perspective of the dominant group, and a "rediscovery of culture" is essential. Some of the teachers' comments in this study made reference to a "rediscovery of my language and culture." Teachers in this study mentioned their failure to consider language and culture as powerful tools for teaching. Several mentioned that their own language and culture had been absent in their educational history, and they are now aware at this stage of their careers of the need to draw on the culture of their students.

Linguistic competence subsumes the basic assumption that teachers must be able to communicate with students in order to transmit knowledge. Teachers should be equipped to investigate and discover other cultures by communicating with their students and their students' parents; they also should be knowledgeable of cultural differences and the importance of their interactions with students and parents. As mentioned earlier, an important finding from this study is that Spanish proficiency is a variable that enhances teachers' understanding of the language and culture of Hispanic students. Thus, the expectation of proficiency in the students' language merits closer scrutiny and consideration. Reinstating foreign language requirements for graduation from high school and college would help prospective teachers understand the experience of learning a second language and might make teachers more cognizant of the cultural capital of linguistic minority students. Accordingly, the findings of this study strongly argue in favor of mandating second language proficiency for teachers in California.

The findings also point clearly to the need to recruit and train Hispanic teachers. The significant effects for ethnicity that emerged show that teachers who share the linguistic and cultural background of students are more likely to hold more favorable attitudes toward the cultural capital of linguistic minority students. Thus, efforts made to identify promising Hispanics and recruit them to the teaching profession are well worth the time and effort involved (Wong & Valadez, 1986; Yzaguirre, 1981).

It is also important to consider how student teachers from different training institutions perceive the language and culture of minority students. Teacher training institutions are implementing different pedagogical models, including culturally relevant or responsive pedagogy. Research that examines student–teacher interactions in culturally diverse classrooms is needed to provide information on the instructional skills teachers trained at different institutions possess (Jackson & Cosca, 1974). Finally, since a high percentage of linguistic minority students come from low-income households, and bilingual teachers frequently come from different social strata, examining the influence of factors such as the socioeconomic status of teachers and students also may shed new light on teacher perceptions and the kind of teacher preparation experiences teachers need.

CONCLUSION

Cultural capital and Freire's theory of education are used in the study described here to analyze the situation that linguistic minority students encounter in school. The chapter emphasizes the need to understand how teachers perceive the role of language and culture in the educational process overall and then specifically in bilingual programs. Increasingly, educators support the position that sharing and understanding the students' cultural capital enable the culturally relevant teacher to communicate and interact more effectively with them. There is a compelling need to systematize and maximize our effort to train teachers for all students in our culturally diverse society.

4

Removing the Mask of Academia
Institutions Collaborating in the Struggle for Equity

VALERIE OOKA PANG, MARY GRESHAM ANDERSON,
AND VICTOR MARTUZA

One warm summer night, a group of about 20 professors sat outside our dormitory talking. We were part of a consortium of 15 colleges/schools of education. All of a sudden Mary, one of the professors, got up and said, "Come on everyone, get up. Let's dance."

Some of us looked around and thought, "But what will my dean think?" However, most of us thought, "Why not?" Mary cranked up her boom box and danced. We probably looked like fools dancing around the pool, with no obvious partner. We didn't care. Then Mary called to everyone, "Come on, get in a circle. I want to show you something."

We all got in a circle, and she sang, "Heah—we go loopty lou. (clap) Heah—we go loopty la. (clap) Heah—we go loopty lou (clap), all on a Saderday night." We joined in and sang with Mary, clapping the rhythm of the song and placing different accents on words than in the traditional version. Mary taught us a southern African American version of the song.

It was an unbelievable sight, university professors shaking all parts of their bodies and turning around just like children and singing in black vernacular. We had a great time, giggling, smiling, and enjoying each other's company.

The story above describes an important element of effective professional development for university professors. Like any other group, they need to feel safe, happy, and validated to be open and flexible. For several participants it was difficult to feel safe in a professionally mixed setting because of their positions as assistant professors. However, in the context of teaching about cultural issues, it is imperative that professors be actively involved in their learning because their cultural orientation may differ from that of others. Learning occurs in a cultural context, and it is important for participants not only to grapple with intellectual and political issues but also to understand that cultural differences include deeply embedded emotional and aesthetic factors. The above example provided the professors with a cultural experience that did not center on an academic issue but rather created a bridge from scholarly understandings to an emotional, creative, and spiritual involvement in the cultural activities of others.

A PROFESSIONAL DEVELOPMENT PROGRAM
FOR PROFESSORS

Creating professional development for university faculty is challenging because professors are socialized to believe they are societal experts in their chosen fields and often wear the mask of omnipotence. Removing that mask is not always easy because it can threaten an individual's security and institutional power. The professor may be a dean who feels it is best not to show her weaknesses to those in her college. Another professor may feel apprehensive about revealing personal beliefs, fearing what others may think of him.

The purpose of this chapter is to explore the questions: "What are the most effective ways to train university professors in the emotionally laden and controversial areas of multicultural and bilingual education?"; "How can institutions be encouraged to form collaborations?"; and "What are the obstacles to structural change in higher education?"

The challenge of providing professional development to 64 professors—assistant professors, associate professors, full professors, chairs, deans, and assistant deans—from 15 institutions was difficult. The 15 institutions, ranging from small private colleges to large land grant research universities, formed a consortium that focused on the infusion of multicultural and bilingual education into teacher education.

The consortium arose from a philosophy that incorporated critical theory (Bowles & Gintis, 1976; Brameld, 1955; Freire, 1970/1968; Giroux, 1988b; Greene, 1993; Luke & Gore, 1992; Sleeter, 1991), the ethics of caring (Noddings, 1992), and a pedagogy of liberation and social justice (Banks & Banks, 1989; Cummins, 1986; Sleeter & Grant, 1987; Trueba, 1989). Professors were presented a wide range of ideologies and allowed a personal choice of philosophies. The goal of the professional development was reflective thought, not indoctrination. The aim of the consortium was to support structural changes in schools and colleges of education for the incorporation of multicultural and bilingual education throughout their teacher education programs. The training focused on institutional policies, organizational structural change, research-based content area strategies for use with English learners and culturally diverse students, and incorporation of multicultural and language acquisition strategies appropriate for preservice and inservice teachers. Professors were continually challenged to clarify their beliefs about issues of race, class, gender, and sexual orientation as they relate to institutional practices and policies, and as these beliefs affect their own teaching. A great deal of discussion centered about Sleeter and Grant's (1987) five approaches to multicultural education and how those approaches would be implemented in a teacher education program.

The groundwork for the consortium was built during professional development seminars where institutions sent teams of three or four professors. The overarching theme was the challenge to become an institution where issues of equity are at the forefront of all aspects of teacher education, such as student admissions, college policies, curriculum, instructional strategies, research, faculty retention, and allocation of resources. Not only did the seminars present content knowledge focusing on culture, language, and cognition; the curriculum also required participants to grapple with issues of equity and social justice. No one wanted to appear racist, sexist, classist, homophobic, or prejudiced against physically and mentally challenged, or religiously different people. The content of the seminars needed to be shaped so that emotions, values, philosophy, and teaching content were addressed during the 2-week training session. During the seminars each university team developed an institutional plan for the implementation of multicultural and bilingual issues into their teacher education programs. In addition, professors reviewed and revised their course syllabi to incorporate issues dealing with the struggle for equity and cultural liberation.

KEY ELEMENTS OF THE PROFESSIONAL DEVELOPMENT PROCESS

We found that most institutions of higher learning are gatekeepers for the status quo and that organizations are slow to change. Issues of equity and culture are complex, and the power structure of colleges and schools is built upon a social hierarchy of exclusion. Although professors of color may be recruited or new books with cultural content added to the bookstore shelves, the power structure remains solidly in place; this structure is based on the legitimacy of the Western construction of knowledge, value orientation, and historical tradition.

Transformative Learning

Change is a complicated process that must have meaning to each individual within the organization (Fullan, 1993). Professional development aimed at helping professors learn about multicultural and bilingual education may require them to change their viewpoints or understandings. Key to this change is professional development that not only attempts to "sensitize" professors to the ugliness and obstacles that oppressive behavior produces, but also explains how the ideology of the dominant majority has been legitimized in educational policies and practices and knowledge construction (McCarthy, 1993). Moreover, many professors need opportunities to discuss how Western hegemony is continually supported. The dominant ideology for many people is painful to examine because they have accepted this orientation not as an alternative, but as the norm. Luke and Gore (1992) discuss this in terms of being patriarchal and sexist.

> The master narratives that have written Truth, Logic, Reason, History, and the Individual to the center of Meaning and the Real, have been constitutive of Anglo-European male experience and "consciousness" at the expense of constructing and positioning negative identities outside the masculine positivity. . . . Universal "man" is a rational impassionate thinker, a builder of civilizations and military strategist, an objective lawmaker and observer, a writer and speaker of doctrine and truth. (p. 207)

The standard for thinking, doing, being, and acting is European, American, and masculine.

Helping professors remove their masks or give up their beliefs was a struggle. Since such change was difficult, we saw it as a long-term process that demanded a safe and accepting environment where trusting relationships could be constructed. Trusting relationships between teacher and student and among students are the building blocks of learning (Noddings, 1992). Like college students, professors responded to a safe, supportive environment in which they could ask questions, try out their ideas without being ridiculed, and validate their worth as people and as professionals. Noddings (1992) believes that the ethic of caring is crucial to great teaching. The environment should be motivating, interesting, and, of course, a caring place where masks can be removed.

The next important component of transformative learning is modeling (Pang, 1994). Professors of education benefited from instructors who modeled good teaching. It was crucial to have instructors who were interesting presenters, cared about their participants, used different strategies, and knew how to motivate their audience to ask questions and share their knowledge about multicultural and bilingual education.

Experiential Learning

A crucial element of the seminar process was to provide professors with numerous opportunities to engage in hands-on, real-world learning, such as the experience described at the beginning of the chapter. Another example of experiential learning occurred when several consultants used languages other than English. Many professors spoke only English and had little affective understanding of the frustration, confusion, and isolation that many students may experience as they struggle to become proficient in English as a second language. Professors need to have a personal point of reference regarding the emotional impact that learning a second language may have on students. As part of the seminars, one instructor used Cantonese and another spoke in Spanish, giving the professors a minute sense of how difficult it is for students who have not mastered English. This scenario also was used to explain how important it is for students of color to know the "culture of power" (Delpit, 1988). It is frustrating to students who may not understand the expectations, language, behaviors, and value system of mainstream teachers. They do not have access to the power structure and the privileged knowledge base of mainstream society, which act as "gatekeepers" to their full participation in society. Such experiential learning fostered understanding of how we as professors can act as "gatekeepers" or advocates for our students.

In other hands-on sessions professors assessed what they were teaching, how they were teaching, and the effectiveness of their teaching. Professors shared their syllabi with each other. They identified important issues, and looked for representation in the readings, instructional strategies, curriculum, and films used in their classes. This set the stage for the continued development of interuniversity collaboration.

Problem-Posing Dialogue

Dialogue was the key instructional strategy for the seminars. It is facilitated by heterogeneous grouping, which redefines the social organization of learning so there is a greater degree of interdependence and respect among participants (Johnson, Johnson, & Smith, 1991; Slavin, 1989/90). In professional development for faculty, about one-half of the time should be devoted to dialogue. Professors seemed to enjoy thoroughly the problem-posing approach to education (Freire, 1970/1968). According to Freire, real learning takes place when people tackle social problems, design solutions, implement the solutions, and re-evaluate their progress. Professors became actively involved in the issues covered, whether the discussions dealt with the resistance of universities to change or affirmative action as a viable aspect of social change. Social problems tackled during the seminars included white privilege (McIntosh, 1989), prejudice in the academy, and cultural learning styles. Other less controversial topics included reviewing approaches to multicultural education (Banks & Banks, 1989; Sleeter & Grant, 1987), the process of language acquisition (Tharp & Gallimore, 1989; Trueba, 1989), and sheltered strategies for content area instruction. The use of an issues-centered approach allowed participants to reflect upon the complexities of equity issues and encouraged the serious examination of personal and professional viewpoints.

Problem-posing education is open-ended and facilitates higher-order thinking. In addition, since each person is seen as having equal status, multiple perspectives are prized and validated. Problem-posing education often requires individuals to examine local problems and use culturally familiar knowledge to create bridges to broader social issues. This approach brings community issues (which may represent intolerance toward culture, ethnic, class, gender, or handicapping conditions) to the forefront. This issues-centered approach does not include indoctrination but supports the standard of equity and social justice as core values in education. Not all perspectives can be agreed upon, especially if opinions do not support cultural diversity or the self-determination of oppressed people.

Dialogue emphasizes collaborative discussion, clarification of values, and group action. When dialogue is central to the training process, a stronger sense of community can be created among participants. Dialogue helped sharpen and clarify seminar participants' thoughts. In addition, it forced them to examine their own values and biases. Many of the decisions we make every day involve competing values. Professors often see themselves as liberal individuals who support the values of social justice and equality. Yet, often they may not have had the chance to see whether their actions in their personal lives are consistent with their ideals. The seminars were constructed so that complex questions were addressed, such as, "What does white privilege look like?" and "How does white privilege impact a person's life chances?" Speakers like Henry Trueba, Christine Sleeter, and Geneva Gay challenged participants to examine the social realities described in Kozol's book *Savage Inequalities* (1991).

Professors needed ample opportunities to examine issues they thought they understood, but had not looked at from a real-life point of view. For example, many professors believed in equal educational opportunity and that all students should have a chance to follow their dreams. Professors also believed that many African American students encountered more obstacles, which led to lower admission and retention rates in college. Most professors believed that educational experiences were enriched when the student population was diverse. Nevertheless, when professors were affected personally, they were unsure whether they supported admissions programs that allowed for a diverse population. Dialogue can assist individuals to seek new ways to look at issues and help them clarify their own positions on complex social issues that impact their personal lives.

Theoretical Frameworks for Learning and Teaching

The curriculum foundation for the seminar was built on four philosophical orientations. Two theoretical frameworks focusing on social reconstructionism and critical theory were presented (Banks & Banks, 1989; Bowles & Gintis, 1976; Brameld, 1955; Cummins, 1986; Gay, 1994; Giroux, 1988a; Greene, 1993; Sleeter, 1991; Sleeter & Grant, 1987). The sociopsychological framework, based on the work of Vygotsky, focused on the cultural context of learning and the importance of relationships within the classroom environment (Tharp & Gallimore, 1989; Trueba, 1989). The fourth framework was Noddings's (1992) moral foundation of caring. With the use of these frameworks, the seminar was shaped to help teacher educators understand that content, instructional pedagogy, and climate form an interconnected whole. These frameworks suggest that learning and teaching involve the creation of a collective consciousness and interconnectedness within a cultural context. That is, students should be prepared to be active participants in our democracy; ultimately, they should be prepared to tackle social problems and work toward the betterment of all citizens.

Theory and Practice

Theory and practice linkages were introduced in the readings, followed by an examination of prejudice reduction at both personal and institutional levels. For example, one article described racism in young children and the racist behavior of their teachers (Pang, 1988). Pang's vignettes emphasize why prejudice reduction is important in our daily school lives. Another reading not only asked teachers to understand and validate the real-world experience of children but also described how a teacher's cultural ignorance can destroy a culturally different child's trust in schools (Lake, 1990). After reading an article by Reyes and Halcon (1988) professors discussed institutional racism. The article describes the way academy members devalue the college degrees, research, and specializations of their colleagues of color, often challenging or even rejecting research exploring equity issues as meritless. Speakers used videos depicting their research projects in schools to bridge theory and practice. Shirley Brice Heath, a consultant, brought relevancy to the training by addressing issues of exclusion and equity in an elementary education research project. Heath described a cross-age tutoring program in which fifth-grade Latina girls tutored first-grade students in reading (Heath & Mangiola, 1991). The younger children's improved reading ability was impressive, and the fifth-grade tutors increased not only their reading skills but their self-esteem as well.

Visits to culturally diverse communities brought further relevance to the seminar. Unfortunately, this snapshot view of culture can serve only as an initial introduction to a community of color. Professors must become involved with culturally diverse communities in their cities. It is through personal contact that professors can develop a comprehensive understanding of deeper aspects of culture such as family relationships, language development, education, gender roles, and social, economic, and political status.

Trusting Relationships

Creating trusting relationships among participants was key to the seminar's success; participants did not always agree but it was essential that they were willing to hear and respond to other points of view. Unfortunately, the structure of the tenure and promotion process acted as a barrier to open discussion; assistant professors were reluctant to express views that conflicted with their deans' views. We found the hierarchical nature of higher education to be antithetical to the goals of an inclusive and culturally diverse community of learners. Although the goal of the seminar was to empower professors to become actively involved in the struggle for equity, honest discussion was not possible because of professors' unwillingness to put aside their titles or power.

VOICES OF PARTICIPANTS

The following two sections provide views from two consortium participants. The first profile was written by a white professor with almost 25 years in teacher education and extensive experience in global education. The second profile was written by a professor of color with a background in issues of equity.

A Teacher Education Professor: Reflections and Changes

Like many undergraduate teacher education programs across the country, ours has been slow to respond to the changing demands and challenges created by recent demographic trends and the steadily increasing cultural diversity they have produced. More often than not, meaningful curricular change occurs only when the "writing on the wall" becomes so salient that it can no longer be ignored. In our case, this came in the form of a state-level change in certification requirements that mandated a three-unit multicultural course for all students in the secondary teacher education program. Although a similar requirement was not set for the elementary teacher education program, the inevitability of such an action seems undeniable.

As a result, the faculty responded by deciding to recast its "School and Society" and "Sociological Foundations of Education" courses into multicultural offerings. These courses became the cornerstone for change within the college. I restructured the foundations course—my primary teaching responsibility—around the issue of culture. My students examine the meaning of culture and the influence it has on (1) how we regard ourselves and others; (2) what we believe and value; (3) how we feel; and (4) how we construct our version of reality, with particular attention to the role of schooling in the cultural socialization process. My syllabus also focuses on issues of power, marginalization, equity, cultural diversity, and prejudice.

I created a case-based course that clearly bears the footprint of my experiences in the consortium. The course is highly interactive and encourages students to become involved in a community with which they may be unfamiliar. Using critical pedagogy and social reconstructionism as the frameworks for the course, I utilize discussion rather than lecturing as the major instructional strategy. The case-based teaching approach uses ethnographic or narrative selections based on real events that stimulate discussion. In addition, I use videotapes, small-group discussions and whole-group debriefings, and a portfolio-based grading procedure, which requires students to submit a book review, a film review, a cultural plunge report, and a detailed account of a 20-hour public service activity.

Every semester preservice teachers participate in two different service learning activities. Many students connect with inner-city schools to provide tutoring, mentoring, and other services. In addition, they visit international organizations, effective schools, and culturally diverse communities. The preservice teachers experience intellectual growth and affective changes, which are reinforced by selected readings that discuss prejudice in the classroom (Pang, 1988), cultural knowledge (Lake, 1990), and African American language (Williams, 1991).

My involvement in the consortium provided a great deal of new information, ideas, theoretical insights, and practical experiences. Guest experts addressed a wide variety of diversity issues (e.g., language proficiency, juvenile gangs, and critical pedagogy). The formal program contributed greatly to my course revision project.

Perhaps of greater value, however, was the informal component. This consisted of spontaneous gatherings where we voiced our dissatisfactions (e.g., about the rigid daily schedule), chewed on the meaty ideas the presenters liberally dispensed, and talked about our personal goals and frustrations. The informal interactions helped me integrate the new and the old, get a clearer picture of the peaks and valleys of my knowledge base, and discover the rich knowledge of my colleagues who had been laboring in the multicultural vineyard much longer than I.

As a member of an institutional team, we wrote a mini-grant and conducted extensive literature searches, purchased materials, and sponsored a faculty multicultural and bilingual education workshop. As a result of these efforts, participating faculty in these areas are considering ways of infusing a multicultural dimension into existing courses as well as creating new courses to address content-specific diversity issues. Discussions have progressed from rhetoric to action. Colleagues are more willing to enter into dialogues about sensitive issues, and there has been a conscious attempt to focus on effective practice. In addition, we hosted a weekend conference for other teams within our region. Six university teams made an agreement to explore ways of collaborating in curriculum development and an international exchange program. The consortium has contributed to course revisions at my university as well as to the creation of a regional consortium that will continue to facilitate interinstitutional collaborative efforts.

A Professor of Color: Experiencing the Difference

Cultural plurality exists on the planet Earth. Unfortunately, professional efforts to accept and respect the reality of human diversity often have served to deter rather than facilitate the achievement of a socially valued multicultural society. During multicultural training sessions, college and university professionals are expected to collaborate to change monocultural policies and practices through professional development efforts. When professionals themselves dismiss, ignore, deny, or reject ways of knowing and living that are different from their own cultural views, they also are sabotaging their own efforts to empower each other to serve as change agents within university settings. Consequently, relationships between professional efforts and personal, cultural worldviews directly influence outcomes that too often reflect a lack of authentic institutional change. The following discussion, however, illuminates the unexpected impact of a professional multicultural training effort on my professional development, my ability to survive within a university setting, and my understanding of the fundamental need to ground multicultural education preparation in real-world views.

My participation in the consortium seminar was hindered by predetermined standards for behavior and expectations of involvement. When I recognized that I was expected to play a passive rather than an active role in the learning process, my first reaction was to challenge the premise upon which the seminar was established. It was difficult for me to understand how a seminar, designed to encourage multiple views and listen to multiple voices that represent cultural plurality, could be so restrictive. When I suggested examining the oppressive structure of the seminar, I was extremely surprised by the anger, hostility, and personal rejection I felt from some colleagues.

Although initially I regretted my decision to participate in the seminar and consortium, the personal and professional relationships that developed during this process proved to be invaluable. Living together in close quarters facilitated informal discussions about individual strengths, concerns, and expectations. The sharing phenomena created a bonding reality that transcended my skepticism about possible benefits. Genuine interpersonal relationships were not promoted explicitly during the formal seminar sessions; we sought and maintained these relationships as individuals because of our personal need to connect with each other around common issues of concern, professional growth, and survival. Many of the participants were junior faculty who were concerned about the tenure process. These sincere relationships helped to empower us to achieve our professional goals. The excitement and the joys of these efforts greatly outweighed the negative aspects of the seminar and consortium.

I believe that professional development means professional enhancement, which implies some level of individual or group change. As professors acquire skills and competencies that facilitate their roles as change agents, the benefits gained from professional development experiences are expected to influence the direction and nature of institutional change. Unfortunately, too many professional environments are themselves based on the premise that those invited to participate in the learning process bring an inadequate or deficient knowledge base with them. When program planners structure workshops, institutes, or inservices in the name of professional development, they promote traditional "expert–novice" classroom interactions, rather than the sharing of professional expertise. A fundamental flaw of this expert–novice approach is that the professional's role as novice is problematic. The novice position places participants in a situation of powerlessness rather than empowerment.

Usually, the expert expects the novice to be receptive to the new information and incorporate the acquired content into future individual and professional endeavors. Hence, the results of such professional development efforts have little to do with the development of change agents and more to do with the maintenance of traditional models of knowledge access, knowledge creation, and knowledge use. Consequently, traditionally administered professional development efforts often leave the novices less empowered to initiate, influence, or support authentic institutional change than they were *before* the training experience.

Within large- and small-group sessions, professors shared cultural perspectives that differed from those of their peers. For example, one participant explained how Asian Pacific Americans perceive the painted yellow faces in the picture book, *The Five Chinese Brothers* (Bishop, 1938), as derogatory and discriminatory. Another participant, whose first language is Spanish, explained her thinking process for translating and using English as a second language. Participants appreciated learning about rhythmic patterns and tonal changes in African American dialects through my reading of a picture book about the jazz musician, Charlie Parker (Raschka, 1992). These professional exchanges brought new ways of understanding how educational barriers affect learning. The multiple perspectives shared were critical for redefining what teacher educators concerned with establishing an inclusive, pluralistic society needed to know. Consequently, participants were empowered to think and respond differently to the ideas presented and discussed within a sensitive, safe, and accepting climate of interaction.

Reflections on the Voices of Participants

The reactions of the two professors indicate the difficulty of addressing institutional change. Although each university team includes a college administrator, the process of dialogue and change is a long-term one. The overall structure of higher education often impedes honest discussions about issues of oppression and culture. Although the goals of individuals and institutions may be admirable, it was apparent that real change was not understood or embraced by many participants. Problem-posing education, since it is not indoctrinating, takes a great deal of dialogue and reflection. A 2-week foundational seminar was not enough time to put new structures in place. The two participants whose voices we heard have indicated that although many individuals made minor adjustments in their thinking and some made serious revisions in their teacher education courses, institutional change was minimal.

OBSTACLES TO THE PROFESSIONAL
DEVELOPMENT SEMINAR

There were many successes in the professional development seminar but there were also many disappointments. Discussions with deans and teacher education directors emphasized the importance of organizational change that would support cultural diversity and equity. Although we found that the masks of individual professors could be lowered, and many were willing to infuse bilingual and multicultural content into their courses, their institutions were slow to move forward.

Institutional Power Structure

The institutional power structure and academic hierarchy can pose substantial obstacles to successful collaboration. All the institutions represented in the seminar used the historical tenure and promotion process and ranks of assistant, associate, and full professor. Each institution was asked to send a team of approximately four people who would be responsible for creating an institutional plan for change. The team was to include a dean, assistant dean, or director of teacher education. Since deans, chairs, and other administrators were members of various teams, the consortium gained important administrative support for institutional change. On the other hand, this prevented junior faculty from giving honest views and challenging the comments of those in higher positions. This obstacle, which was never addressed by the entire group, crippled the seminar process. Administrators were reluctant to provide too much direction in the creation of the team plan. In order for other faculty at the institution to agree, it had to be a "bottom up" effort, said one assistant dean. He was concerned that this consortium would be seen as another attempt by administrators to push faculty into a program they had not chosen.

Conflicting Expectations

The training program could not fulfill the goal of every participant. The administrators came to the training for different reasons. Some deans were interested in promoting multicultural and bilingual issues in their colleges and felt that this training program provided their faculty the opportunity to receive professional development from a federally sponsored project. One dean felt that it gave her faculty a chance to develop a multicultural literacy project because the professors came together for an extended period of time to organize a new class. Some of the administrators felt that their attendance enhanced the perception of their work by their faculty as being culturally aware and supportive of equity.

Professors also had various reasons for attending the professional development program. Some wanted the chance to share ideas with national experts and clarify their thinking about complicated cultural issues. Others thought a trip to southern California would be a great way to get in some swimming, golfing, and good eating. Still other faculty wanted to appear to be team players within their university setting to influence future promotion, tenure, or other opportunities. Some professors were hoping that attending this program would help to push their colleges toward real change.

Changing Ways of Thinking

The most difficult obstacle of any professional development regarding multicultural and bilingual education is challenging individuals and institutional leaders to change their way of thinking. Most institutions are designed to support the status quo and not to encourage change. Coupled with the impact of both covert and overt forms of prejudice, changes on both an institutional and a personal level are extremely difficult. The most challenging obstacle was dealing with people and institutions and their unwillingness to look at attitudes and practices that may act as gatekeepers to the inclusion of culturally diverse people. Such inclusion may take the form of changing admissions policies, incorporating a socioethnic requirement for teacher educators, and providing financial resources for research centering on students of color.

Cultural Dimensions

Many professors did not understand the impact of culture on the learning process. Since many were European American, the professors generally did not have the opportunity to examine the impact of culture on their own lives. This posed problems in assisting professors to understand how culture is a mediator of worldview. However, some of the participants understood the "culture of silence" in an academic setting. Most participants accepted the hierarchy of positional power and did not feel comfortable challenging it. When faculty felt disempowered to speak up for fear of losing possible points for promotion, they were willing participants in this system. Professors who challenged the status quo were often seen as overly sensitive or aggressive, not as individuals who were struggling to remove the mask of oppression in the academy. The culture of silence was pervasive throughout the consortium.

OUTCOMES OF THIS PROFESSIONAL
DEVELOPMENT PROGRAM

Differences of race, class, gender, religion, handicapping conditions, and sexual orientation do matter in the United States. The consortium of 15 institutions provided individuals and colleges and schools of education the opportunity to begin or to continue their efforts at integrating cultural diversity issues into their teacher education programs. The primary focus was to assist professors in personal and professional change. The 2-week foundational professional development seminar allowed faculty time for personal reflection, opportunities for dialogue with peers, and the chance to create relationships with colleagues from other institutions.

Professors have shown in their syllabi and through discussions that they now include a more comprehensive selection of readings dealing with race, class, gender, sexual orientation, and handicapping conditions in their classes. In addition, professors have added activities that engage students in community outreach. Some financial and human resources, which may not have been available in the past, are being directed toward preparing teachers for a culturally diverse society and world in many colleges and schools of education. Unfortunately, little institutional change occurred in most institutions. Without administrative support for multicultural research and the infusion of bilingual issues into courses and community projects, coupled with consideration of these issues in the tenure and promotion process, the system remains static.

Informal Networking

Nevertheless, one of the most important outcomes of the professional development program was the informal network. More in-depth learning took place after class, during meals, and in the evening than in the formal lecture sessions. The experience of living together for 2 weeks gave participants many opportunities to build trusting relationships, and dialogue developed naturally. The sharing was sincere and genuine rather than contrived and forced. Many found that they could remove their masks and let the real person come through.

Interinstitutional Collaboration

The seminar promoted collaborations between institutions and among individual team members. For example, the 3-day regional conference that one team hosted for six other institutions one year after the initial seminar served to extend and continue the dialogue of the foundational seminar. During this regional conference professors shared reading materials and syllabi, and discussed issues ranging from Afrocentric curriculum to the weaknesses of critical theory.

Interinstitutional connections between individual members of different university teams also arose and promoted continuing professional development and interuniversity collaboration. A group of professors from three different institutions presented, at the American Educational Research Association's annual meeting, their collaborative study on the ethics of conducting research in the African American community. Other professors contributed to a consortium newsletter that announced planned activities of the consortium and also included articles written by members. In addition, a Publications Committee was formed and a monograph of teacher education articles is in progress.

Institutional and Personal Bias and Identity

One of the most persistent challenges we found was dealing with personal and institutional racism. Professors often commented that they were not racist because they believed in equal educational opportunity for all students. Most professors skirted around issues of personal prejudice and institutional exclusion; they were reluctant to talk about their feelings, fearing they might be seen as closed-minded. The complex interplay of personal prejudice, institutional culture, and the sociocultural belief in the superiority of professionals with advanced degrees formed a large psychological wall for some professors.

When people have the opportunity to discuss their fears in safe and accepting environments they are more able to see their biases and then move beyond them. Several professors who came to new understandings about racism initially were embarrassed that they had not identified their prejudices prior to the seminar. They had a better sense of how racism and classism dehumanize people and treat victims as the cause of our social problems.

Personal prejudice is difficult to challenge because of the different ways people define themselves. European American professors were unable to see themselves as part of a collective. Although most professors from culturally diverse groups, like African Americans, Pilipino Americans, Puerto Rican Americans, and Mexican Americans, felt an association with an ethnic group or knew that others categorized them as being from a community of color, most European American professors had not dealt with their ethnic identity or involuntary membership. Some would say, "But I'm an American. I don't see myself as Irish." Others would comment, "I'm a mutt. I don't know what ethnic group I should be identifying with. I'm an American." This is not an unusual reaction.

Scheurich (1993) observed that European American professors believe prejudice is alive and well in the university community, yet they feel personally detached from acts of discrimination. European American professors believe that racism represents acts carried out by individuals, not by groups. Furthermore, they have difficulty seeing themselves as part of a collective. Since racist acts are perpetrated by individuals and not by any conspiracy on the part of a community, racism cannot be charged to the white collective. When European Americans perceive racism in this way, as acts of individuals, and do not feel that they are part of a racial group or understand how they label others as members of racial groups, then they do not perceive any responsibilities for eradicating racism. As Scheurich (1993) further explained:

> We Whites, however, experience ourselves as nonracialized individuals. . . . We do not experience ourselves as defined by our skin color. We especially do not experience ourselves as defined by another race's actions and attitudes toward us because of our skin color. (p. 6)

The issue of entitlement is difficult for members of the dominant group to understand. If professors continue to refuse to see their own racism and the racism of institutions, equity in higher education and schools will not be possible.

Racism and other kinds of oppression are not easy topics to face and resolve. The struggle for equity is a long journey. As West (1993) has observed:

> To engage in serious discussion of race in America, we must begin not with the problems of black people but with the flaws of American society—flaws rooted in historic inequalities and long-standing cultural stereotypes. How we set up the terms for discussing racial issues shapes our perception and responses to these issues. White America has been historically weak-willed in accepting the humanity of blacks. (pp. 3–4)

Continued dialogue regarding issues such as racism, sexism, classism, and other areas of difference is extremely crucial for change to occur. The focus for these changes needs to include the attitudes, knowledge, and practices of individual teacher educators, for it is only through deep reflection that change in institutions will occur.

CONCLUSION

Although it is possible to create programs that "sensitize" professors to the need for cultural literacy, the basic structure of universities remains largely dominated by Western thought and an entrenched system of control. The hierarchical nature of higher education is thus an enormous obstacle to real change. The mask of control and power exercised by administrators must be removed to advance systemic reform in teacher preparation. We need leaders who have deep ethical convictions and the moral courage to move forward in the face of oppressive conditions. They must be willing to risk questioning, isolation, animosity, and hostility from others. Movement toward a socially just, transformed society in which marginalized groups are included within an expanded definition of community (Greene, 1993) is a slow process that will not occur without grave pain. The struggle is a difficult one.

Explicating Theory: Processes and Parameters for Redesigning Teacher Preparation for Diversity

In Part II critical attention is focused on theory related to processes that transform teacher preparation practice. As in Part I of this volume, the three chapters in this section address individually, and in an holistic fashion, the theoretical underpinnings for redesigning two important parameters of teacher preparation: how preservice teachers gain knowledge of the lives of diverse others, and how to enable them to incorporate this understanding into their pedagogy.

In Chapter 5, "Preparing Teachers for Tomorrow's Children: Cross-Cultural Training for Teachers," Darlene Eleanor York reviews the literature, including theories, methodologies, and models of cross-cultural training for teachers. This chapter analyzes these training models and organizes the diverse body of research in order to draw conclusions about common findings in anthropology, psychology, and intercultural communications. The difficulties of teaching culturally diverse students, designing cross-cultural programs to enhance pedagogical effectiveness, and establishing standards both between and among programs are reflected in the diversity of models and methods that have evolved. Chapter 5 also addresses ethical questions related to cultural conflict and cultural relativism and offers suggestions for resolving these concomitant problems.

Cynthia B. Dillard, in Chapter 6, emphasizes the importance of another parameter for redesigning teacher preparation for diversity: "Placing Student Language, Literacy, and Culture at the Center of Teacher Education Reform." This chapter is a critical examination of competing theoretical orientations and, in contrast to conservative calls for education reform, recommends including the voices of women and people of color. Chapter 6 explicates several instructional strategies that facilitate teacher development along these lines, such as dialogical teaching, critical literacy, ethnographic inquiry and cross-cultural communications, and interdisciplinary and participatory learning approaches. Dillard's notion of centering students responds to a central concern of several authors in Part I, the lack of mutuality and respect in the relation between teacher educators and their students, which contributes to dominating practices in teacher education.

Chapter 7, entitled "Directed Inquiry in Preservice Teacher Education: A Developmental Process Model," further explicates the theoretical possibilities and practical exigencies of redesigning teacher preparation. The process model that Etta R. Hollins delineates is based on research and theory in the literature on "learning-to-teach." This model engages preservice teachers in several processes: directed inquiry, examining the centrality of culture in school learning, and constructing what Hollins defines as an *operating knowledge base* for "productive classroom practices." Hollins addresses the theoretical underpinnings of each of these processes. This process model operationalizes Dillard's emphasis on centering students' learning in their own experience: It constitutes a structured, theoretically grounded, developmental process for acquiring cross-cultural competence and culture-centered knowledge that is directly related to teaching and avoids some of the pitfalls identified in York's chapter.

Chapters 5 and 6 reflect the balance that is maintained throughout this volume between larger, social-contextual issues—whether related to theorizing, models of intervention, or calls for reform of education—and specific processes and problems of practice involved in the redesign of teacher preparation. The emphasis on *processes* in Chapter 7 is another recurring concern in this volume. The model program and practices presented in other chapters represent integrated, holistic approaches to the redesign of teacher preparation programs, not single courses or curricula. Finally, Part II provides support for another concern of this volume: An important outcome of the redesign of teacher preparation is not just to enable preservice teachers to learn about the diversity of others but to change schools.

5

Preparing Teachers for Tomorrow's Children
Cross-Cultural Training for Teachers

DARLENE ELEANOR YORK

The emphasis on excellence in education coexists with a widening gap between white and non-white academic performance (Center for Education Statistics [CES], 1987; Jencks, 1988; National Assessment of Educational Progress [NAEP], 1985; National Center for Education Statistics [NCES], 1989). At the same time, federal, state, and institutional remedies for the problems of minority education have been directed primarily toward the treatment of students rather than the training of teachers. Teachers who enter the teaching profession with few or no cross-cultural experiences and who receive little or no cross-cultural preservice training demonstrate high levels of antagonism and bias (Law & Lane, 1987), inadequate knowledge of other cultures (Yao, 1985), and a lack of pedagogical preparedness (Irvine, 1990; Sleeter, 1989), and experience culture shock (LeCompte, 1985).

Determining whether cross-cultural teacher training is an effective method to prepare teachers for culturally diverse classrooms centers around two fundamental questions: (1) Can a particular training method be designed, developed, extrapolated, and evaluated to supersede cultural differences within schools, thus allowing "equal opportunity" for effective cross-cultural teaching performance among all preservice teachers? (2) Can a particular standard of cross-cultural teaching performance be defined and measured to supersede differences in cross-cultural training programs?

Theory and Research on Culture in Classrooms

Historically, questions about culture have been problematic in education. For example, the theory of cultural relativity—still somewhat troublesome within the field of anthropology—continues to raise philosophical questions within education (Stocking, 1968). Cultural relativity assumes that the ways people experience the world, act within it, and give meaning to life depend on culturally conditioned cognitive, affective, and behavioral processes, including the linguistic modalities that shape discourse (Hall, 1973). If teachers' and students' "ways of knowing" are culture-bound (and if the culture of teachers and students differs), then there is no way of knowing what is "true," since to determine truth we can each invoke nothing but our own cultural standards. The immigrant student who explains disease as the work of demons appeals to a culturally defined, relative standard for truth that differs in kind, but not in philosophical authority, from the majority culture science teacher who explains disease as cell dysfunction (Hatch, 1983; Phillips, 1984). Ways of interpreting experiences and events in learning—of knowing which is the "true" explanation—are not merely inappropriate, they are impossible, for there exists no standard for validity. Thus, one difficulty with cultural relativity among culturally different teachers and students is the relativity of knowledge, particularly when each knows a very different "truth."

A second difficulty surrounds the determination of what is good, what should be, what ought to be. Moral injunctions are endemic in all human societies. Each culture values and rewards certain beliefs and behaviors, and censures and punishes others. These are not privately held opinions about the nature of right and wrong; these operate as public sanctions. A difficulty arises when the moral and ethical systems of cultures clash, since none can appeal to an absolute standard. Cultures display and honor certain values and not others. Yet in classrooms, where the teacher serves as moral mediator who must define and enforce a moral code—as well as suppress violations against it—which code to use in a culturally diverse classroom can prove to be a difficult choice. In daily classroom interactions involving cheating, giving students a fair chance to participate, taking turns, and settling disputes, social and cultural privileges may be accorded to students whose cultural values are most congruent with the teacher's code. Others, whose cultural values may be disregarded or ignored, not only may be confused by a new set of values they neither embrace nor understand but also may be shunned by teachers and peers who believe that "goodness" in behavior and thinking should be axiomatic. Even more compelling is a teacher's call for the tolerance of diverse values and perspectives. Such a call may impose a moral standard antithetical to that of the child's native culture (Howell, 1981).

Finally, if cultures are relative and contextually defined, then it may be difficult to make generalizations about different human societies—even different schools and classrooms across cultures. It could be argued that cross-cultural training for teachers must be conceptualized and conducted on a culture-by-culture, perhaps even a school-by-school, basis. On the other hand, the concept of the teacher as a cultural mediator—who can shift between and among cultures easily and effectively—may provide a more suitable paradigm for training.

Research on the effects of cultural difference and teaching effectiveness is difficult to conduct. In addition to the philosophical difficulties discussed above, methodological problems exist as well. Researchers often fail to stipulate in advance the precise role of culture, thus undermining the validity of *post hoc* explanations. For example, intercultural communication theorists study communication events, with the "level of interculturalness" functioning as an intervening variable between communicators, such as a teacher and student (Sarbaugh, 1988, p. 37). However, this research requires *a priori definitions* of cultural differences and predictions of communicative behavior relative to the magnitude of the differences. A misidentification or overgeneralization of cultural difference provides a poor predictor of intercultural communication competence (Collier & Thomas, 1988). In contrast, cross-cultural psychology theorists assume that culturally different teachers and students operate from mismatched conceptual references: Culture then serves as an independent variable. This concept, however, is difficult to generalize since social status, gender, personality attributes, or social class may intervene or interact with culture to detract from or magnify the cultural differences (Kagitcibasi & Berry, 1989). Finally, cultural congruence theorists, who emphasize a view that is hospitable to cultural constructivism, have difficulty separating "culturally congruent" teaching behaviors from other appropriate teaching behaviors (such as the use of a repertoire of instructional styles) and substantiating a claim that children whose teachers exhibit culturally sensitive behaviors have more positive educational experiences than those whose teachers do not (Kleinfeld, McDiarmid, Grubis, & Parrett, 1983).

Because culture is unquestionably a multidimensional variable, it further becomes important in cultural research in schools that cultural subcomponents be particularized so that the significance of cultural effects can be clearly substantiated. Beyond the difficult process of defining culture as a variable, the specific cultural dimensions under examination (such as participation structures) must be operationalized if relationships and variations are to be measured. Otherwise, although culture may be specified as an independent variable, poor conceptualization and measurement techniques may reduce culture to a residual variable.

Finally, the measurement and interpretation of effects are problematic. Defining educational "benefit" through a myopic cultural lens is clearly unacceptable, yet some standard for successful change must be established. If change requires the relinquishment of specific cultural norms and values— for example, if children whose native culture values cooperation rather than competition are taught to be competitive in schools—then the cultural consequences may be profound and unintended. Although somewhat abstruse, these difficulties with culture research not only influence current scholarship, but affect cross-cultural teacher training programs as well.

CROSS-CULTURAL TEACHER TRAINING MODELS

Cross-cultural training, in education as well as in other fields, begins with two fundamental assumptions: (1) that people living and working in one culture have difficulties when they enter another culture; and (2) that proper cognitive, affective, or behavioral training (or some combination of the three) can ameliorate the difficulty (Landis & Brislin, 1983). The knowledge base for training is derived from analyses of research concerning the difficulties experienced by cultural sojourners (those who leave one culture to enter another). Researchers outside the field of education have sought to do the following to enhance cross-cultural training:

1. Identify degrees of cultural strangeness among people whose worldviews, values, or languages differ (Sarbaugh, 1988)
2. Generate models of cross-cultural adaptation (Adler, 1981; Church, 1982; Gullahorn & Gullahorn, 1963; Rhinesmith, 1975)
3. Specify research paradigms appropriate to cross-cultural studies (Kim, 1988)
4. Develop theories to explain cross-cultural conflict, identity, behavior, and adaptation

Despite these efforts, there is far from universal agreement among educational researchers about the need for preparatory training for teachers or the type of training that should be administered. This lacuna exists in part because of the theoretical and methodological difficulties discussed earlier and because of the difficulty of defining cross-cultural teaching effectiveness in the classroom. However, Mahan (1984), and more recently York (1993), have attempted to specify differences in outcomes between conventional teacher training and cross-cultural teacher training. At this relatively early stage of educational research, however, it is unclear whether the training should generalize among cultures or be confined to specific cultures, and whether the training should be composed of a combination of cognitive, affective, and behavioral training (and, if so, in what degree) or emphasize one or two components.

The literature on cross-cultural teacher training reveals five models that are used: (1) the social exchange model; (2) the intellectual model; (3) the awareness model; (4) the interactionist model; and (5) the environmental training model. A description of each model will be given and, when sufficient data exist to answer them, four questions about each model will be explored.

1. Does the training prepare teachers for entry into one particular culture (culture-specific training) or into any cross-cultural context (culture-general training)?
2. What are the goals of the training? What changes does the program emphasize in trainees? How are these changes defined and measured?
3. What are the outcomes of the training?
4. What are the strengths and limitations of the model?

The Social Exchange Model

Sometimes referred to as "cognitive-behavior modification training" (Landis & Brislin, 1983), the social exchange model uses the principles of behaviorism and behavior modification and applies them to aid in cultural adjustment. This frequently operates in one of two ways. First, elements of operant conditioning can be used in some social context. For example, in a study outside the field of education, subjects were asked to identify which aspects of their own culture they found most pleasurable (positive reinforcement) and which most disagreeable (negative reinforcement) (David, 1972). These were then analyzed culturally until another culture tending to emphasize and downplay similar aspects of life could be found. For example, a man who enjoys American football may equally enjoy watching a soccer tournament in another country. In multinational corporate overseas transfers, cultural "equations" may be tested to match domestic employees with foreign cultures (Befus, 1988; Grove & Torbiorn, 1985). Matching teachers to children's cultures, though possible, remains untested. However, another aspect of behaviorism, social exchange theory, can be used.

Social exchange theory differs from operant conditioning in that an individual's interactions within a culture are measured during encounters with other individuals rather than in nonpersonal or group contexts. Social exchange theory posits that individuals will measure the potential "profit" from individual cross-cultural encounters, will seek to increase the profit margin if possible, and will disregard or avoid exchanges when the "cost" is too high (Thibaut & Kelley, 1959). When the profit-and-loss equation is imbalanced, the law of equity (Blau, 1964) or the law of distributive justice (Homans, 1974) demands that the offended individual seek redress or terminate the exchange.

This kind of training has been used with teachers to help them maintain a positive margin of interaction with culturally different students. Teachers are taught, for example, to gain desired responses from minority students (Pedersen, 1984; Wendt, 1984) and to utilize shame, guilt, and "sarcasm with good will" (Paulson, 1980, p. 25) to control the behavior of minority children. While reliance on these kinds of techniques may require only brief and inexpensive training, this training can be used unethically. For example, if teachers are taught only to recognize a positive profit margin for themselves in every encounter with minority students, it is possible that the treatment of those students may become coercive, manipulative, and insensitive. Such training does not focus on the climate of exchange between teacher and student, nor does it take into account the "profit margins" for children who are required to attend school and are assigned to a particular teacher. Furthermore, research on the effectiveness of this method requires both sufficient knowledge of a particular culture and the measurement of training effects within the actual cross-cultural context—a step rarely, if ever, taken in cross-cultural teacher training research.

The Intellectual Model

Also called the "university model" (Harrison & Hopkins, 1967) and "information or fact-oriented training" (Landis & Brislin, 1983), this model has dominated cross-cultural training in many occupational fields, including education. Predicated on the assumption that learning about a culture equips the trainee to live and work in that culture, a number of reasons account for this model's popularity. It (1) offers the trainee a breadth of knowledge, although it is culture-specific in nature; (2) requires minimal staffing; (3) addresses the trainee's need to "know" about a culture; (4) is transmitted in a classroom setting that is comfortable and familiar to teacher candidates; and finally (5) is rooted in cognitive theory. This theory stresses that mental processes (e.g., ideas, knowledge, perceptions, and attitudes) are determinants of behavior, and it assumes that increased knowledge is linked to maturation processes that direct social actions (Bandura, 1977).

Some disagreement exists in education about what specific knowledge should be imparted to teacher candidates who will enter cross-cultural classrooms. Researchers have selected (1) social and historical information (Barker, 1986; Byram, 1988; Cere, 1988; Chu & Levy, 1988; James, 1980; Sims, 1983); (2) cross-cultural sensitivity, conflict, and assimilation theory and information (Boyer, 1983; Chu & Levy, 1988; Lieberman, Kosokoff, & Kosokoff, 1989; Thiagarajan, 1988); (3) information about specific cultural patterns of thought and behavior (Allameh, 1986; Bickel, 1985; Cere, 1988; Donmall, 1985; Johnson, 1983; McKenzie & Ross, 1989; Singer, 1988); and (4) culturally derived instructional and evaluation strategies to use with minority children (Bell, 1986; Boyer, 1983; Byram, 1988; Dege, 1981; Knight, 1981; Rivers, 1988; Simpson & Galbo, 1986; Singer, 1988). Generally, the inclusion of social and historical information is found uniformly throughout this literature; other information selected seems to originate from personal preferences, except for that cited in Chu and Levy (1988).

The limitations of this model stem from the incongruence between the classroom learning environment and the work environment. There is reasonable consensus among teacher educators that academic success among preservice teachers does not necessarily produce effective teachers. This same inability to translate increased knowledge into improved teaching performance exists with inservice teachers who are provided with information-oriented, cross-cultural training (Yao, 1985).

Another approach that shares the theoretical base and general goal of information-oriented training is the cultural assimilator, which consists of a collection of vignettes representing culturally ambiguous events. An example of such an event would be a culturally conditioned practice of averting one's eyes in certain situations, which in some cultures might be interpreted as a sign of respect, and in others, as a sign of disinterest. In this exercise, the respondent (trainee) uses a paper-and-pencil method that requires consistent participation (Albert & Adamopoulos, 1980; Triandis, 1990). In the 2- to 5-hour training session, the trainee reads each incident, chooses among several "explanations" of the event, and checks which explanation is appropriate in the culture under examination. The initial goal is purely cognitive: to help the trainee develop ways of perceiving events as they are perceived in the new culture. The assimilator has been used somewhat infrequently in education in recent years, perhaps because of the difficulty of validating each vignette (Cushner & Brislin, 1986; Davidson, Hansford, & Moriarty, 1983; English, 1980; Kramsch, 1981; Lambert, 1989). Furthermore, although Cushner and Brislin (1986) and English (1980) report positive results from using the assimilator—including increases in cross-cultural understanding, increases in desire for cross-cultural encounters, and increases in sensitivity to minority students—the results are self-reported by participants and tend to be gathered immediately after training rather than during actual cross-cultural interaction. This means that the cultural assimilator tends to be used largely within the familiar environment of the academic classroom where trainees encounter no real person or situation from another culture.

The Awareness Model

A radical departure from the social exchange and intellectual models is the "human relations" or "cultural awareness" model of cross-cultural training (Landis & Brislin, 1983). Arising from the popular T-groups of the 1960s, the awareness model has been used extensively in many different kinds of occupational and social groups. Freudian psychoanalytic theory, which assumes that unconscious or subconscious states of mind determine behavior, underlies the concept of the group in this model. In clinical settings, psychoanalysts have used instruments such as the Thematic Apperception Test and the Rorschach Test to reach the unconscious. By releasing these unconscious states and bringing them to the surface of the conscious mind, advocates believe that significant affective changes are possible. In cultural awareness training groups, the trainer encourages participants to explore their own cultural identities, to unearth areas of prejudice or discrimination, and to share these with the group in order to develop attitudes and feelings that are more culturally sensitive.

In education, this training has been used to explore levels of respect for other cultures (Cummings & Bridges, 1986); awareness of behavioral and value conflicts (Delgado-Gaitan, 1985); cultural sensitivity (Dubin, 1985; McGroarty, 1988); consciousness of racial prejudice (Feldman, 1985; Rozema, 1982); anxiety and attitudes toward authorities (Gayles, 1988; Lane, 1980); ethnocentrism (Howell, 1981; Tafoya, 1981); and discrimination (Laughlin, 1980). While the training does encourage honest confrontation with significant and perhaps unconsciously felt cultural barriers, the model has three significant limitations. First, although this method may dislodge deeply rooted convictions and beliefs, unless the facilitator is highly trained, participants may not progress into higher states of sensitivity and, in fact, may regress into deeper states of ethnocentrism and prejudice (Starosta, 1990). Second, the emphasis on "genuineness" and "openness" may appeal to those Americans who share such values, but not all cultural groups respond well to such a climate (Bennett, 1986). Candidates who might be effective in cross-cultural environments may resist enforced vulnerability. Finally, groups fail to show evidence of continuing growth in the prediction and control of results. In other words, the specification of outcomes is nebulous at best, and trainees may not be able to shift from a culture-general, affectively oriented training session to the social behaviors and psychological interpretations required in a specific culture.

The Interactionist Model

Similar to the intellectual model because of its grounding in cognitive theory and its emphasis on cognitive goals, the interactionist model differs significantly only in that, rather than cultural "experts" (such as professors, trainers, or facilitators) to disseminate information, cultural representatives or veterans of cross-cultural experiences are used instead. It is assumed that this interaction lowers the anxiety levels of trainees and enables them to move more easily into a new culture. Much of the literature in this vein is anecdotal, focusing on personal testimonies or on recommendations to potential sojourners. Advice on teaching abroad (Hansen & Hansen-Krening, 1988; Miller, 1988; Wallace, 1980); on ways to avoid racism (Taylor, 1987); on teaching students who have limited English proficiency or who are minorities (Dodge, 1985; Wang, 1984); on how white teachers should interact with students of color (Jenkins, 1990); and on how teachers for cross-cultural environments should be selected and trained (Mayne, 1980) forms part of this literature.

The strengths of this culture-specific method are that (1) it uses an informal method of personal exchange, which may allay trainee fears, and (2) the speakers are not disinterested authorities but people who actually have lived and worked in the foreign culture. However, the drawbacks are numerous. The model provides little opportunity for empirical verification. The application of the method is fragmented—many different kinds of people provide often folksy, homespun advice garnered from widely different kinds of experience. Perhaps this kind of advice is to be anticipated when veterans are asked to share openly about an experience, and the immediacy and intimacy of their revelations may carry more power to prepare trainees than the objectivity of a prepared training program. However, the research results from this training are necessarily disjointed and incomparable.

Another serious and unintended outcome is described by Osborne (1989). In a study of white teachers on a Zuni reservation, the teachers avoided all but essential contact with members of the foreign culture, choosing instead to live in a white cultural enclave. Representatives from another culture may communicate hostility or disinterest toward the newcomer. They also may provide too little information about the new culture or inaccurate information, which will have to be unlearned. Cross-cultural veterans unintentionally may instill or encourage cultural misperceptions and reinforce stereotypes. This may result in a preference for cultural isolation rather than cultural immersion.

An interesting and impressive use of interactive training was made by Kleifgen (1988), who videotaped interactions between white preservice teachers and minority children. Explanations for each interaction were gathered from the preservice teacher, the child, the parents, and the supervising teacher. She found that frequently, the explanations of the child, the parents, and the supervising teacher were similar, but those of the preservice teacher were markedly different. Using these differences as opportunities for cross-cultural training between the veteran teacher and the preservice teacher allowed differences in subsequent teaching encounters to be measured. The interaction of supervising teacher (as cultural veteran) and preservice teacher (as trainee) served as the catalyst for change. Critically important in this study was that the subsequent cross-cultural learning was measured in behavioral, not solely cognitive or affective, outcomes.

The Environmental Training Model

This model, also referred to as the "simulation" model (Bennett, 1986) or the "experiential learning model," emphasizes affective and behavioral goals. Unlike the other models, which require little or no contact with the foreign culture, the trainees are active participants in the learning process from within the foreign culture or a simulated foreign culture. The training fosters the growth of cultural attitudes and skills that arise from and are legitimated by actual experience. Although frequently culture-specific in nature, the model relies on a pattern of adaptation that may be applied universally.

Drawing primarily from symbolic interaction theory, environmental training requires maximum trainee participation in a culturally different context. Symbolic interaction theory, like cognitive theory, stresses mental processes as determinants of human behavior. However, symbolic interaction theory posits that exchanges between people are mediated by a symbolic world; people imagine possible reactions to behavior and use this information to act (Mead, 1934). In cross-cultural environmental training, participants are encouraged to explore possible solutions to cross-cultural difficulties, act, assess the consequences, acquire additional cultural information, explore further possibilities, and so on. Merely immersing trainees in a different culture, when immersion is divorced from other training methods, seems to have neutral or negative effects and does not seem to foster affective, cognitive, or behavioral effectiveness in a cross-cultural environment (Berman, 1982; Flemming & Ankarberg, 1980; Osborne, 1989; Pang, 1981; Wilson, 1983; York, 1993).

However, when environmental training is (1) used in conjunction with other forms of cross-cultural training as preparation for a supervised cultural immersion experience; (2) used by an institution (such as a university) that can promote a stable, ongoing relationship with a cultural group; and (3) used in a systematic and goal-oriented program of training, the results seem to suggest positive changes, despite idiosyncratic differences in program requirements (Grubis, 1985; Kincheloe & Stanley, 1983; Kleinfeld & Noordhoff, 1988; Mahan, 1982; Ryan & Robinson, 1990; Torney-Purta, 1986). For example, Reusswig (1981) conducted a study of the Bay Area Bilingual Education League (BABEL) training program in San Francisco, California. In this program, 90 trainees who were experienced educators with little or no cross-cultural experience were selected by the California State Department of Education for a 2-month summer training program at the Universidad de Guadalajara. The training sequences during the immersion were varied, were carefully monitored, and were designed to improve cross-cultural knowledge, intercultural communication, and foreign language skills. At the end of the training, all but one of the candidates who tested for the California Bilingual Certificate of Competence received it. Furthermore, in pretests and posttests, candidates showed a 40% gain in cultural and linguistic knowledge, a 13.8% gain in positive attitudes, and a 150% gain in knowledge of bicultural psychology.

In a similar environmental training study, Mahan (1982) surveyed 291 preservice teachers who had completed varied predeparture cross-cultural training exercises and who had successfully completed a 17-week cultural immersion preservice teaching session on a Native American reservation. Results showed that cross-culturally trained teachers were more likely to experience success in subsequent teaching (measured by teacher evaluations and employment records) at a rate of 83% compared with 52% for those conventionally trained. Furthermore, cross-culturally trained teachers received offers for the teaching positions they sought at a rate of two-to-one compared with their conventionally trained peers. Finally, more than 40% of the cross-cultural teachers sought and accepted employment in schools with minority populations. The dropout rate for the cross-cultural teaching program is less than 4%, a low figure compared with a 20% failure rate for Peace Corps volunteers and a 40% failure rate for corporate overseas transfers (Baines, 1987; McCaffrey, 1986; Tung, 1981).

CONCLUSION

The need for competent, cross-culturally trained teachers has prompted the emergence of a variety of cross-cultural teacher training models. However, the increase in training programs has not produced uniformity of goals, training content, theory, or outcomes. A common understanding of cross-cultural teaching effectiveness is needed as well as a standard for measuring the effects of different kinds of training. This analysis has not attempted to integrate existing training models but to separate them. Distinguishing outcomes and models provides necessary clarity to the current research; the inclusion of a hierarchical pattern of cross-cultural trainee relationships serves to emphasize and specify the intensity and importance of human relationships in the training of teachers for work in cross-cultural classrooms.

Further research needs to be conducted to examine differences in the kinds of teacher training for teaching students from different ethnic and immigrant groups. Whether the same methods can be equally effective for different students, or whether cultural differences warrant the development of different training programs for teachers, is an important and unexamined aspect of this training. Finally, while specific programs were not evaluated in this analysis, it is clear that certain training methods are widely used, frequently without developing or employing a standard to measure results. Additional research in this area will, no doubt, provide needed clarification.

6

Placing Student Language, Literacy, and Culture at the Center of Teacher Education Reform

CYNTHIA B. DILLARD

The teacher's theoretical orientation guides his or her pedagogical decision making, goals, and classroom interactions. There is a critical need for teacher education reform that is informed by diverse voices, specifically the critical voices of women and people of color. This chapter provides several recommendations for a more democratic and multicultural teacher education that is clearly centered in the language and culture of diverse students.

COMPETING CALLS FOR EDUCATIONAL REFORM: FROM CONSERVATIVE TO CRITICAL

Education, as a social activity involving significant side effects, does not merely change individuals; it also changes the relationships among them. Schooling unifies or divides people, just as it elevates or subordinates them. It highlights some languages, customs, and historical viewpoints and downplays others. It creates "expert" elites and "lay" citizens. It even affects those who do not get it, since they will be considered relatively more ignorant as more people become educated. Thus, when people choose one sort of schooling over another, they are in part choosing among the forms of social life they hope to reinforce and bring into being (Bredo, 1988, p. 70).

What Bredo describes is a reality of education: Schools are places where ideas as well as ideals are transacted and transformed. In relation to teacher education, the reform movement, beginning with the 1983 report, *A Nation at Risk*, created the context for discussions on the need to restructure programs of teacher education. However, several competing ideologies underlie these calls for restructuring reforms, which warrant examination and critique.

The Conservative Calls

Some of the most powerful and vocal proponents for school reform have come from outside of schools themselves, namely, from industry and traditionally conservative organizations within the United States. Their argument goes something like this: Managers complain that the quality of labor (our graduates) is inadequate, lacking the discipline and literacy skills necessary for employment. Thus, from their perspective, reforms in education must focus on increasing the skills of students so that they can compete and perform in the economic arena. Shor (1986) asserts that a shortage of math and science labor in the 1980s lead to drastic changes in the school curriculum, which focused major resources on math, science, and computer skills instruction. Further, this led to a shortage of trained teachers in these subject matter areas and consequent out-of-license and emergency credential problems in the 1990s. Other official reports besides *A Nation at Risk* (National Commission on Excellence in Education, 1983), such as the Paideia Proposal (Adler, 1982), and a number of popular critiques (Bloom, 1987; Hirsch, 1987; Ravitch, 1990) began to blame teachers and students, suggesting growing mediocrity, the need for higher standards, and very strict definitions of what literacy development should be for students in U.S. classrooms. However, what was missing from these reports was attention to and an examination of the underlying political, social, and economic realities of both society and schools, and the contributions of these factors to the problems within the educational system (Dantley, 1990).

Several researchers suggest that these conservative calls for educational reform also have signaled a concurrent retreat from democracy and democratic ideology within public education (Apple, 1988; Finkelstein, 1984; Giroux & McLaren, 1986; Greene, 1984, 1986; Jordan, 1992). They describe this retreat as a shift of paradigms, from the ideology of schools as shapers of citizens able to participate actively in a democracy, to schools as producers of labor. Finkelstein (1984), one of the most vocal challengers of the current conservative reform movement, describes this retreat.

> Those calling for reforms in American education have purposively disconnected their calls for reform from those more liberal and just calls for a redistribution of power and an acceptance and celebration of pluralism and democracy. . . . Americans, for the first time in a 150 year history, seem ready to do ideologi-

cal surgery on their public schools—cutting them away from the fate of social
justice and political democracy completely, and grafting them instead onto elite
corporate, industrial, military, and [narrow] cultural interests. (p. 280)

She goes on to state that in order to persuade the U.S. populace of the need
for educational reform, conservatives such as Bloom (1987), Hirsch (1987),
and Schlesinger (1992) have created a common discourse and symbolic
structure using economically based arguments that add to the national and
cultural insecurities and the fears of the mainstream American public. These
fears have managed to set a collective course of action away from the democratic principles in education that Dewey suggested in 1959. According to
Dewey, one of the prime pedagogical tasks of schools and education is to
prepare an articulate public—one capable and articulate enough to work and
act cooperatively in a democracy.

The absence, masking, or total disregard of the voices of women, new
immigrants to the United States, speakers of languages other than English,
and people of color in the conservative call for educational reform is equally
disturbing. Conservative proponents of school reform advocate a return to
basics, stressing the need for very narrow definitions of literacy and the belief that the responsibility for and decisions about what will be learned, when,
and by whom rightfully should rest with the teacher. Little consideration is
given, as is pointed out by a growing number of researchers, to the social
inequality and the authoritarian pedagogy necessitated by the use of such
models in education, where students with differing economic situations,
abilities, and learning styles receive differential instruction and educational
opportunities (Anyon, 1980; Apple, 1988; Fine, 1991; Freire, 1970/1968;
hooks, 1994; Kozol, 1991).

These conservative arguments encourage teacher education programs
to provide preservice teachers with considerable *technical* expertise but with
little understanding of the structure, language, history, and culture of schools.
That understanding is needed so that teachers can then question, challenge,
and ultimately transform the educational system to more appropriately serve
the needs of increasing numbers of diverse students.

A More Critical View of School Reform

There are more critical voices calling for teacher education reform specifically and for educational reform in general. Giroux and McLaren (1986)
describe the need for teacher education programs to function as developers
of transformative intellectuals who are tightly linked with critically transforming schools and the wider society. Further, transformative intellectuals

exercise forms of intellectual and pedagogical practice which attempt to insert teaching and learning directly into the political sphere by arguing that schooling represents both a struggle for meaning and a struggle over power relations. . . . [Transformative intellectuals] are those whose intellectual practices are necessarily grounded in forms of moral and ethical discourse . . . and who are capable of articulating emancipatory possibilities and working toward their realization. (p. 215)

Giroux and McLaren also outline the need for reforms specifically related to language. They suggest that preservice teachers as well as teacher educators need to be encouraged to develop a language of critique—of society, schools, and the politics of both—as well as a language of possibility. In order to develop such a language, examinations and dialogue about the personal, philosophical, and political backgrounds, culture, and language (as well as other elements of identity, including social class, ethnicity, gender, orientation, etc.) of both the teacher educator and the preservice teacher must be undertaken. Further, there must be encouragement to examine and question that with which we engage (texts, other teachers' perspectives, education literature) in order to make appropriate decisions about classroom practice and curriculum development for diversity.

Zeichner (1983) is another voice calling for more inquiry-oriented and critical teacher education reform in order to help prospective teachers develop their reflective abilities, for example, and to help them examine moral, ethical, political, and instructional issues that are embedded in their everyday thinking and practice. In Chapter 2 of this volume, Melnick and Zeichner discuss the cultural insularity of teacher education faculty—one obstacle that must be overcome.

Greene (1984), criticizing conservative educational reform proposals, suggests that the view of what is appropriate or "right" (to be taught and to be learned) is limited in the conservative call for "relevance," "excellence," or "efficiency." Greene states further that those of diverse populations, such as limited-English speakers, women, immigrants, or others, are virtually ignored or are only marginally a part of these calls. In other words, those who are situated as "different" have not yet been recognized educationally or culturally as part of the mainstream of American society, including schools. As such, Greene's more critical call for reform is based on the need to "cultivate the imagination" in teacher education, by helping students and professors look at different and alternative realities in order to understand their own perspectives more clearly. She calls for making a broad range of languages available to students, while respecting and fostering their own languages and culture, versus the learning of a discrete set of lists as advocated by Hirsch (1987). Goodman, Smith, Meredith, and Goodman (1988) echo this position: "Students [and teachers] should no more be excluded from the rich range of personal language . . . they must be given all of their world. All teachers assume this mission" (p. 24).

We turn now to a discussion about teacher education that includes and acknowledges the voices of women and people of color in their various theoretical and experiential forms. Although emerging from people of various racial and cultural backgrounds, geographic locales, ages, and academic and linguistic traditions, this discussion is certainly not to be taken as representative of all of the possibilities.

MISSING VOICES IN TEACHER EDUCATION REFORM: WOMEN AND PEOPLE OF COLOR

> Teachers need to allow themselves to be affected by alternative voices. . . . Listening to alternative voices is not easy. It is painful as well, because it means turning yourself inside out, giving up your own sense of who you are and being willing to see yourself in the unflattering light of another's angry gaze. It is not easy, but it is the only way to learn what it might feel like to be someone else and the only way to start the dialogue. (Delpit, 1988, p. 297)

Delpit's words highlight three themes that emerge in the voices of women and people of color and that can shape educational reform generally and teacher education reform more specifically. The first theme is that education must be seen as the practice of freedom (Freire, 1970/1968), with freedom defined as "the power to act and to choose" (Greene, 1986, p. 432). This includes inventing languages and pedagogies in the context of schools that enable people to overcome their own oppressions and to extend their own understandings (Casey, 1993; Dillard & Ford, 1992).

The second theme is that education is experienced as both a personal and social endeavor, and the affirmation of a multitude of different voices is a critical factor in the struggle for freedom in and through education (Dillard, 1994; hooks, 1994). Finally, education must be centered in the lives of students. This suggests that preservice teacher education needs to be situated in relation to the lived experiences of the students themselves, while also attending to the lived experiences of those whom preservice teachers wish to know more about.

These three themes suggest that teacher education reform needs to begin with an explicit examination of the goals of school and schooling. Why do we "school"? What purposes should an education serve for an individual? Is it possible to meet the needs of the individual in the social context of schools, and vice versa? The voices of women and people of color provide very personal responses to these questions and an extended examination of the three themes introduced here.

Education as the Practice of Freedom

In a "Talk to Teachers" Baldwin (1988) points to what he calls a paradox in the educational system of the United States: Once individuals develop a critical consciousness, they begin to examine and question the society and system in which they are being educated. Although an important purpose of education is to help individuals develop the ability to look at the world for themselves and to make their own decisions, Baldwin suggests that society is not very eager to have these individuals around. Instead, society wants a group of "educated" citizens who will obey the current rules and order of society. Further, if society succeeds in this, then the society is also about to perish. The obligation of those who see themselves as responsible (teacher educators) is to examine society and try to change it no matter what the risk.

hooks (1989) believes that struggle for structural change in society is a necessary part of education toward the practice of freedom. Generations of living in a racist society have taught ethnic minority people what it means to see education as the practice of resistance against domination and the practice of freedom to choose and to act. Nowhere is this clearer than within the walls of academe where there remains a culture of domination and white supremacy that reinforces racist, sexist, classist, and homophobic values, beliefs, and underlying assumptions in policy, curriculum, and teaching practice (Bell, 1992; hooks, 1989, 1994; James & Farmer, 1993). In relation to teacher education, hooks (1994) specifically suggests that it is essential for teachers and professors to explicitly emphasize, discuss, and rethink issues of race, class, gender, domination, and supremacy in teacher education. In addition, hooks believes that true academic freedom is realized most fully when diversity of intellectual representation and perspectives is available within these discussions.

It is important to note that critical education toward freedom, with all of its struggles, is not necessarily an enjoyable pursuit. For those who promote teacher education as a practice of freedom, the requisite critical, political, and pedagogical stance often has serious consequences, such as being viewed as a troublemaker or "radical" by colleagues, or not being liked by students. Greene (1988) discusses education as the practice of freedom in a broader societal context. She suggests that all educators need to reexamine those basic principles that are supposed to be part of our heritage. If we do that, our perspectives on the meaning, possibilities, and understandings of freedom for our more particular university settings will become both more specific as well as more expansive. Greene (1988) concludes:

> If we are seriously interested in education for freedom as well as for the open-ing of cognitive perspectives, it is also important to find a way of developing a praxis of educational consequence that opens the spaces necessary for the re-making of a democratic community. For this to happen, there must of course be a new commitment to intelligence, a new fidelity in communication, a new regard to imagination. It would mean the granting of audibility to numerous voices seldom heard before and, at once, an involvement with all sorts of young people being provoked to make their own the multilinguality needed for struc-turing of contemporary experience and thematizing lived worlds. (p. 127)

Education as Personal and Social: Affirming Voices of Difference

The second theme relative to school reform focuses on the personal and social nature of education through the concept of voice. Voice here is de-fined as the manifestations of lived experiences within socially constructed contexts. In educational settings, voice is both a medium of expression and a product of power. To discover or find one's voice is an ongoing process of making explicit the rather implicit ideological and social assumptions of power, and considering these assumptions in relation to the cultural, social, political, and historical contexts in which they were constructed.

Consideration of social context is crucial to understanding the concept of voice, as voice is created and constructed through and out of such con-texts. In the sense that individual voices are socially constructed, they are distinct and personal, inseparable from the lived experiences of the indi-vidual. To have a voice is to name your world, including what is oppressive, unequal, or unjust. To discover one's voice is necessarily to examine one's background and culture and to view one's life in relation to the larger soci-etal context. In concert with other voices, social relationships are altered and serious personal and social understandings begin to demand answers.

Authenticity is a critical issue in the personal and social nature of voice. One way to create and affirm authenticity is to have spaces throughout teacher education that value a multiplicity of voices. Students and those who teach them should not feel as if their personal language and literacies are less authentic than their more "academic" or intellectual voices (hooks, 1989; Lorde, 1984). Rather, authenticity in teacher education is seen through the construction of social realities that celebrate, acknowledge, and respect dif-ferences and accept them as valid ways of knowing. Fundamentally, authen-ticity in education may have a very different meaning for those groups of people who have been oppressed or exploited: It is both a revolutionary act

(Shor & Freire, 1987) and an act of recovering one's humanity (Freire, 1970/1968).

Educational institutions also have tended to emphasize learning, thinking, writing, and speaking in ways that shift attention away from personal experience (hooks, 1989; Lorde, 1984) and theoretical and critical perspectives that help individuals see and understand differences and commonalties (Bateson, 1989; Belenky, Clinchy, Goldberger, & Tarule, 1986; Lorde, 1984). Too often in university contexts, according to hooks (1989), speaking about one's personal experiences—to allow a wider audience the accessibility of one's thoughts—is considered as a sign of intellectual weakness. In teacher education, when we consciously set up dichotomies—between the voices of children in public schools and the more informed voices of preservice teachers, between voices in English and voices speaking other languages, between the lived experiences and expressions of teachers and our more "scholarly" renditions of a similar phenomenon—we also set up divisions that not only are false, but discourage dialogue and sharing. It is, therefore, important that teacher education students and faculty have as many languages and literacies on hand as possible. Maybe most important, spaces must be made within schools of education to provide for the multiple expressions of such literacies to be a part of the personal and social dialogue of teacher education.

Centering Education: Including Multiple Realities

Centering the pedagogy and practice of education involves including and situating pedagogy and practice authentically in relation to one's own culture and background experiences. In my own graduate classes in multicultural education, one of the most difficult problems I have stems from my desire, as an African American woman, to center African American women's experiences and to help my students center those experiences as well. However, moving students beyond years of normative notions of life's experiences and a particular way of looking at the world—primarily as white, middle class, and Western in nature—is a very difficult task. I have come to understand, as has Brown (1988), that this is not simply an intellectual process for students but is "about coming to believe in the possibility of a variety of experiences, a variety of ways of understanding the world, [and] a variety of frameworks of operation, without imposing consciously or unconsciously a notion of the norm" (p. 10). Brown's practice of centering suggests a restructuring of both the content of teacher education and the structure of participation and interaction. This is reminiscent of Nachmanovich's (1990) examples from jazz music: Any individual who is part of a jazz group brings her special skills and talents to the musical event. The expectation is that as a member of the group the individual will provide her input and talent in concert with the group. However, this person is allowed, even required at times, to render individual solos or improvisations—to use her individual background and talents within the context of the group. Aptheker (1989) describes another example of centering, using the game of basketball as an analogy. She describes the engaged student as one whose pivot foot remains stationary (in his own culture and experiences) while the other foot pivots the center, able then to "center" itself in a number of other places and positions. This is not meant to suggest that preservice teachers or teacher educators can learn to actually be a Chicano, a woman, or the like, but it is a way in which they can learn to center in another's experience and judge it by its own standards without necessarily having to co-opt or adopt those perspectives as their own.

Attempts to restructure teacher education and pivot the center challenge the notion that teacher educators as "professors" know better than the students themselves what or how preservice teachers need to learn. Restructuring requires teacher educators to recognize that the learning process lies instead in the hands of the real authorities: the students. Only then can preservice teachers and teacher educators begin to learn how realities are shaped and personal lives created. Further, such centering reinforces the idea that individuals are only authorities of their *own* experiences and understandings. Experiencing one's own authority, states Brown (1988), better enables an individual to hear the authority in the various voices of those whom they may teach. As the call for reform begins to include these voices, the possibilities for real change in teacher education also may be forthcoming.

SOME CONSIDERATIONS IN REFORMING CONTEXTS, METHODS, AND CURRICULUM

Including in this examination of teacher education the voices of those who traditionally have not been heard, provides a way to reform the underlying goals of education, presented here as the practice of freedom, as a personal and social endeavor, and as a way to affirm diversity and center in another's experience. However, it also raises two very important questions. To use Goodlad's (1990b) terminology, What should preservice teachers "reasonably expect" from their programs of teacher education? and, What are we providing? Although many important insights can be gained from these voices, several points seem particularly salient in their implications for teacher education.

First, preservice teachers should expect honest, trusting, more egalitarian relationships with teacher educators and significant others during their teacher preparation. These relationships must be built on mutual respect and value the personal attributes, language background, and orientation of both the preservice teacher and the teacher educator. Second, knowledge and understanding of the political nature of schools and schooling are critical in programs of teacher education. This should include direct experiences, discussions, and reflection on the social, cultural, historical, and pedagogical issues that construct the multiple realities of education and the role of the teacher in the endeavor. Learning how to live and teach through diversity, including the inevitable struggles and contradictions, seems especially important. Finally, the sense of embracing diversity is developed through ongoing opportunities for personal interactions and transactions with people and contexts that are diverse in traditions, beliefs, language, and thought. Thus, becoming a literate teacher, in relation to diversity, means doing more than writing and reading *about* culture—it means learning to *be* diverse in perspectives, skills, and knowledges. It means understanding, influencing, and participating in the lives of diverse students, schools, and the wider society. Thus, the integration and valuing of diverse and multiple literacies is crucial to the philosophy, pedagogy, and practice of teacher education and preparation.

However, as Goodlad (1990b) states, since public school education does not contain all of the elements necessary for continual renewal, there is a need to be guided not by what *is* with respect to schooling, but by what *should be*. Given the voices included and the perspectives set forth in this chapter, the following suggestions provide a framework for a more situated pedagogy in teacher education, one that models a truly literate multicultural environment and places preservice teachers' language, literacy, and culture at the center of their teacher preparation.

Toward a More Situated Pedagogy

The goal of situated pedagogy in teacher education is to integrate the conceptual with the experiential, including the life experiences of both student and teacher. While individual institutional contexts and needs must be taken into account in any discussion of educational reform, the following pedagogical elements provide a framework that colleges or schools of education might use when evaluating their own educational practices.

Dialogical teaching, which consists of posing problems followed by critical discussion, encourages high-level critical thinking and dialogue. It also results in students' awareness that in order to solve problems of interest to them and to the field of education, their participation is expected, valued, and needed.

Critical literacy refers to the ability to question aspects of literacy, including reading, writing, speaking, listening, and thinking. A critically literate teacher helps students to move beyond simple memorization of information, teaching them to strive to understand the origin, structure, assumptions, and consequences of the process or subject being studied. Thus, critical literacy ought to be modeled by the teacher educator and enacted through the teacher preparation pedagogy and curriculum.

Two closely related elements, *ethnographic inquiry* and *cross-cultural communications*, seem crucial to the preparation of teachers in a diverse society. Opportunities for preservice teachers to interact with others of diverse backgrounds and cultures are critical, and bilingualism and bidialecticalism should be encouraged in teacher education. The study of literature and cultural representations outside traditional offerings—women's literature, literature of various ethnic and cultural groups, developing world literature, labor and industry studies, among others—should play an important part in the strategies and materials used in teacher education. Further, study of and engagement in ethnographic research models and techniques, such as Heath's (1983) study of language use, Ladson-Billings's (1994) study of successful teachers of African American children, and Paley's (1979) study of her own critical pedagogy and ethnic understandings in her kindergarten classroom, might be employed to provide preservice teachers glimpses into the realities of school and schooling and the usefulness of such models in informing their own future teaching.

For preservice teachers to see themselves as *change agents*, as catalysts for educational reform, debate and discussion on the political nature of education are important. Preservice teachers must have opportunities to study and participate in community change projects, school advocacy organizations, school policy and law, and the politics of the teaching profession. Everhart (1983) suggests that linking students with relevant networks in this way brings about contradictions that can force students to examine the underlying assumptions of educational issues and to become more critically aware of the social context of the educational system.

Interdisciplinary approaches within teacher education will strengthen both the conceptual and pedagogical development of preservice teachers and teacher educators. Studying history, foreign languages, sociology, art, music, economics, political science, and other social sciences will assist students in their development of a more critical and informed pedagogy.

Dramatic and visual arts, music, poetry, public speaking, and other modes of *creative* and *literate expression* should be integrated into teacher education programs. Preservice teachers should have multiple opportunities to present and share important research, knowledge, and understandings about education to broader publics and in creative ways that more closely represent the diversity in literacy that their future students will bring to the teaching and learning endeavor.

Finally, *participatory learning* should be the guiding approach in reforming teacher education programs. The democratic ideals modeled by cooperative group projects, self-designed learning plans, discussions, and seminars are an effective and appropriate way to prepare teachers capable of critical thought and action.

CONCLUSION

The pedagogy and practice in programs of teacher education must reflect the importance of language and cultural diversity in the teacher preparation process by integrating more participatory methodology, multiple contexts for learning, and interdisciplinary curricula. This framework for a more transformative teacher preparation program encourages preservice teachers to examine the moral, ethical, political, and educational issues embedded in their everyday thinking and practice as teachers. This includes fostering a deep regard for and recognition of the ways that their own personal language, literacy, and culture influence—and possibly even limit—multicultural learning, teaching, and classroom practice. Finally, through such a program of teacher education, preservice teachers may come to understand themselves better in relation to others, as well as to recognize a variety of ways in which their future students will understand the world. This is vital today, as Greene (1988) suggests, precisely because "a teacher in search of his/her own freedom may be the only kind of teacher who can arouse [students] to go in search of their own" (p. 14).

7

Directed Inquiry in Preservice Teacher Education
A Developmental Process Model

ETTA R. HOLLINS

Schools in our society are called upon to perform two distinctive functions:
(1) enculturate the young into a social and political democracy, and (2) introduce the young to those canons of reasoning central to intelligent, satisfying
participation in the human conversation. If schools are to perform these two
functions well, teachers must be thoroughly grounded in the understandings
and beliefs necessary for carrying them out. They must (3) learn the pedagogy
essential to the enculturation and trait development of the young, and (4)
possess the knowledge and skills necessary to participate in the continuous
renewal of the schools for which they are the stewards. We viewed these four
sets of requirements as the underpinnings of the teaching profession. (Goodlad,
1991, p. 5)

Goodlad's concept of schools as agents for the "enculturation of the
young into a social and political democracy" and introducing "the young to
those canons of reasoning central to intelligent, satisfying participation in
the human conversation" does not specify whose culture should be central
to this process. Enculturation that forces one group's culture on another can
have devastating effects.

For example, at the turn of the century enculturation in government-
supported schools that forced Native Americans to conform to European
ways was particularly painful and destructive (Adams, 1988). Presently,
many of the same practices are evident in urban inner-city schools serving
African American and Mexican American youngsters where the curriculum
content, instructional approaches, and social context are all based on Euro-

pean American culture. Many of these schools are centers of conflict and disharmony where order is maintained by punishment, metal detectors, and security guards. The threat that this deterioration will escalate is fueled by the increasing discrepancy between the culture of teachers and that of their students (Zeichner, 1992), and research showing that teacher preparation programs have little impact on preservice teachers' beliefs and images of themselves as teachers and of the pupils they will teach (Kagan, 1992).

I believe it is possible to alter the course of public schools and to better prepare teachers for diverse populations of students. The purpose of this chapter is to propose a developmental process model for teacher preparation engaging preservice teachers in directed inquiry, examining the centrality of culture in school learning, and constructing an operating knowledge base for productive classroom practices. In this process model, teacher preparation is more than a series of loosely connected courses designed by individual professors. Designing a developmental process for teacher preparation requires careful deliberation and collaboration among teacher educators and the use of findings from research on learning-to-teach and educating teachers for cultural diversity.

The proposed process model is based on research discussed in several recent reviews of the literature on learning-to-teach (Borko, 1989; Burden, 1990; Carter, 1990; Kagan, 1992), educating teachers for cultural diversity (Gomez, 1993; Zeichner, 1993), my own work in conceptualizing teaching and learning-to-teach culturally diverse populations (Hollins, 1982a, 1982b, 1990a, 1991, 1993, 1995, 1996; Hollins & Spencer, 1991), and extensive deliberation with colleagues. In analyzing reviews of the literature on learning-to-teach, it is immediately apparent that discussions of culture and diversity are marginal. It is also evident that the literature on learning-to-teach and educating teachers for cultural diversity is not subsumed in dialogues on redesigning teacher preparation programs. This is particularly troubling given the centrality of culture in human existence and teaching as an act of cultural transmission or enculturation.

The proposed process for preservice teacher preparation consists of four interrelated components: (1) constructing an operating knowledge base for productive teaching; (2) preparing for student teaching; (3) experiencing teaching; and (4) synthesizing and integrating knowledge about teaching. The operating knowledge base in this context refers to the schemata constructed by individual teachers for use in making decisions about classroom practices. Preparing for student teaching involves data gathering for the purpose of constructing a profile of the pupils, the school as a whole, and the community of which the pupils are members. Productive student teaching involves developing and testing hypotheses and formulating theory by using data from profiles of students and their communities in planning learning experiences, monitoring students' responses, and attending to the relationships and social interactions between and among students and their teacher(s) (Hollins, 1996).

CONSTRUCTING AN OPERATING KNOWLEDGE BASE

Kagan (1992), in a review of the literature on learning-to-teach, references research reported by Cochran-Smith (1989) in which it was concluded that experienced teachers "construct their own private pedagogical theories," which are used to make cause–effect linkages that explain student behaviors and responses to instruction. There is no indication that these "private theories" are directly related to content or procedures included in a teacher preparation program. Teachers who develop private theories without the benefit of guided experiences that challenge and correct erroneous beliefs and assumptions, are at risk for validating and operationalizing these notions. It is important to include in a teacher preparation program a process for constructing an operating knowledge base that is valid and reliable for designing productive classroom instruction for students from different cultural and experiential backgrounds.

Based on recent reviews of the literature, research reports not included in these reviews, and my own work in conceptualizing teaching and learning-to-teach culturally diverse populations of students, five common elements associated with constructing an operating knowledge base for teaching are evident: (1) defining culture; (2) examining and reflecting on significant personal experiences for self-understanding; (3) inquiring into the experiences of others; (4) examining the ideologies and purposes undergirding school practices; and (5) observing productive teaching and learning experiences. While these elements are not exhaustive, they are basic in developing an operating knowledge base for productive teaching. These elements are interrelated and overlapping, although they are not necessarily sequential.

Defining Culture

Gomez (1993) describes different approaches to challenging prospective teachers' perspectives about others, including programs, courses, and field experiences focusing on diversity. The common thread in each of the approaches identified in Gomez's literature review is the essential goal of changing teachers' attitudes, beliefs, and knowledge about those different from themselves. These approaches address teachers' knowledge of biases related to race, social class, and gender; awareness of inequities within the larger society; and awareness of the ways schools reinforce social inequities and stratification. However, the author does not identify programs in which preservice teachers struggle with the meaning of culture in their own lives and in the lives of their pupils, or the linkages between culture and learning in school.

In my own work with preservice teachers, I have observed problems with understanding the centrality of culture in human existence. Many European American preservice teachers identify themselves as middle-class Americans without reference to any particular external geographic origin or cultural heritage. The same preservice teachers identify people of color by race or external geographic origin. These color- or race-based descriptions usually do not include social class status and present nationality. Culture usually is described as observable artifacts or functions, rather than as the basis for making sense of and responding to the physical, social, and spiritual world. In many preservice teachers' conceptualizations, culture is not directly linked to teaching and learning in school, nor are school practices viewed as culturally derived.

It is important for prospective teachers to begin their preparation for teaching by constructing a working definition of culture that will direct their work with children from different cultural and experiential backgrounds. This definition of culture will be revised and reconstructed throughout the preservice program as new experiences and information are acquired. A beginning point might be an examination of what typically is referred to as "American culture." This would include a critical analysis of the ideological underpinnings as well as their manifestations in social institutions.

Understanding Self

The schemata used to make sense of the physical and social environments are based largely on culturally framed interpretations of personal experiences. The vitality of these schemata is supported in research showing that the attitudes and beliefs held by prospective teachers remain unchanged after they have completed preservice teacher education programs (Kagan, 1992). These studies indicate that creating dissonance is important in challenging erroneous assumptions and beliefs.

Four different approaches are presented here for helping prospective teachers understand self. Each approach examines self from a different perspective: (1) naturalistic exploration of the deep meaning of educational experiences; (2) examination of images of self as teacher; (3) examination of racial identity; and (4) examination of cultural identity. Each of the approaches to self-understanding presented here is important in teacher development, and they may be used together in the same program. The scope of this chapter does not permit an analysis of the relationships among these approaches.

Krall (1988) reports on a technique for assisting graduate students in education to recover their personal educational experiences as a "method for identifying and understanding broad curricular and pedagogical issues" (p. 467). Krall concludes that

> The journey inward becomes an ongoing process that leads outward to a more complete understanding of the human condition. Self-understanding is not merely a reflection on what we are but on what we are in relation to the world. Self-understanding comes to us via our unique perceptions of the world which are dependent on our inherent individual abilities as well as on our particular sociocultural histories. (p. 478)

The approach Krall (1988) uses is a naturalistic journey inward that allows individuals to recover the deep meaning of their past experiences. This is a holistic examination of one's own educational experience.

In contrast, Bullough, Knowles, and Crow (1992) are concerned with preservice teachers' conception of themselves as teachers. They contend that

> The meanings attached to the teaching schema function as an interpretive lens through which beginning teachers selectively respond to the content and activities offered to them. Generally, their aim in responding is to seek confirmation of what they already believe to be true. (p. 186)

It is not clear whether the teacher development practices these authors advocate address cultural and societal influences on perceptions of teaching and schooling. It is also not clear whether changing teachers' images of themselves as teachers and of their students involves challenging biases related to race and ethnicity manifested in instructional approaches, the framing of curriculum content, and the social context in the classroom.

Hollins (1996) describes two heuristics for increasing self-understanding related to culture and racial identity. The first is the use of Helms's (1990) stages of white and black racial identity. Preservice teachers can be encouraged to reflect on the various stages of racial identity, their characteristics, and the social factors influencing them. They can be shown examples of behaviors and statements indicative of each of these stages. They can be encouraged to document examples of each of the stages of racial identity observed in their daily lives. This is a process of introspection for preservice teachers from different racial groups, rather than an examination of the behaviors and lives of others.

The second heuristic involves a surname search that takes prospective teachers on a journey revealing aspects of their own personal identity and connection to the past (Hollins, 1990b). This is a form of family history research emphasizing identity with a particular name. Preservice teachers are encouraged to explore the origin of the name and to describe the culture and lifestyles of its earliest users. Some individuals will be able to identify elements of the past in their present values and practices. Some individuals experience cognitive dissonance when realizing that societal pressures and other factors resulted in name changes that permanently disconnected them from their own heritage. Sharing their discoveries, experiences, and feelings during the surname search helps preservice teachers understand the cultural nature of human experiences. This learning experience helps prepare preservice teachers to examine the cultural and experiential background of their pupils.

Understanding the Diversity of Others

Understanding cultural diversity means revealing the deep meaning of culture. This requires conscious knowledge of the influence of culture on the way we personally make sense of and respond to the physical, social, and spiritual world. It requires eliminating unconscious and egocentric perspectives of the world as an extension of oneself. When prospective teachers have arrived at this point, it is possible to begin the study of cultural diversity.

Time constraints in most teacher preparation programs make it necessary to limit the examination of cultural diversity to those issues most directly related to supporting the development of an operating knowledge base for productive teaching. Like many other scholars, I certainly agree that teachers need broad-based knowledge of societal issues related to diversity and about the culture and history of those they will teach. However, in the past such knowledge does not seem to have improved outcomes for underserved populations of public school pupils or the productivity of instruction in culturally diverse classrooms. What teachers need to understand is the relationship between pupils' home culture and school learning. Teachers need to understand how cultural perspectives influence approaches to learning, the curriculum content valued, and supportive social situations for learning. They need to understand how to incorporate cultural knowledge and knowledge about culture into daily classroom practices.

Several approaches are presented in the research literature on helping prospective teachers acquire knowledge about pupils from diverse cultural and experiential backgrounds, including (1) reflecting on their own beliefs about specific ethnic groups; (2) interacting with those different from themselves through community field experiences; (3) studying the cultural experiences and history of specific ethnic groups; (4) identifying learning styles; and (5) identifying culturally sensitive curriculum content and instructional strategies

(Zeichner, 1992). The descriptions of these approaches do not make explicit the linkages between the pupils' home culture and school learning.

Hollins (1996) presents an approach to learning about students' cultures and experiential backgrounds in a way that informs classroom practices. This approach, referred to as reflective-interpretive-inquiry (RIQ), relies on ethnographic techniques for data gathering and analysis. RIQ involves seven categories.

1. Teachers' beliefs about students reflect personal beliefs about students.
2. Teachers' beliefs about instruction reveal biases in beliefs about instruction that favor specific cultural perceptions, practices, and values.
3. The social context of instruction facilitates the examination of similarities and differences between social interaction in the classroom and in the students' home culture.
4. Students' experiential background indicates significant experiences students have had within and outside of school.
5. Ethnic and cultural group identifies practices and values characteristic of the students' cultures.
6. The local community examines the political and social structure within the student's local community.
7. Societal context reflects a particular culture in relationship to the larger societal context.

Using RIQ, preservice teachers study one cultural group extensively, rather than dealing superficially with several that are different. Intensive study of one cultural group facilitates constructing a working definition of culture, helps reveal the relationship between culture and school learning, and supports developing an operating knowledge base for teaching diverse populations of pupils. As preservice teachers learn more about the relationship between culture and school learning, they may begin to question the cultural basis of school practices.

The Underpinnings of School Practices

Assisting preservice teachers in examining the cultural basis of school practices requires studying relationships among ideologies, the purpose of schooling, school practices, and the research and theory constituting the knowledge base for existing school practices. One approach to this type of study is to develop two interdependent and overlapping categories, which, for the purposes of this discussion, will be labeled the essential schema and the collateral schema.

Essential Schema. The economic, political, and social ideologies from which the purposes of schooling are derived are included in the essential schema. Ideologies are the products of specific cultural beliefs, practices, values, and worldview. These ideologies and the corresponding purposes of schooling constitute the essential schema for designing the curriculum, learning experiences (instructional methodology), assessment approaches, social context within schools, and school–community relationships.

An example of an essential schema can be found in Adams's (1988) description of the ideologies and purposes that formed the basis for Native American education from 1880 to 1900. Adams describes fundamental ideologies as including Protestantism, capitalism, and republicanism, which appeared thematically as Protestantism, individualization, and Americanization. The primary purposes for providing formal education for Native Americans included (1) acculturation, (2) subordination, and (3) dispossession of the land.

The school curriculum reflected the fundamental ideologies and corresponding purposes of schooling for Native Americans. The Protestant ideology was reflected in the curriculum in the McGuffey Readers, classroom prayers, and hymn singing. Americanization involved redefining the Indian's political organization by replacing tribal loyalties with individualization. Citizenship education included language instruction and political socialization.

Collateral Schema. The collateral schema consists of the research and theory supporting school practices and constituting the knowledge base for designing the curriculum, learning experiences, assessment approaches, social context within schools, and school–community relationships. There is a reciprocal relationship between the essential schema and the collateral schema. The essential schema is primordial and initially frames the collateral schema; however, it also may be influenced by the collateral schema.

Contemporary debates over the canon present an example of the interrelatedness of essential and collateral schemata. Both multiculturalists and traditionalists claim democracy as the undergirding ideology for their positions. However, the multiculturalists advocate cultural pluralism, while the traditionalists advocate a common culture. The multiculturalists contend that the school curriculum should include the culture and heritage of all ethnic and cultural groups (Banks, 1991/92). The traditionalists argue that this is not the function of schools (Ravitch, 1991/92). This debate brings to the forefront the interrelatedness of political ideology, the purpose of schooling, and school practices exemplified in curriculum content. However, other aspects of school practices are products of essential and collateral schemata, and preservice teachers should be provided opportunities to examine them as well.

Multiple Exemplars of Productive Practice

Preservice teachers need to examine multiple exemplars from different perspectives when constructing an operating knowledge base for productive teaching. One perspective is acquired by examining the underlying essential and collateral schemata. Another perspective is acquired by examining the relationship between the pupils' cultural and experiential backgrounds and classroom practices. Exemplars of productive practice may be documented or operative.

Documented Exemplars. Useful exemplars of productive teaching may be carefully documented and contextualized situations, allowing preservice teachers to examine curriculum content, learning experiences, and the social context of classroom learning. Documented exemplars may be presented in different formats, including videotapes, audiotapes, or ethnographic field notations. Particularly useful examples of ethnographic accounts of teaching practices include Anyon's (1981) study of social class and teaching practices, Au and Mason's (1981) study of teaching practices for Native Hawaiian pupils, and Lipka's (1991) study of teaching practices for Yup'ik Eskimo pupils.

Operative Exemplars. The actual spontaneous and undocumented occurrences that can be observed by physical presence in the classroom, through two-way mirrors, or by means of closed-circuit television provide excellent opportunities for prospective teachers to observe and analyze productive teaching. Operative exemplars also may provide opportunities for preservice teachers to engage in dialogue with the teachers and their students prior to and following the observation.

PREPARING FOR THE PRACTICUM

Preparing for the student teaching practicum builds upon and extends the process of constructing an operating knowledge base for productive teaching. This preparation includes building profiles, analyzing data, and constructing theory. The process is facilitated when preservice teachers are assigned early in the program—in teams of 3 to 5 members—to the schools where they will student teach. This does not mean they will immediately begin student teaching, but rather that these school sites will be the focus of their inquiry and data gathering. Early school assignments allow time for compiling data and developing familiarity with a particular site.

Building Profiles

The preservice teacher needs to develop profiles of the pupils at the appropriate grade level or in the content areas included in the student teaching practicum to which he or she has been assigned, of the school as a whole, and of the local community of which the pupils are members. A profile of the pupils at a particular grade level or in a particular content area will include demographic information on their ethnicity and social, political, and economic status; academic performance as indicated by standardized tests and other assessments, advanced placement or awards, and success at subsequent levels of education requiring application of the knowledge acquired in the particular content or grade level under consideration; social interaction patterns and responses in the school context; and attendance patterns, including mobility, suspensions, and expulsions.

A profile of the school as a whole will include demographic data about the number of pupils in attendance and their culture/ethnicity and social class status; social climate as indicated by relationships among all groups of participants (pupils, teachers, parents, administrators, and support staff); awards and recognition for pupils and teachers; truancy, suspensions, and expulsions; academic performance as indicated by standardized tests and other assessments, advanced placement or awards, and success at subsequent levels of education; characteristics of the teachers such as years of experience in the profession, years of service at the particular school, advanced degrees, and perception of the school; and governance practices and policies at the school.

A profile of the local community will include demographic data about its social, political, and economic status. It will include information about traditions and values manifested in social organization, relationships among groups, practices within institutions and agencies, distribution and uses of power, individual and group recognition, and civic and social concerns. The profile of the community also should include its relationship to the larger society. For example, the images of the community portrayed in the media and governmental affiliations should be noted.

Data collected in building profiles of the pupils, the school, and the community will be analyzed and used to construct theories to guide framing curriculum content, designing productive learning experiences, and creating a supportive social context for learning for the particular population under consideration. All information gathered should be carefully categorized and filed for analysis in the second phase of preparation for the practicum. A summary of the information should be compiled in the form of charts or graphs for quick reference.

Analyzing Data

Preservice teachers need to complete a detailed analysis of the data compiled on the pupils they will teach, the school, and the local community prior to beginning the student teaching practicum. This analysis should (1) link major patterns, problems, and issues identified in compiling the data to a review of related literature; (2) describe the data gathering approaches used; (3) present a narrative summary of the findings; and (4) discuss the implications of this study for productive teaching and learning for the designated pupils. When possible, preservice teachers should be organized in teams (3 to 5 members) to develop these profiles, analyze the data, write the report, and construct theory to guide their planning.

Constructing Theory

Constructing theory involves five phases and requires application of all aspects of the operating knowledge base developed so far. The phases of constructing a theory for teaching a designated population of students include (1) formulating testable hypotheses; (2) preliminary testing of hypotheses through observations in classrooms; (3) revising hypotheses; (4) testing hypotheses through planning instruction and teaching the designated population; and (5) summative review and revisions.

In the initial phase of constructing theory, preservice teachers will formulate testable hypotheses about teaching the designated population of pupils. These hypotheses will be presented as generalizations systematically drawn from patterns identified in the data collected. Preservice teachers will extrapolate explanations for their hypotheses from related research literature, interpret their findings from the data they have collected, and discuss the implications of their findings for teaching and learning in the classroom. Specifically, the hypotheses should address framing the curriculum for the designated pupil population, designing or selecting meaningful and productive learning experiences, and creating a supportive context for learning.

In the second phase of constructing theory, observations are designed specifically to test the conclusions drawn from and the inferences made about teaching and learning for the designated pupils. In this instance preservice teachers are permitted to observe both productive and less productive teaching. This permits opportunities to critically examine hypotheses from different perspectives. Notations should reveal examples of what is observed in the classroom that supports and conflicts with what has been hypothesized.

These notations are used in the third phase, re-examining and revising hypotheses as necessary.

The fourth phase, translating hypotheses into plans for facilitating learning for the designated pupils, requires collaboration among team members. This phase involves designing or selecting learning experiences, reframing curriculum content, and identifying approaches to creating a supportive social context for learning based on the hypotheses developed. Summative review, the final phase of hypothesis building, is completed after the student teaching experience.

THE STUDENT TEACHING PRACTICUM

The student teaching practicum is an integrative and collaborative process where teams of preservice teachers apply and test the knowledge they have acquired by teaching in real classrooms. This part of the teacher preparation program is led by experienced teachers who serve as coordinators, and university professors who serve as facilitators.

An Integrative Process

The student teaching practicum is an integrative process that brings together the operating knowledge base for productive teaching and classroom practices. The practicum begins with the initial phase of hypothesis building. At this point preservice teachers initiate the use of their operating knowledge base for productive teaching by applying it directly to a designated population. This type of active engagement should help preservice teachers understand the importance of knowing their pupils well before planning or selecting learning experiences, framing curriculum content, or deciding on the protocol for social interaction in the classroom.

A Collaborative Process

In the proposed model, student teaching is a collaborative process involving a team of preservice teachers, one or two experienced teachers, and a university professor. Collectively, this group is referred to here as a student teaching unit. The experienced teachers are referred to as coordinators, and the university professor as a facilitator. These new labels indicate changes in roles and relationships.

The coordinator arranges or schedules teaching segments for team members, engages in discussing plans, and participates in reflecting on learning outcomes, pupils' responses to learning experiences, and the social context within the classroom. Prior to scheduling teaching segments, the coordinator reviews the profiles developed by the preservice teachers, their written reports, hypotheses, and teaching plans. This helps the coordinator prepare for participating in ongoing dialogue and reflecting on the preservice teachers' classroom experiences. While coordinators share their knowledge and beliefs about teaching and the pupils they teach, they are not necessarily expected to serve as models of productive teaching nor are their thoughts accepted as absolute truth. The coordinators and members of the team engage in mutually supportive and reciprocal professional growth.

The role of the facilitator is to assist team members in re-examining and refining their operating knowledge base for productive teaching, testing hypotheses, and identifying the need to adjust their theories and teaching plans. The facilitator uses her knowledge of schools and preparation as a scholar to challenge, question, and exhort preservice teachers to more advanced levels of analysis, observation, and synthesis in reflecting on and planning for teaching.

Team members make use of their collective experiences when collaborating on planning for instruction, assisting each other in reflecting on personal feelings of comfort and anxiety while teaching, and in reflecting on pupils' responses to learning opportunities and the relationships among pupils.

SYNTHESIZING AND INTEGRATING KNOWLEDGE

At the conclusion of the student teaching practicum, each team should complete a summative review of their teaching experience, the hypotheses formulated, and their operating knowledge base for productive teaching. This summative review will provide opportunities for synthesizing and integrating knowledge constructed during the entire preservice program. Questions to guide the summative review include

1. What basic principles of teaching and learning have been revealed or validated through inquiry and teaching?
2. How do these basic principles relate to teaching different populations of pupils?
3. How were the profiles you developed helpful to you in your work with the specific population of pupils to whom you were assigned?
4. To what extent were the hypotheses you formulated validated or invalidated by your teaching experiences?
5. What basic ideologies undergird educational practice in the school where you were assigned and how were they manifested? How were you influenced by these ideologies?

6. What conclusions have you drawn about the role of collaboration in professional development?

CONCLUSION

This chapter addresses the need for an operating knowledge base for productive teaching. The components presented are not to be interpreted as exhaustive, but rather illustrate that the process for developing a valid and reliable operating knowledge base for teaching requires deliberate and systematic attention to specific factors.

Consistently providing productive learning experiences for pupils from diverse cultural and experiential backgrounds requires a well-constructed operating knowledge base. Teachers need to understand themselves, their pupils, and the underpinnings of school practices, and to have exposure to multiple exemplars of productive practice. They also need to have carefully selected information about the pupils, their home cultures, and their communities. Teachers need to know how and when to use specific information to enhance learning. These skills can be acquired through a teacher preparation process based on directed inquiry and reflection on practice such as that described in this chapter.

The centrality of culture is a critical component of the proposed teacher preparation model. It is evident in discussions related to understanding self, understanding others, and examining the underpinnings of school practices. Ignoring the centrality of culture supports the perpetuation of cultural dominance, the replication of existing school practices, and a high probability that existing inequities in schooling outcomes will persist.

PART III

Developing and Assessing Culturally Responsive Competence: Models of Program Practice

The four chapters in Part III describe examples of transformed program practices that teacher educators are using to develop the ability and to assess the competence of preservice teachers to meet the needs of culturally diverse students. The authors provide comprehensive descriptions of the professional development outcomes their programs expect preservice candidates to acquire and demonstrate. These chapters describe the course content, the role of faculty as facilitators of learning, and several phases of teacher development, as well as teaching and assessment methods.

In Chapter 8, "A Model Program for Educating Teachers for Diversity," Peter Murrell, Jr. and Mary E. Diez describe how "majority culture" teacher candidates can develop the cultural knowledge and teaching ability necessary for effective work in ethnically, racially, and linguistically diverse communities. Using case examples, these teacher educators explain how the program design at Alverno College conceptualizes and assesses broad-based abilities for teaching effectively in diverse urban communities. The chapter concludes with an analysis of the abilities and competencies associated with the transformation of Alverno's teacher credential candidates into reflective, culturally responsive teachers.

Next, in Chapter 9, "Transforming Teacher Education: Including Culturally Responsible Pedagogy," Tonya Huber, Frank M. Kline, Linda Bakken, and Frances L. Clark explain the reasoning behind the major revisions that were involved in transforming instruction in a traditional teacher education program at Wichita State University that now includes "culturally responsive pedagogy." The new program design is a block of integrated foundations courses and field experiences that are designed specifically to prepare teachers to address the cultural and educational needs of diverse students. The authors describe in detail Block I, the program segment that has primary responsibility for addressing diversity issues using data gathered after the implementation of the program with one cohort of students.

In complementary chapters Sara S. Garcia (Chapter 10) and Joyce E. King (Chapter 11) describe the theoretical rationale and transformative pedagogy they have used in a foundations course sequence at Santa Clara University. In Chapter 10, "Self-Narrative Inquiry in Teacher Development: Living and Working in Just Institutions," Garcia describes several forms of reflective thinking in teacher education. This chapter provides examples of student teacher development using a process of self-narrative inquiry, a mode of critical, reflective analysis that enables students to engage and critique their cognitive and affective schemata. Garcia also provides information that other teacher educators can use to build reflection-through-inquiry processes and to assess the impact of these instructional strategies that facilitate teacher self-development.

In Chapter 11, "'Thank You for Opening Our Minds': On Praxis, Transmutation, and Black Studies in Teacher Development," King discusses instructional processes that enable preservice teachers to recognize and transcend their own miseducation with respect to diversity, equity, and justice issues. Thus, transmutation refers to an order of change in the conceptual knowledge, thought, and practice of credential candidates that enables them to assess critically their own self-understanding and the needs of diverse learners. King illustrates the grounding of this form of transmutation in the Black Studies epistemological critique of knowledge and schooling.

Each of the chapters in Part III discusses the transformation of teacher preparation programs in terms of specific characteristics of the students in these programs. Thus, these program developers are modeling a key instructional principle for any learners: Start where the learners are.

8

A Model Program for Educating Teachers for Diversity

Peter Murrell, Jr. and Mary E. Diez

What teachers need to be capable of . . . is gaining information from their own students and the local community, and learning how to transform it for pedagogical use. (Zeichner, 1992, p. 23)

This chapter describes how largely middle-class and suburban teachers in training at Alverno College can develop the cultural knowledge and teaching ability necessary for effective work in ethnically, racially, and linguistically diverse communities. We illustrate with case examples how our program develops broad-based abilities and diversity-related sensibilities by integrating classroom learning with field experience in culturally diverse field sites. We conclude with an analysis of the abilities and competencies associated with the transformation of our predominantly white, middle- and working-class women into reflective and competent teachers of diverse populations.

FRAMING THE KNOWLEDGE BASE
FOR TEACHING TO DIVERSITY

For us the central issue for the design of teacher education programs that prepare teachers for diversity is epistemological: Can we authentically define professional knowledge in diverse settings in ways that clearly point to the knowledge, abilities, and dispositions that undergird effective teaching practice with children of diverse backgrounds? We agree with a growing number of researchers who argue that the capacity for effective teaching in culturally diverse urban communities requires multiple exposures to the educational lives and perspectives of the children and immersion in and teaching practice in those urban communities (e.g., Delpit, 1988; Foster, 1989; Hollins, 1990b; King & Ladson-Billings, 1990; Ladson-Billings, 1990; Meier, 1989; Meier & Nelson-Barber, 1989; Murrell, 1991, 1993, 1994). When teacher preparation programs view the knowledge base for effective teaching in diverse settings as information content to be inserted into course sequences (whether in a class lecture or in a published source), it is of little value for developing the capacity for effective work in diverse and urban classrooms. This approach is problematic because it obscures any clear articulation of effective practice in these settings. For instance, content knowledge not acquired in the contexts within which it has meaning and utility likely will not become pedagogical knowledge that teacher candidates draw upon in actual practice. A teacher candidate "learning about" Hispanic learning styles in a college text may find little application to effective work in her classroom consisting of working-class Mexican and Puerto Rican children (see Murrell, 1990).

A related problem that an information-centered model causes, especially for teacher education programs with enrollments of predominantly white, middle-class students, concerns developing appropriate professional dispositions. For students who may already question the value of teacher preparation for diversity, requirements that do not have a noticeable impact on their practice in student teaching and field assignments merely confirm negative dispositions toward diversity.

The third and perhaps most critical problem that this model causes is the neglect of deep understandings of how cultural and racial differences are embedded in a social, historical, and political context in our society. While there are calls to integrate "multicultural competence" (e.g., Dilworth, 1992; Hixson, 1992) into teacher preparation, a clear articulation of what that competence actually consists of remains elusive and rarely is situated in praxis. It is not sufficient merely to be aware of cultural learning styles. Teachers must understand and analyze institutional racism and come to terms with their own complicity in its various forms (Sleeter, 1994). To fulfill their responsibility to promote healthy and integrated self-images of all children, teachers also must develop an actively antiracist curriculum and not be satisfied with an "add on" approach merely to ensure that all groups are "represented" in pictures on the walls or in text materials.

Our alternative epistemological position is based on an integrative-generative model that requires instantiation and integration of theory, principles, and skills in actual teaching performances—performances that demonstrate the ability to teach effectively and responsively in diverse contexts. Future teachers do not simply learn principles and skills, but *integrate* them with teaching practice so as to *generate* situation-specific knowledge necessary for effective teaching in diverse urban schools. The knowledge base for working effectively with children of diverse backgrounds is, therefore, generated through praxis in diverse classrooms, guided by expert supervision and performance assessment, and then refined through extensive critical self-assessment.

The goal of Alverno College's teacher education program is to create for the future teacher an actively generative knowledge structure that includes a solid understanding of theory and its application in practice, specific professional skills required for teaching, and specific professional dispositions. In an integrative-generative model, learning about cultural diversity is not kept separate but is linked to all other aspects of the knowledge, skills, and dispositions required for teaching. Learning is seen as having multiple sources, including one's own observations, and the learner's experience provides the impetus for ongoing modification of understanding. Thus, our thesis is that a teacher education program that prepares teachers who will demonstrate an understanding of cultural diversity and manage instruction for children of diverse backgrounds must (1) be designed as an integrative, rather than additive, process; (2) view the knowledge base for teaching as generative, not static, and as acquired through integrating theory and practice; and (3) critically interpret the cultural politics of teaching and learning in diverse settings. The approach we will describe adopts the perspective of the development of teacher candidates in these three frameworks.

We advocate forms of culturally responsive teaching expertise based not merely on specific knowledge of individual cultural and ethnic groups, but on pedagogical ability to promote social, cultural, and intellectual inclusion of *all* students in the classroom. This pedagogical ability includes, in addition to specific cultural knowledge, skills of interaction, ethnographic inquiry, and critical reflection that enhance prospective teachers' likelihood of understanding their classrooms as cultures and as communities. At stake is whether teacher candidates can promote academic achievement and social development by learning to create learning environments in their classrooms that are culturally inclusive, developmentally appropriate, socially inviting, intellectually enticing, and democratically organized. In the next section we present our program's developmental ability-based model of teacher education.

THE MEANING OF TEACHER
PREPARATION FOR DIVERSITY

The principles undergirding the teacher education program at Alverno, as well as the entire undergraduate program, reflect the belief that teaching must be dedicated to the development of learners' abilities in the context of the disciplines and domain-specific professional knowledge. Instruction is founded on the belief that learning involves using knowledge—to think, critically interpret, discover, interact, and create (Diez, 1988/90). Learning capacity increases developmentally, even in the serendipitous discoveries one makes in unfamiliar cultural contexts, because the learner monitors what she sets out to learn and formulates explicit standards that she must meet. This view of learning in cultural contexts is similar to Hymes's (1981) notion of "ethnographic monitoring."

Our ability-based curriculum is central to developing diversity-relevant teaching knowledge because it addresses the need to interrogate one's own epistemology regarding issues of race and diversity. Moving beyond the epistemological belief that knowledge can be "owned" by virtue of access to texts is a difficult developmental task that is frequently grappled with by European American teacher candidates. In the beginning stages of the developmental trajectory, white students often are demonstrably uncomfortable and seem unable to participate in the examination of "racial stuff." In advanced stages of the developmental trajectory, these students understand that some of the most valuable cultural understandings about the children, families, and communities they serve is arrived at through immersion in a social context. Therefore, they begin not only to respect alternative ways of knowing and being but to use them to establish intersubjectivity with people of diverse backgrounds.

The ability-based curriculum and an ability-based epistemology of professional teacher knowledge permit the development by *both* faculty and teacher candidates of greater expertise in diverse settings. Such development is made possible by explicit goals articulated in terms of abilities. The educational literature suggests a number of such abilities that teachers must have in order to teach diverse children effectively. Among these are the ability to (1) develop an *inclusive curriculum* incorporating the intellectual, historical, and literary traditions of different cultural groups; (2) orchestrate an *inclusive classroom community*, where every child is a full and advantaged participant in the social, intellectual, and cultural life of the classroom; and (3) coordinate an *inclusive family and community network*, where parents are invited to become extensions of the intellectual and social life of the classroom. The Alverno Education Department encourages development by teacher candidates of these diversity-relevant abilities through five advanced outcomes that guide our work—*conceptualization, diagnosis, coordination, communication,* and *integrative interaction.*

A MODEL OF THE DEVELOPMENT
OF TEACHING ABILITY

While the Alverno College teacher education program is fully described elsewhere (Diez, 1988/90), we briefly describe the five abilities that are the framework for the program. By ability, the faculty at Alverno mean an integration of knowledge, professional skill, and professional dispositions that define what a practitioner knows and is able to do. The concept of development assumes that the beginning teacher will, with increased experience, study, and mentoring, refine and expand her or his abilities.

Conceptualization is the ability to integrate content knowledge with frameworks and a broadly based understanding of the liberal arts in order to plan and implement instruction. Essential here is the teacher candidate's ability to link various frameworks from the content knowledge base in, for example, language arts or literature, developmental psychology and learning styles, and liberal arts approaches (e.g., taking multiple perspectives, reflecting on one's beliefs, etc.). Students design language-focused lessons for a particular elementary level and are asked to justify their choice of materials and activities as developmentally appropriate, sensitive to variations in modality/preference, and inclusive of diverse cultural experiences. Follow-up activities, which vary this assignment, call for the integration of language activities in a science or social studies class.

Diagnosis is the ability to relate observed behavior to relevant frameworks in order to determine and implement learning prescriptions. Observation is an essential skill that most teacher candidates have not mastered at the beginning of their program. Over four semesters of fieldwork prior to student teaching, candidates spend 2 to 3 hours a week in field placement, observing teachers and students as well as working with individuals, small groups, and whole classes. For each visit, they respond to specific questions in their field logs, a type of guided journal.

Teacher candidates develop their observation skills by beginning with a framework (e.g., comparing observations of discipline and students' behavior in their third field assignment with expected patterns). They begin to develop flexibility in applying theory and a disposition to question when faced with discrepant information by addressing differences between the generalizations of a framework and the experiences of individual children. As they progress to more complex observations, candidates record teachers' responses to students and patterns of student verbal and nonverbal behavior following the teacher response. Faculty feedback and assessment are critical in developing candidates' observational skills, a disposition toward careful gathering of data, as well as a meta-awareness of candidates' biases and preconceived ideas during observation.

Coordination is the ability to manage resources effectively to support learning goals. The Alverno faculty view resources broadly, including time, space, persons, activities, concepts, and media. A central resource for the child, and by extension for the teacher, is the child's parent(s) or guardian(s). The fourth field experience seminar, as well as other class experiences, address the role of the parent in a child's education as another method of development and assessment.

Based on their interests, pairs of candidates prepare role-plays of a parent–teacher conference that relate parent and teacher collaboration and to additional resources for the good of the child (e.g., school social workers or psychologists). Issues of cultural difference often are addressed, with candidates examining again their own feelings as well as their skills related to working with persons whose backgrounds are different from their own (e.g., putting parents at ease or asking questions in a nonthreatening way). In a class focused on assessment and evaluation teacher candidates use data from students' classroom performance and special testing to take part in a simulated multidisciplinary team evaluation. The group puts into practice the ability to evaluate the needs of the student and also how the various roles—from parent and teacher to psychologist—function in the multi-disciplinary team (a formal hearing process to evaluate educational needs and prescribe appropriate services in the public schools).

Communication is using verbal, nonverbal, and media modes of communication to establish the environment of the classroom in order to structure and reinforce learning. This ability builds on the college's general educational ability, which focuses on reading, writing, listening, speaking, and the use of media. One of the educational frameworks that distinguishes communication as an ability developed in the teacher education curriculum relates to conceptualization because each candidate needs to show command of the subject matter she is teaching. This ability is developed with a gradual strengthening of the various aspects across all courses.

The classroom interactional framework involves students' use of Cazden's (1988) IRE pattern of teacher initiation, student response, followed by teacher evaluation of the response. Students interrogate and discuss possibilities for expanding the contingencies of teacher remarks and student responses, from simple reward (e.g., brownie points) to the social reinforcement of inclusion, and ultimately to discourse as the medium of learning in the classroom.

The most complex of the abilities, *integrative interaction*, draws the other four into its meaning: "Acting with professional values as a situational decision-maker, adapting to the changing needs in the environment in order to develop prospective teachers as learners." The final fieldwork seminar, including student teaching, in which integrative interaction becomes the core of the development of generative, diversity-relevant teaching ability, is the most important context for developing this ability. Both the experiences of teacher candidates and the practical expertise of cooperating teachers inform the "wisdom of practice" component of our ability-based program. In the student teaching seminars and the cooperating teacher workshops, candidates discuss with both their college and site supervisors issues of effective teaching practice in culturally diverse settings. The value of bringing together cooperating teachers and candidates in these dialogues has been important for generating practical knowledge regarding teaching in diverse settings, from different perspectives, to which Alverno's Education Department would not otherwise have access. The discussions help to extend and broaden the experiential component of the integrative interaction ability.

Using the theme, building classroom communities, a recent workshop examined family, culture, and democracy as metaphors for classroom communities that are responsive to students of diverse backgrounds. Such metaphors permit education faculty, practitioners, and candidates to articulate critical professional knowledge and envision what classrooms look like when they are culturally inclusive, developmentally appropriate, socially inviting, intellectually enticing, and democratically organized, and promote learning and development.

PERFORMANCE ASSESSMENTS AND TEACHING PRACTICE

The portfolio-interview assessment in the semester prior to student teaching draws upon the full range of the candidate's performances across her coursework. Candidates review their past work and select specific items that the assessment requires (e.g., a videotape of the candidate working with students, sample lesson plans, subject area work, instructional materials, and reflective writing such as a philosophy of education statement or a journal entry). A pair of candidates is assigned to a pair of practitioners, usually a principal and a classroom teacher. The candidates review their choice of portfolio materials with their Alverno advisor, and on assessment day the candidates and their practitioner/assessors have a discussion on questions prepared by the department. One typical question is related to the ability to work with diverse students. The practitioners give the candidates feedback on criteria related to both the portfolio and the interview and then review with the candidates their goals for student teaching. The department uses the recommendations of the practitioners as part of the data for admission to student teaching. In both the final fieldwork seminar and student teaching, candidates must prepare whole-class lessons (including special lesson plan formats for reflective analysis). The final field assignment is in a culturally diverse classroom, and one or both of the two 9-week student teaching placements are in an urban, public school classroom. Students of color account for 70% of enrollments in the Milwaukee Public Schools, thus also ensuring experience with diversity.

The program's use of performance assessments situated in authentic contexts promotes an integrated professional knowledge base in three ways. Performance assessment (1) integrates theory and practice by requiring students to apply knowledge developed in program courses to their concomitant clinical field experiences; (2) integrates the five professional abilities (conceptualization, diagnosis, coordination, communication, and integrative interaction); and (3) requires students to adopt professional roles and dispositions as they perform learning tasks. Thus, content knowledge, skill, and professional demeanor are always integrated in the students' exhibition of their learning.

Performance assessment also creates an actively generative knowledge structure that includes the application of theory to practice, specific professional skills required for teaching, and specific professional dispositions. Prospective teachers learn the meaning of culturally responsive teaching "from the ground up"—grounded in their own teaching performance, shaped by expert feedback, and clarified by their own critical reflection. Times for critical self-reflection and review of teaching performance, according to culturally responsive teaching criteria, occur at several points in the program (e.g., the portfolio-interview assessment prior to student teaching).

THE POWER OF PRAXIS AND THE ABILITY-BASED INSTRUCTIONAL FRAMEWORK

Preparing expert teachers to effectively teach children from linguistically, culturally, and economically diverse backgrounds requires the development and integration of particular culture- and class-specific foundational knowledges in, for example, human development, social behavior, and moral reasoning. In addition to pedagogy, there are issues of professional consciousness and ethical conduct in relation to the social and economic plight of many urban students. What are the political and ideological contingencies that good teachers respond to in order to educate and empower poor children and children of color? How do skilled teachers develop a shared perspective with students that permits them to communicate effortlessly across the lines of unequal power (Delpit, 1988) drawn by poverty, racism, and differences in cultural expression? How do good teachers particularize their understanding of human development—cognitive, linguistic, social, moral, and emotional—in terms of the culturally distinct socialization patterns and teaching traditions among African American, Native American, Hispanic, and other marginalized ethnic groups in urban settings? These questions go directly to informal knowledges and pragmatic pedagogies not found in textbooks, but that are critical to effective practice for teaching diverse populations. The remainder of the chapter discusses how we work with students to develop these pragmatic pedagogical understandings.

In essence, we problematize the dilemmas, conflicts, and challenges teacher candidates experience in their fieldwork. Candidates integrate theory with practice by viewing their teaching experience in culturally diverse and urban field placements as a self-study of their professional growth as a culturally aware teacher. The shared thinking and cross-cultural understanding that develop in the seminars help preservice teachers to identify teaching problems in their field sites, especially those that emerge from difficulty in communicating across race, cultural background, and language differences. The prospective teachers learn to analyze situations by viewing knowledge as problematic and socially constructed. Each participant situates herself in a cultural scene or frame (Goffman, 1974) as she analyzes her teaching experience in the field, including "frozen-frames" of her teaching performance on videotape.

To assist the candidates in adopting culturally sensitive practices, the instructor inserts into the candidate's "frame" (perspective) specific information about culture, communicative styles, or issues related to racism that are relevant to the problem, dilemma, or situation the teacher candidate presents to the group. By bringing to light culturally relevant considerations that did not occur to the teacher candidate in the moment of teaching, the instructor links culturally responsive teaching to the teacher candidate's experience. The goal is to scaffold and shape the candidate's ability to adopt a more culturally sensitive and developmentally appropriate perspective of the problem than the candidate originally "framed" (when pausing the videotape at a particular point, for example) for the rest of the group.

The following excerpt from a class session illustrates the ability-based pedagogy and the power of praxis in our program. A candidate (RN) shared a situation from the second-grade classroom where she had begun, on occasion, whole-class instruction.

> Well, I had an incident with one boy last week. I am doing something different I don't think anybody else is doing. . . . I'm going to have them have their own little news programs . . . with music . . . their favorite songs. And I told them it could be anything you like except any kind of M. C. Hammer or 2–Live Crew. I said, "Nothing like that," because this is a second grade. . . . One little boy raised his hand and asked, "Can I have M. C. Hammer?"
>
> And I said, "No," and he said, "Can I ask you why?"
>
> And I said, "Would you want your children . . ." (pause) I said . . . "*I* personally don't like M. C. Hammer, and I know you probably do. But do you think you're at the right age where you should listen to this?"

There are a number of things that might be inserted into RN's frame that would deepen her understanding and improve the appropriateness of her response to the student. For instance, candidates in field seminars understand well how important it is for teachers to be in touch with the lives, experiences, and cultures of the children they teach. In this case, it was simply a matter of being aware of the difference between rap artists. M. C. Hammer (now known simply as "Hammer") is popular among younger students, due in part, perhaps, to his being a featured Saturday morning cartoon. 2–Live Crew, on the other hand, have been criticized for their vulgarity and exploitation of women, and have been the subject of a nationally publicized freedom of speech court battle as a result of a concert they gave in Florida.

On a deeper level, a perspective the instructor inserted into RN's frame concerned what she communicated to the child about a symbol with which he identified: She made it clear that she considered M. C. Hammer inappropriate music for him to listen to. Most significant for future action in RN's setting is the cooperating teacher's nascent racism and her unspoken standard about what was appropriate, as we see in the continued discussion among several teacher candidates and the supervisor (PM):

GP: A lot of M. C. Hammer is not that bad. . . .
RN: No? But I know this teacher. I mean there was no way . . . when he said M. C. Hammer, she almost jumped all over his back.
KB: I think there is really a misconception. . . .
PM: Perhaps a rule of thumb. . . . If it's a Saturday morning cartoon . . . [laughter]
RN: Well, I didn't know how to handle that.
PM: How do you know what to do? How do you know what standards of behavior and expression to have in your classroom? The reason why this is an aspect of exemplary practice is that an exemplary teacher knows how to draw . . . [to] discover the interests of the community. What would parents want?

Note that in this interchange, relevant information was inserted by another teacher candidate. However, the real work regarding how that incident might have been handled with greater racial and cultural sensitivity required the insertion of another concept by the supervisor (PM), which reframed RN's problem. PM questioned what constituted the experience of "not knowing" how to handle the boy's request. In particular, did RN want to, in fact, grant permission to the little boy to use M. C. Hammer, but did she not know how to negotiate the disapproval of the cooperating teacher? Did she feel that she was upholding community standards regarding children and rap music? Or does her quandary stem merely from not having a foundation for deciding what to do—independently of the cooperating teacher's disapproval? The supervisor continues:

> There is a wide range of interests among parents, and you also have to work within the administration's code. But . . . you have to come up with a vision of what the "community of your classroom" needs to be like . . . and decide appropriateness from that standpoint. How will you do that?

The elements of the instructional process as described above are illustrated in this excerpt. The participants provide analytical discussion of teaching and the insertion of relevant interpretations for each other. Although the seminar participants explored various plans of action appropriate to RN's current situation and the interests of the child, she was encouraged to decide her future actions. The goal of the instructional process is to maximize prospective teachers' ability to read important meanings regarding their relationship to the cultural scene of the classroom and to act intelligently and ethically on them. This requires access to and understanding of the classroom "underlife" (Erickson & Schultz, 1991) or the informal social organization of the classroom. It also requires access to situation-specific understandings about racial dynamics, cultural expression, and the life experiences of one's students.

Teaching is a complex act requiring moment-by-moment adjustments of plans to fit continuously changing and uncertain conditions in a situation. This kind of instruction is designed to induce in prospective teachers "adjustment expertise"—the ability to use and apply what they discover through detailed examination of classroom interactions. One develops that expertise primarily from *experience* and by obtaining practice in working through difficult moment-to-moment teaching situations. The knowledge teachers use in making these adjustments is contextual and interactive, as is the way teachers *acquire and use* knowledge (Lampert & Clark, 1990, p. 21).

In the case of another teacher candidate (TJ) in her third field assignment, she works out issues regarding her racial stereotypes regarding Puerto Rican youngsters over time and through guided, critical conversations about her teaching with peers and Alverno faculty. TJ's field placement was a third- and fourth-grade bilingual classroom in a predominantly Hispanic elementary school. Her problem concerned establishing a presence in the class and working effectively with the other teachers. TJ's early conceptualization reflected her concern and uncertainty. In response to a prompt question in her journal, TJ remarked:

> Do all Hispanic children talk excessively and out of turn in all
> situations, especially in the classroom? (Journal entry, September 10,
> 1990)

TJ's early diagnosis reflects an attempt to connect aspects of ethnicity, culture, and community to the behaviors and performances she observed in the classroom.

> There are some children that lack self-worth because of their home
> environment, and, therefore, "act out" in class to gain attention.
> Moreover, when these few "act out" in class, they are yelled at, and,
> therefore, do not have a high self-esteem. In comparison to previous
> field experiences, the children in this class are very similar to that of
> my first field placement. In these two fields, I worked with Hispanic
> children who come from backgrounds in which their self-worth is not
> always boosted, but still, even given their backgrounds, most of the
> children seem to have good self-esteem within the classroom. In
> comparison to my other field placement, the children in this field
> have lower self-concepts which is probably due to their different
> backgrounds. The children in my other field came from the suburbs
> and had a more stable background, whereas these children do not
> always have stable backgrounds. (Journal entry, October 4, 1990)

In order to work with TJ's ability to view herself in relation to her classroom, a professional conversation situation was set up with another field student who had already taught in a diverse urban setting. The goal for engaging TJ in an analytical conversation was to insert, in a nonthreatening way, alternative conceptualizations and diagnoses of her ineffectiveness in her classroom. The other student participant, BD, assumed the role of a teacher colleague. In the following excerpt, the faculty (one of the authors) is designated as PC.

PC: My role is primarily to resurface and reinsert some of the issues surrounding adjusting in a multicultural setting . . . [as] sort of moderator, re-inserter, shaper of the conversation. The primary focus will be between the two of you as colleagues.

(To TJ): Yours is one of a professional having identified an area that you'd like to work on—concentrating on the knowledges, skills, and dispositions that you want to work on to become a more multiculturally competent teacher. And so, one of the things you'll be doing in the conversation is talking about particular instances in which you've seen that as an issue . . . as a problem . . . you're

getting feedback here from BD, whose role is that of one who is more experienced in a multicultural setting.

TJ: Over the last 8 weeks or so numerous things have occurred in my field placement that seem a little out of the ordinary for a normal classroom, to me. . . . The fact that the classroom is bilingual is probably really tough for me, even though I have had a Spanish background. . . . Any tips?

BD: Well, the first thing that I heard you say is that it is not a "normal" classroom. . . . Well, my ears perked up about that. It's like, well what's "normal"? Is "normal" a classroom where all the children speak English? . . . If that is not your experience then it won't seem normal to you. I think in our culture now that's really changing. And as we get more in touch with who our students are, "normal" may, in fact, mean more diversity.

In her remarks, BD managed to surface for TJ the way she had been characterizing her problem, namely, as differences in language rather than as the nature of the relationship she had established with her students. TJ was pushed further in her diagnosis when PC asked her to describe the nature of her interactions with her students.

TJ: I know that part of their culture is to talk excessively out of turn. And I can only take that to a certain extent. It's like overwhelming to me. And then of course you want to yell. . . . Where do you draw the line?

BD: . . . that's a tough one. Let's see . . . I had a couple of things come to my mind, again as far as just the terminology that you mentioned—that they were talking excessively. Again, that's an interpretation of *your* standards compared to their standards. I would say, try to look more as . . . "they're more outgoing than I am," or "they're using their verbal communication more than I want," or something like that and try not to make a value judgment. Try to look at it as a different style but without a judgment. And another thing I would see—and I have that too because I am more understanding maybe than a lot of my students who are more outwardly expressive—body language is different in different cultures. . . . It's a challenge. I try not to comment on it, when it's not interfering in a major way.

The perspective TJ was gaining as a result of BD's feedback helped her begin to interpret her difficulty in a wider framework of her relationships. For example, when she indicated that she was inhibited from even attempting Spanish because she did not want to say the wrong thing, BD responded:

> I have been trying this now [risk-taking about using language]. I
> challenge myself to take the risk and just botch up and they laugh.
> But I see them actually getting closer to me just interpersonally. I
> found that makes all the difference as far as, you know, the tone of
> the class.

Following the professional conversation situation, TJ began to make
inferences based on the connectedness she had with her students and
began to reflect on ways she needed to change to be effective teaching these
children.

> Since my background is not the same as the Hispanic culture, I have
> found that it has been very hard for me to create a link between my
> teaching abilities and the values of the Hispanic culture, but I do
> need to become more knowledgeable about Hispanic culture, so that
> I can make a stronger link between my values and those of Hispanic
> children. (Journal entry, October 11, 1990)

In TJ's situated self-assessment, she followed up on this entry by focusing
on the question: What specific knowledge about the lives, histories, and
cultures of these children do I need to teach them effectively? The most
important outcome of the situated self-assessment from the standpoint of
TJ's performance was a change in her conceptualization of her approach to
teaching in the setting.

> Even though all the fears have not gone away, I have learned to
> handle my fears and not let them control all of my behavior and
> attitudes toward Hispanic children. Little by little, I have taken this
> weakness of being apprehensive and turning it to become a strength
> in myself. (Journal entry, November 6, 1990)

In her reconceptualization TJ began to see the connections between her
effectiveness in the classroom and expanding her role. The case of TJ by no
means provides a complete picture of a prospective teacher developing the
integrative interaction ability that supports culturally competent teaching
for diversity. However, it illustrates the movement that is initiated by the
practice of instruction through which the prospective teacher sees for herself what about her practice is problematic and what she needs to do next.
The most powerful technique for self-discovery is "frozen-frame" analysis
of videotaped segments of the candidate's teaching.

In summary, the seminar sessions support the development of the integrative interaction ability by

1. Engaging individual candidates in an analytical conversation and inserting information, interpretations, foundational knowledge, and theory that assist them in formulating culturally sensitive and appropriate responses to their issues
2. Guiding candidates in the development of their skills as observers engaged in inquiry
3. Encouraging the formulation of plans of action that are based specifically on the context of the participants' teaching/observing situation and that are never apart from that context in the abstract
4. Articulating plans of action that are appropriate for candidates' current level of ability, making progress more likely as they work to negotiate successfully the problematic relationships in their teaching/observing sites
5. Encouraging candidates to define for themselves the actions they need to take, given the potential gap between actions appropriate for a culturally responsive teacher and the actions appropriate for the level of ability of the candidate
6. Encouraging problem solving, decision making, and self-analysis upon evidence

CONCLUSION

Preparing teachers for diverse settings requires a program of "learning in action" that integrates *foundational professional abilities* (e.g., cross-cultural developmental theory, communicative skills, critical self-assessment, and community sensibilities), together with the *teaching contexts* in diverse and urban communities where the abilities will be applied. The key element in our program for preparing competent teachers for diversity is an epistemology of professional knowledge grounded in the concept of generative abilities. Rather than viewing professional knowledge required for teaching effectively in diverse settings as content material to be studied, we view this knowledge in terms of abilities to be developed—what teachers must *actually do* in order to develop culturally responsive teaching practices and professional sensibilities. Prospective teachers, therefore, develop their conceptions of effective, culturally responsive teaching out of their own teaching experience and assessments of their own teaching practice, not out of text material about multicultural education.

This ability-based epistemology makes possible several powerful pedagogical features of the program that prepare preservice teachers to "learn how to learn" in diverse settings and to develop the ability to articulate standards of effective culturally responsive teaching. Teacher candidates are continually problem solving around issues of race and culture as they experience them in their fieldwork.

Integrative interaction is the key advanced outcome for organizing the development of expert teaching ability in diverse settings. Candidates in the Alverno teacher preparation program develop pedagogical knowledge associated with culturally diverse settings in the context of integrative interaction and the four other advanced outcomes already described: conceptualization, diagnosis, coordination, and communication. The case study of TJ illustrates how this experience provides avenues for improvement that candidates might not otherwise have had, given their initial biases, fears, and dispositions toward diverse cultures.

9

Transforming Teacher Education
Including Culturally
Responsible Pedagogy

TONYA HUBER, FRANK M. KLINE,
LINDA BAKKEN, AND FRANCES L. CLARK

Celebrating the storytelling and oral literacy common to so many of America's peoples, this discussion of diversity will begin with a story printed a long time ago in the *Northern Cheyenne News*.

In a time that existed before the continent looks as it does now, long before the Europeans came to the "American" shores of Mother Earth, the animals decided they must do something heroic to meet the problems of a "New World." They decided to organize a school. They adopted an activity curriculum consisting of running, climbing, swimming, and flying. To make it easier to administer the curriculum, all the animals took all the subjects.

Duck was excellent in swimming; in fact, better than his instructors, but he made only passing grades in flying and was very poor in running. Since he was slow in running, he had to stay after school and also drop swimming, in order to practice running. This was kept up until his webbed feet were badly worn, and he was only average in swimming. But average was acceptable in school—so nobody worried about that—except Duck.

Squirrel was excellent in climbing until she developed frustration in flying class where her teacher made her start from the ground up instead of the treetop down. She also developed "charley horses" from over-exertion and then got a C in climbing and a D in running.

Eagle was a problem child and disciplined severely. In the climbing class she beat all the others to the top of the tree, but insisted on using her own way to get there.

At the end of the year, an abnormal Eel that could swim exceedingly well and also run, climb, and fly a little, had the highest average and was valedictorian.

The Prairie Dogs stayed out of school and fought the tax levy because the administration would not add digging and burrowing to the curriculum. They apprenticed their children to a Badger and later joined the Groundhogs and Gophers to start a successful private school.

Educationally "disadvantaged," "at-risk" children are those who are most likely to achieve only minimal success in school systems as these school systems are currently organized (Fradd, Weismantel, Correa, & Algozzine, 1990). Many of these children (approximately 17% of the total student population) are of non-English language backgrounds (Hodgkinson, 1990), many others have been identified as having a disability. Between 1976 and 1985, there was an increase of 1,000,000 children diagnosed with mildly handicapping conditions (Hagerty & Abramson, 1987). Major factors contributing to the dynamic population change include sizable immigration, overall population increase (Lindholm, 1990; Sing, 1989), and increased numbers of ethnic minorities (Cortes, 1986), whose average age is about 5 years younger than the national average (Seelye, 1993). Also, increasing numbers of special education students are being served in regular classrooms (Shepard, 1987). As other authors in this volume have noted, the academic performance of minority students is considerably below majority norms, and the gap grows wider with each school year (Alatorre Alva & Padilla, 1988).

A CULTURALLY RESPONSIBLE PEDAGOGY FOR TEACHER EDUCATION

To be educators, as Brendtro, Brokenleg, and Van Bockern (1990) point out, requires teachers to be aware of and willing to put themselves at risk: at risk to care, to be rejected, and to fail. Perhaps Urbanski (1988) indicated the challenge best.

The problem with today's schools is not that they are no longer as good as they once were. The problem with today's schools is that they are precisely what they always were, while the world around them has changed significantly. Schools must be restructured as centers of inquiry and reflection, not of unexamined tradition. (p. 48)

How then can we, as educators, recognize the natural abilities and talents of students frustrated by a system that prizes the status quo and standardization? How can we, as teacher educators, help preservice teachers develop a pedagogy that takes responsibility for the ducks, the squirrels, the eagles, and the prairie dogs?

All "Americans," through birthright and/or citizenship, inherit the story of America's first people, the Native Americans, and the subsequent treatment of peoples—Indian, African, Mexican, Asian, Islander, economically or socially destitute, female, of different religious orientations or abilities—by conquering colonizers and nation builders. Since the 1954 Supreme Court decision in *Brown* v. *Board of Education*, the Black Power movement fed the Red Power (American Indian) movement's claims to cultural recognition and equal rights in education. In 1974 *Lau* v. *Nichols* (Reutter, 1985) mandated programs for Asian children, which resulted in achieving bilingual programs to meet the developmental needs of Asian and Hispanic Americans. Largely unnoticed has been the awakening of white ethnic groups—most notably, eastern and southern Europeans—who began to examine their own unique experiences in the United States and concluded, correctly, that much of their own histories and cultures were ignored in American education. They joined the movement toward culturally relevant education, but largely as a conservative element (Dilworth, 1992, p. 4).

What is needed is a culturally sensitive and responsible pedagogy for all students to maximize learning in American education. Culturally responsible pedagogy is not color-bound or language-specific but subsumes all diversities to ensure sensitivity to and responsibility for all learners. Based on this holistic orientation, the Block I faculty at Wichita State University incorporated the framework Smith (1991) developed for a culturally responsible pedagogy.

Smith (1991) categorized the knowledge base for teacher education into 13 parameters. An explanation of each parameter follows.

Parameter One: Theoretical, Ideological, and Philosophical Foundations of Education in a Global Society. Theory and policy are tested and applied through interview and observation as students employ the tools of the ethnographer to explore the *enculturative* process of their own culture as it is influenced by the *acculturative* process of schooling. When school culture conflicts with home culture, the learner may suffer. It becomes critical to educational effectiveness for those involved in the educational process to recognize the scholastic ethnicity (Bennett, 1990) of their program and institution and how that culture matches or conflicts with the traditional or home culture of learners participating in that acculturative process (Foerster & Little Soldier, 1981).

Parameter Two: Psychosocial-Cultural Contexts of Human Growth and Development in Nonmainstream Ethnic/Racial Cultures. Psychosocial-cultural contexts add components regarding similarities and differences in child rearing, interaction, gender role identification, parenting roles and responsibilities; definitions of disability; and other psychosocial-cultural patterns affecting the way people learn and respond to teaching. Teacher education programs need to espouse and model the tenet that classroom activities should "retain the school's goal of specific forms of educational achievement and simultaneously take advantage of various unique configurations of children's background experience" (Laboratory of Comparative Human Cognition, 1986, p. 1057).

Parameter Three: Cultural and Cognitive Learning Style Theory and Research. This parameter embellishes the traditional knowledge base of such cognitive theorists as Piaget and Vygotsky and provides a brief, but thorough, overview of the history and application of cognitive theory and human learning in which cultural learning frameworks are acknowledged in curriculum and instruction. Gardner's (1983, 1991) research on multiple intelligences has significantly influenced teachers' conceptions of teaching and testing during the past decade. Humans can "know" in a number of ways. Recognition of cultural characteristics, combined with a thorough understanding of learning style theory, enables the teacher to maximize instruction. Several influential works in this area invalidate teaching all children the same way (Armstrong, 1994; Hale-Benson, 1988; Huber & Pewewardy, 1990; Morris, Sather, & Schull, 1978; Shade, 1982).

Parameter Four: Foundations of Culturally Responsive Curriculum. This parameter includes research on preparing teachers to be responsive to and responsible for cultural issues in the explicit, implicit, and null curricula (Eisner, 1985). Much of what happens in classrooms is incongruous and "out of sync" with what happens in home and community experiences.

Parameter Five: Foundations of Effective Strategies. One of the implicit objectives of this parameter is that students and teachers understand that the way they have experienced education is but one of many ways. Coupled with ethnographic explorations of school culture and an expanding understanding of scholastic ethnicity, this is a powerful growing experience. The parameter pushes teachers beyond the traditional acceptance that "methods" involves learning a bag of tricks and list of steps to be executed without regard to the dynamics of learners and contexts.

Parameter Six: Foundations of Culturally Responsible and Responsive Diagnosis, Measurement, and Assessment. At the root of this parameter is a rethinking of the traditional view of intelligence as a physical substance, a measurable entity, and a subsequent focus on measurable, easily quantifiable constructs focusing on linguistic and logical-mathematical intelligence. Instead, a broader understanding of cognitive theory stresses how humans (as diverse individuals) think. We need to redefine "intelligence tests" currently used to support cultural bias in diagnosis, measurement, and assessment (resulting in over- and underplacing children in such programs as special education and gifted classes). Intelligence needs to be reinterpreted to include an understanding of the different and varied ways in which humans learn ("how students are smart," not how smart they are).

Parameter Seven: Psychosocial-Cultural Influences in Subject-Specific Learning. Escalante's success (Mathews, 1988) with Hispanic students at Garfield High is attributed largely to his understanding of their culture and his ability to connect mathematical concepts to cultural pride and history. Cocking and Mestre (1988) and Orr (1987) also have explored the influence of culture and linguistics on the learning of math. Adding information regarding underrepresented groups is an initial step (e.g., Oakes, 1990) that must be followed by recognition of and instruction for specific cultural influences (e.g., Bowen & Bowen, 1992).

Parameter Eight: Language, Communication, and Interaction Styles. Teachers need to learn about communication and interaction styles, both verbal and nonverbal, within and across cultures. For example, in some cultures it is inappropriate to pat a person on the head, make direct eye contact when being scolded, cut hair, wear sunglasses when communicating, appear without an escort—the list goes on. Learning all the rules is impossible, especially since culture is an ongoing development, not a static entity. Acquiring the skill to find out what is appropriate and inappropriate behavior or action is not only possible but necessary.

Parameter Nine: Essential Elements of Cultures. This is one parameter of the knowledge base that has enjoyed some exploration in traditional classrooms and teacher education programs. However, the essential elements cannot be represented by "Indian week in November, black history month in February, and tacos on Tuesday" (Huber, 1992, p. 28). Ancient through contemporary cultures that make up the American mosaic in the global quilt must be looked at as similar but unique—each offering its unique ways of dealing with the essential problems of being human (Robarcheck, 1992). America has not melted into a monolithic shape; all of her features should be equally recognized.

Parameter Ten: Effects of Public Policy on the Distribution of Power and Success. This parameter requires critical reflection on the impact of the differential effects of policy and practice on race, class, gender, ability, and culture regarding such issues as teacher expectations, ability grouping and curriculum tracking, desegregation and integration, discipline and suspension/expulsion, and dropout/pushout factors (e.g., Adair, 1984; Carrier, 1983; Duran, 1983; Kozol, 1991; Lomotey, 1990; Shepard & Smith, 1989).

Parameter Eleven: Foundations of Racism (Including Handicapism). This parameter departs completely from the traditional teacher education knowledge base to look specifically at issues of racism, handicapism, slavery, genocide, prejudice, bias, stereotyping, and discrimination, and their effects on both microcultures and American macroculture. An area of some confusion encircles this parameter since many teacher candidates have a hard time conceptualizing that both sides lose out when racism flourishes (Hidalgo, McDowell, & Siddle, 1990).

> Although the situation of oppression is a dehumanized and dehumanizing totality affecting both the oppressors and those whom they oppress, it is the latter who must, from their stifled humanity, wage for both the struggle for a fuller humanity; the oppressor, who is himself dehumanized because he dehumanizes others, is unable to lead this struggle. (Freire, 1970/1968, p. 32)

Parameter Twelve: Experiential Knowledge Base. This parameter of the knowledge base actually must be extracted from life and supervised clinical experiences that include personal, cross-cultural, and multicultural experiences, and supervised demonstration of culturally responsive/responsible teaching in clinical school settings with culturally diverse student populations. Field experiences and critical reflection on personal life components specifically address this aspect of the knowledge base.

Parameter Thirteen: Foundations of Craft Wisdom. This parameter is a recognition of the growing body of professional knowledge about how teachers teach effectively and responsibly in multicultural classrooms representing diversity issues. The work in this area often is attributed to anthropologists and, more recently, to ethnographers, those who do "educational anthropology," particularly Spindler and Spindler (1987; Spindler, 1982).

UNDERSTANDING HUMAN DIVERSITY

Teachers need to develop a broad understanding of humans and their diversity. As teacher educators, we need to *enculturate* preservice teachers with an applicable theory of human development and to *acculturate* them to the breadth of divergent cultures that are represented in our school systems. Further, the culturally responsible pedagogical program needs to nurture in teacher education students an understanding and caring about the realities and challenges of children with exceptionalities, differing abilities, handicapping conditions, and other diversities.

For those of us who look at human growth and change from a developmental, social, multicultural, and special education view, the notions of *intraindividual* change and *interindividual differences* are of central interest. Intraindividual change refers to the development of one individual over time; interindividual differences in development address the differences among individuals of the same age or group at one point in time (Greenfield & Cocking, 1994). Using this perspective to describe and explain human development and human diversity, posits the need to understand "the changing individual in a changing world" (Lerner & Hultsch, 1983, p. 12).

What the Developmentalists Say

Over the past 30 years, two major changes have evolved in social scientists' perspective in defining human development. First, they see human growth and change as a process that occurs over the life span, rather than the traditional emphasis on development that stressed maturation and change during infancy, childhood, and adolescence; stability during adulthood; and degeneration during old age (Baltes, 1973; Baltes, Reese, & Lipsitt, 1980; Baltes & Willis, 1977; Lerner & Ryff, 1978). Lerner and Hultsch (1983) defined the life-span perspective of development as an attempt "to describe, explain, and optimize intraindividual change in behavior and interindividual differences in such change across the life span, that is, from conception to death" (p. 7). This approach stresses the need to understand that there is a dynamic and interactive relationship between the continually changing individual and a continually changing world.

Second, the model of a *contextual worldview* has been increasingly accepted (Lerner & Spanier, 1978; Pepper, 1942; Riegel, 1976). This model posits a continuous interaction between the individual and all the different levels of organization existing in the world. In other words, one not only looks at the inner-physical phenomena (e.g., molecules and organs), or phenomena that characterize the whole individual (e.g., personality); one also needs to address the outer-physical phenomena (weather, pollution) and cultural and historical events (wars, segregation) in order to fully understand human development (Lerner & Hultsch, 1983). Modern developmental theorists increasingly have moved away from the argument regarding which of these two processes is the more important determinant of development to a concern with "how nature and nurture work together to influence" (Berk, 1993, p. 6) the individual's traits, capacities, and character (Berk, 1993; Bruner,

1989; Gibbs & Huang, 1989). For instance, although considerable research supports the theory that such characteristics as intelligence have a biological basis (our genetic blueprint determines the range of possibilities for this construct), the final outcome in terms of achievement gained is affected considerably by the environment (Goldsmith, 1988; Plomin, 1989; Santrock & Yussen, 1992; Thomas & Chess, 1987).

What the Multiculturalists Say

Culturally responsible pedagogy provides a holistic response to the dilemma of responding effectively to the diversity of students in contemporary educational settings. Diversity is here intended to refer to *inter-individual differences*, including, but not limited to, geographic race of origin, ethnic group, regionality, socioeconomic status, gender and sexual orientation, spirituality and religion, abilities and handicapping conditions, language, age, literacy and language development, worldviews, and experiences. Being culturally responsible does not require one to celebrate all diversity; it does require one to recognize the rights of individual learners in an egalitarian, democratic system, particularly in public schools. This explication of diversity is often offensive to those who have viewed diversity as a black and white issue focusing primarily on skin color. The definition is intended to be comprehensive to avoid simplistic generalizations and stereotypes. To be responsive to diversity in the classroom requires starting with where the learner is. Providing the same content and instruction to all students is *not* equity.

What the Special Educators Say

Over the past 30 years, special education has undergone an unprecedented revolution and expansion. Public Law (PL) 94–142 mandated special education for thousands of children who had been physically or functionally excluded by the public schools. Skrtic's (1992) analysis of the structure of special education showed that schools have not been changed significantly to accommodate students whose needs are different; special education students (and to some extent culturally different students) have not been integrated into the fabric of educational service. Instead, they have been served by classes that were added on to the original structure (Deshler & Lenz, 1989; Idol, 1993; Turnbull, 1993). Although students with special needs cannot be said to be functionally excluded any longer (many of them have received significant benefit from their education), one can charge that a dual system has been developed that is analogous to the "separate but equal" system for African Americans.

DESIGNING A PROGRAM FOR CULTURALLY RESPONSIBLE EDUCATORS

The past 20 years have seen two substantial changes in Wichita State University's service area: first, an increase in the Hispanic and African American populations, plus a substantial increase of Asian immigrants to the community; and second, a proliferation of service models for special education needs. The competencies needed to teach a culturally diverse population and those associated with the newer models of service delivery for students with special needs (i.e., inclusion in general education classes) were poorly defined; few of these skills were included in the teacher training program. If these new competencies associated with working with diverse populations were included in teacher education courses, they most often were included as add on elements. As the need for change became more apparent, teacher education program developers added a course or a lecture to accommodate the perceived needs of their graduates. In the same fashion that special education services were added to public schools, all too often no basic changes in the structure of the teacher education program were made. Based on these changes in the service area of our institution and accreditation review, the faculty began to examine the entire undergraduate teaching program.

The Former Undergraduate Teacher Education Program

The undergraduate teacher education program at Wichita State University (which was designed more than 20 years ago) initially included coursework in foundations, growth and development, learning, and evaluation. The courses presenting information about human diversity in public school children were not sequenced with other courses. As a result, preservice teachers could, and did, take these foundations courses during or after their student teaching experience.

Rationale for the Revised Program

In developing the knowledge base and coursework for our program it became clear that if our teacher candidates were to become nurturing educators, they first were going to have to "know" students in order to teach effectively. Knowledge about students allows preservice teachers to recognize differences, each potentially demanding different types of instruction. Teachers must have the skills to use a variety of instructional approaches and strategies to meet learners' needs.

Public schools often try to address differences in individuals through a differentiated staffing model, which attempts to group students with similar abilities and places them with separate teachers who have specialized training. This practice of one teacher for one class is being challenged across the entire educational front. In special education, more and more districts are moving to include more and more severely impaired students in regular classrooms. With this inclusion comes increased team and teaching collaboration. This requires the preservice teacher to have a multidimensional knowledge base about students that integrates each student into a culturally responsible, developmentally appropriate, and least restrictive learning environment responsive to the student's culture, development, and abilities. We suggest that a differentiated teaching model more appropriately meets the demands presented by the majority of the schools in the United States.

The Block Concept

All too often college programs divide the teacher education knowledge base into separate courses taught by faculty with expertise and experience in the appropriate areas. This differentiated staffing plan leads preservice teachers to see a student and the knowledge base as many parts, not a whole. Conversely, Wichita State University's teacher education program has been designed in sequential blocks of coursework. Field experiences integrate the courses within each block, while portfolio development and presentation ensure integration among the different blocks. The revised program is predicated on the belief that "the most important purpose of schooling is the development of integrated knowledge, skills, and values that enable the functioning of students as responsible and productive members of a democratic, multicultural, technological, and global society" (College of Education, 1992, p. 3). The goal of the revised program is to develop nurturing teachers who are knowledgeable and sensitive to the needs of the individual learner. The outcomes statements generated from this goal are sequenced and assigned to courses and/or field experiences. The courses and field experiences are then organized into blocks.

DESCRIPTION OF THE BLOCK PROGRAM

The introductory set of courses, the Pre-Professional Block, consists of a course and its attendant field experience to acquaint the student with the profession before he or she makes a commitment to the program. Students are officially admitted to the teacher education program before they begin Block I.

Overview of the Four Blocks

The first set of professional courses, Block I, addresses human diversity. Courses include Social and Multicultural Foundations of Education, Human Growth and Development, Introduction to Exceptional Children, and a field experience that serves as an integrative platform for these three courses. The second set of courses, Block II, focuses on general issues of curriculum, instruction, and evaluation. The courses in this block include Learning and Evaluation, Curriculum, Instruction, and Management, and a field experience.

Elementary majors have a total of four methods courses that are spread over Blocks II and III. The focus is content-specific curriculum and methods, including a pre-student teaching field experience and a content-specific methods course. The final block of professional courses, Block IV, consists primarily of student teaching and related courses. Although issues of diversity are being addressed throughout the program, Block I is of primary interest to this chapter. This early block provides a firm footing in the understanding of human diversity.

Addressing Diversity Issues (Block I)

In Block I, students examine diversity in humans by exploring: (1) the nature of human growth and development, (2) the exceptionalities and differences in human development, and (3) the nature of education in a multicultural, global society. The field experiences for Block I require students to integrate the content of the three courses through observations, interviews, and data collection in at least three different field placements and in the community at large. Formative development of the teacher candidate is assessed through accomplishments in coursework, collaborative teaming projects, field experiences, and portfolio development and presentation.

Although all of the Block I experiences focus on integration of the major block topics, cultural responsiveness is primarily the responsibility of the Social and Multicultural Foundations course. The stated course purpose incorporates the NCATE (1990) diversity standards, encouraging students to examine education and schools in a changing society. Teacher candidates develop an appreciation for the changing ethnic and cultural characteristics of American schools "to become more responsive to the human condition, cultural integrity, and cultural pluralism in society" (p. 14). Students work in collaborative teams on a major project identified as an *Ethnic/Cultural Group Collaborative* (ECGC) to develop multiple perspectives on the history of education in the United States. *The Quality Learning Experiences* (QLE) plan developed during the final quarter of Block I provides a structured approach to incorporating knowledge of the parameters into an integrated, learner-centered plan (Huber-Bowen, 1993).

The focus of the Introduction to Exceptional Children course is to acquaint students with the ways learners vary in ability. This variance is examined in regard to mobility, general intelligence, specific learning abilities, behavior, and sensory abilities. Its purpose is to assist students in learning to deal with issues of special education. A major assignment for the course is designed to help students understand the impact of limited mobility on the access to common resources.

The Human Growth and Development course focuses on genetic and environmental interaction to describe and explain the changing person. The emphasis is on the host of similarities that are ours because we are human and the resulting stereotyping and overgeneralizing of "differences" in the human condition. Therefore, it provides a foil for the differences portrayed in the other two courses. The integration of the three courses emphasizes the similarities of humankind while it celebrates the differences caused by history, society, culture, and ability.

Field Experience Requirements

Each field experience requirement (FER) is assigned in one of the three nonfield-based classes in Block I. The field experiences are a vital key in the development of students' attitudes toward diversity. Informally, students often cite field experiences as they refer to influences on their attitudes toward diversity. In recognition of this, eight broad-based FERs were devised, five of which are school-based, to help students understand the accommodation (or lack thereof) made for diversity in public school settings. A description of each FER follows.

The Demographic Profile: This FER requires the students to create a demographic profile of a classroom they are observing; students must look beyond the readily observable issues of skin color and reflect on other cultural, ability, and developmental issues.

The Curriculum Resource Evaluation: This FER requires students to examine a teaching resource (e.g., text, video) for cultural representation. Students respond to a series of questions that are designed to direct their focus beyond skin color, names, and obvious cultural issues.

The Preassessment/Multidisciplinary Team Member Interview: This FER consists of two structured interviews: one with a member of the preassessment team in the school and another with a member of the multidisciplinary team. These teams are associated with the prevention of major school-related problems and the identification of disabilities.

Service Delivery Observations and Observations of Exceptional Students: These FERs consist of observations students conduct in a regular education classroom, a school-based special education room (e.g., resource room), and a special day school. With these three observations, students are exposed to a variety of disabilities across a wide range of severity. These observations are followed with short reflective writings about students' impressions of each setting and the individuals observed.

The Whose Culture?: Students in this community- and school-based FER are required to (1) conduct an in-depth interview of a person from a different culture, and (2) observe the culture of a classroom. In a reflective paper, the students are encouraged to compare the culture of the school with the culture of the individual learners in that school. Issues of language, ethnic heritage, work, leisure, and gender roles are explored.

The Cultural Awareness Activity: This FER, a community-based experience, requires the students to attend a cultural event with which they are not familiar. There is a great deal of latitude allowed in their selection of an event. Students have been encouraged to attend events as varied as operas, symphony concerts, pow-wows, ethnic restaurants, and religious services. Part of this experience is to interview a person who regularly attends these events. The students use their observation and interview to identify implications for the classroom.

The Case Study Project: This FER requires students to develop a case study of a child within the context of his or her family. The students are encouraged to find a family (with whom they are unacquainted) from a different culture. The students observe the family in a typical familial situation, interact solely with the child for an hour, interview the parent(s), and assess the child in terms of cognitive or psychosocial development. The case study culminates in an evaluative and synthesized paper reflecting on the experience.

Implementing a Knowledge Base for Culturally Responsible Education

The concepts and elements of the knowledge base for developing a culturally responsible pedagogy have served as guidelines for the embellishment of the revised courses in Block I. The integration of parameter components is represented in Table 9.1. All parameters of the knowledge base are covered at some level but not at the same depth. For example, parameter six, "Foundations of Culturally Responsible and Responsive Diagnosis, Measurement, and Assessment," is examined at an awareness level because of the nature of the field experience structured for Block I. Early application

Table 9.1. Parameters of the Knowledge Base for Teacher Education by Course

	Parameters of the Knowledge Base[1]	Courses			
		SMF[2]	IEC[3]	HGD[4]	FE[5]
One	Theoretical, ideological, and philosophical foundations of education in a global society	✓			
Two	Psychosocial-cultural contexts of human growth and development in nonmainstream ethnic/racial cultures	✓	✓	✓	✓
Three	Cultural and cognitive learning style theory and research	✓		✓	
Four	Foundations of culturally responsive curriculum	✓			✓
Five	Foundations of effective strategies	✓	✓		
Six	Foundations of culturally responsible and responsive diagnosis, measurement, and assessment	✓	✓	✓	✓
Seven	Psychosocial-cultural influences in subject-specific learning	✓	✓		
Eight	Language, communication, and interaction styles	✓	✓		✓
Nine	Essential elements of cultures	✓			✓
Ten	Effects of public policy on the distribution of power and success	✓	✓		✓
Eleven	Foundations of racism (including ableism, classism, sexism, heterosexism, ageism, linguicism)	✓	✓		
Twelve	Experiential knowledge base				✓
Thirteen	Foundations of craft wisdom	✓	✓	✓	✓

[1] The parameters are being expanded to include sexual orientation (see Smith, 1991).
[2] Social and Multicultural Foundations of Education
[3] Introduction to Exceptional Children
[4] Human Growth and Development
[5] Field Experience

experiences of the preservice teachers are limited to observations. Later field experiences increase the application of the principles and concepts learned until the student teacher has full responsibility for the classroom.

Certain parameters of the knowledge base require a fundamental understanding rather than sustained application. It is appropriate for Block I to assume primary responsibility for these parameters, because the field experience of Block I has the resources and structure to allow the key exposures and activities that promote the kind of deep understanding required by parameters one, two, four, nine, ten, and eleven (see Table 9.1). These parameters are covered in depth throughout the Block I courses and are reviewed, but not covered in depth, in any other element of the teacher preparation program. The understanding achieved through Block I serves to shape and inform later practice.

Block Program Potential: Evaluation and Assessment

Huber and Kline (1993) have conducted a program evaluation that seeks to establish the impact of Block I on students' attitudes toward diversity and their preference for culturally diverse settings. Specifically, a revised version of the Social Distance Scale (SDS-R) (Huber, 1991), originally developed by Bogardus (1925, 1933), was administered to the first cohort (110 students) across the blocks in pretest and posttest conditions in order to measure participants' self-reported professional opinions about diversity. Using 6 ordinally scaled professional distance response sets, the SDS-R asks participants to indicate the degree to which they would, as an educator, interact with each of 40 categories of students. The response sets include possible responses from "no contact" to "contact in even the most familiar and personal situation open to a professional," and scoring ranges from "0" for unwillingness to accept students from this particular group in any of the five categories to "5" for willingness to accept students from this particular group in all learning/teaching settings and in community interactions and family settings. Although the totality of items in the scale did not suggest a significant difference between pretest and posttest responses, several logical subscales indicated significant differences. Specifically, teacher candidates were more willing to accept students with disabilities and gang members.

A second measure used to establish the impact of Block I was Ziegler's (1980) Preference for Social Diversity (PSD) Scale. It also was administered in pretest and posttest conditions. The scale asks a respondent to rank 17 items (eight of which are stated negatively) relative to variety in culture. The items include such things as preference for hearing different languages and comfort with people of different backgrounds, as well as a few items more closely related to a general preference for diversity (i.e., preference for shopping in different stores and preference for different destinations for vacations). The sums of the PSD scores were analyzed with a two-tailed t-test for dependent groups. The results indicated a definite increase in the students' preference for social diversity ($t = 20.46$, $p < .001$).

In addition to the formal instrumentation, faculty asked student teachers (who had participated in Block I three semesters earlier) to rate the Block I activities that they found most useful. About 50% (49 students) responded. Students were asked to select from the 15 activities listed (e.g., FERs, class projects, videos, and speakers) and to rank the two that most influenced their view of teaching in a pluralistic society. They also were asked to indicate the activity that was least influential. The top four activities were from the Social and Multicultural Foundations course, the ECGC, and the QLE (class projects), as well as two FERs (the Curriculum Resource Evaluation and the Cultural Awareness Activity). The remaining 11 activities were ranked closely. This suggests that different activities are relevant with different students.

These quantitative data, combined with the anecdotal experiences, begin to build a convincing argument for the effectiveness of the Block I portion of the Revised Teacher Education Program at Wichita State University in helping teacher candidates to understand and accept the array of human diversity they will encounter in the classroom.

CONCLUSION

As with any major change effort, curriculum change undertaken by a college or university faculty must be based on a thorough assessment of the needs addressed by the program and the degree to which the current program is meeting those needs. To be successful, any program must meet the needs of the students as well as those of the faculty who offer the program. New programs as well as old ones have both strengths and weaknesses; what is perceived as a strength by one person may be perceived as a weakness by another.

Adopting a new program presents a number of significant challenges for both students and faculty. It is not an easy process; perhaps Cole (cited in Bateson, 1989) said it best: "To ask faculty to change a curriculum is like asking someone to move a graveyard. It can be done, but it is a funky, messy, complicated, long process" (pp. 97–98). The process of changing curriculum to build a new program created many opportunities for problem solving by students and by faculty.

For instance, the placement of the history and philosophy of education at our institution represented a significant challenge. While generally regarded as part of the foundation needed by students, this course is presently a part of Block IV. Such challenges are obstacles—rather than insurmountable barriers—for which problem-solving strategies can be developed. Developing effective strategies requires cooperation between faculty members and across a college or university campus. Faculty team members must value collaboration and be willing to (1) work together; (2) collaborate on course content and field experiences; (3) communicate openly and frequently; (4) expand their focus from a "course-only" view to a "block" view; (5) coordinate specific course content with other faculty members teaching the same course and with faculty members teaching other courses in the same block; and (6) share responsibility for management and organization of the block.

Some faculty members may feel threatened by this collaborative experience, as courses typically have been organized to function independently of others, even those in the same department. Students also may be threatened by the blurring of lines between courses, as they generally expect each course to be separate from other courses; they expect to keep each course in a separate notebook, and they do not expect that a concept will be discussed in several courses from different perspectives.

The structure of the college or university also poses challenges for curriculum change of this nature. Implementing a block program with extensive faculty collaboration in a system that does not recognize or value collaboration can present significant problems for faculty members; time devoted to collaboration means that time is not devoted to those areas (e.g., research and service) valued by the promotion and tenure systems generally in place. While this collaboration does relate to teaching, it does not necessarily result in more courses taught or credit hours generated.

The collaboration of faculty members within Block I has had a profound effect on the content of the courses within the block, the processes by which information is taught and learned in the courses, and the faculty members involved. This collaboration has evolved to include a mutual sharing of teaching techniques and strategies; that is, we are developing our own learning community.

10

Self-Narrative Inquiry in Teacher Development
Living and Working in Just Institutions

SARA S. GARCIA

> I do not want my house to be walled in on all sides and my windows to be stuffed. I want the culture of all lands to be blown about my house as freely as possible. But I refuse to be blown off my feet by any.
> Mahatma Gandhi (cf., Gaston, 1984, p. 90)

Historically the cultures of certain ethnic groups in the United States have been rendered invisible in school pedagogy. New stipulations for credentialing in California, however, require teachers to reflect critically upon the meaning of cultural difference, including their own thinking and lived experience as well as the lives, backgrounds, and cultural history of the children they teach. To be effective in culturally diverse classrooms, teachers must confront certain contradictions in their own identity. Most teacher candidates have shaped their identity according to a set of mainstream values and beliefs that has denigrated cultural difference. The personal confrontation with difference and self-identity during the professional development process can be frustrating and painful if preservice teachers have never questioned their social position from the perspective of a belief system that values diversity and the cultural agency of ethnic communities.

For preservice teachers, the process of discovering their own identity requires that they take into consideration and honor the histories that are invisible in school pedagogy, especially the cultural histories of the children in their classroom. Hall's (1991) postmodernist articulation of difference suggests that teacher preparation should theorize a dialectical education process—that is, a praxis of discovery in which teachers recover their own history and identity in order to assist children from marginalized groups to recover theirs. This requires

> . . . teachers [to] understand the languages which they've been taught not to speak and revalue the traditions and inheritances of cultural expression and creativity. . . . Ethnicity . . . is constructed in history . . . partly through memory, partly through narrative, [and] . . . has to be recovered. It is an act of cultural recovery. (Hall, 1991, p. 12)

Preservice teachers (and teacher educators) need comprehensive professional preparation that requires transformation in their own thinking and in their lives. However, most faculty have not experienced the process of self-narrative reflective inquiry, particularly with regard to cultural knowledge in ethnically diverse communities. They are not likely to make self-narrative reflective inquiry an integral aspect of teacher preparation and are not prepared to become forgers of change. We must further explore how we, as teacher educators, view ourselves as change agents in teacher education. While we challenge mainstream teacher preparation practices and pedagogy through the discourse of "multicultural education," we also must address the ability of preservice and inservice teachers to foster empowerment and voice (Giroux & McLaren, 1986).

As a teacher educator, I experiment with community studies—research that relates to my own heritage and identity as a Mexican American woman (Garcia, 1994, 1995). My research, like recent ethnographic studies conducted by Limon (1994) and Vasquez, Pease-Alvarez, and Shannon (1994), informs teacher education practice from an interdisciplinary approach that is an alternative to the deficit model that still predominates. This chapter describes the use of self-narrative inquiry to enable teacher education students at Santa Clara University (SCU)—a Jesuit university in northern California—to explore issues of identity and cultural knowledge through the study of community cultural agency. The chapter proposes that self-narrative inquiry may lead teacher educators toward interdisciplinary models of teacher learning and development in which practice (in education and in the community) informs theory dialectically. That is, one is not independent of the other.

REFLECTION THROUGH INQUIRY AT SANTA CLARA UNIVERSITY

Sparks-Langer (1992) presents three approaches for understanding teachers' reflective thinking: Cognitive reflection focuses on the knowledge or processes in teacher decision making; critical reflection emphasizes questioning purposes; and narrative reflection stresses consideration of context factors. Cognitive reflection also includes schemata, an individual's comprehension of the world that is constructed through experience. Knowledge developed through critical reflection is socially and symbolically constructed by the mind through social interaction with others. Finally, knowledge through narrative reflection focuses on teachers' personal interpretations of the circumstances in which they make decisions. Self-narrative inquiry is a form of reflection into one's own "story" that includes making critical, evaluative judgments regarding one's own schemata.

Teacher educators at SCU have integrated modes of reflection that generate cultural knowledge and awareness through critical inquiry (King, 1991; King & Ladson-Billings, 1990). My contribution has been to emphasize various modes of critical introspection or self-narrative inquiry that are more deeply grounded in teacher candidates' learning and experiences, particularly in ethnic communities. As Richert (1992) states:

> As teachers talk about their work and "name" their experiences, they learn about what they know and what they believe. They also learn what they do not know. Such knowledge empowers the individual by providing a source for action that is generated from within rather than imposed from without. (p. 196)

Thus, a larger purpose for using reflection and self-narrative inquiry is to develop candidates' individual agency, critical thinking ability, as well as cultural knowledge of the communities in which they will teach.

Cultural Knowledge and Undergraduate Preparation

The ideal pool of candidates for any credential program in California includes representatives of all ethnic groups in the public schools. Given the low numbers of students of color in most teacher credential programs, it is difficult to design collaborative activities that permit teacher candidates to learn about cultural difference, identity, and community agency from one another.

Typically, credential candidates come into SCU's teacher education graduate (fifth-year) program with diverse levels of cultural knowledge. Approximately 50% of each year's candidates completed their undergraduate studies at SCU; 40% have undergraduate degrees from a University of California campus or a California State University campus; and the remaining 10% are from other states, are second career re-entry students, or are former homemakers. During the admissions interview, we determine whether applicants have worked with culturally and linguistically diverse students. The admissions process does not permit us to assess how well informed applicants are regarding their own culture or other cultures. Experience tutoring inner-city school children, for example, does not necessarily indicate that candidates have developed cultural knowledge that can inform their teaching practice in culturally diverse communities.

Even though credential candidates may have taken undergraduate courses in ethnic studies, cultural anthropology, or sociolinguistics, such courses usually cannot be considered transformative in relation to the candidates' understanding of teaching and learning. Every credential candidate, regardless of ethnic background, should have taken, as a general educational requirement, some ethnic studies courses or had a community-based field experience during his or her undergraduate education. At SCU, the East Side Project offers community-based learning and service experiences that are in keeping with the Jesuit mission's emphasis on social justice. In my experience, students who have this kind of prior preparation for teacher education are better prepared than those who have not had these experiences to respond to readings, discussions, and written essay exams related to critical analysis of social and political issues in foundations courses.

Generally, the lived experience of *ethnically identified* students is a solid foundation from which candidates can begin to reflect critically on issues related to cultural knowledge and community agency. These students often have an intuitive sense of the needs of ethnically and culturally diverse students and demonstrate sensitivity toward other ethnic communities. Still, upon entering our program, these students may have little formal knowledge of their own communities. Listen to the "voice" of one credential candidate:

> As an African American high school student, I never learned enough about the Harlem Renaissance to pass a test on it, nor enough facts and details to formulate an accurate picture of African American life within the United States at that time. Without knowing the historical social climate, without being told how much of the music and writing arose out of that social context, I (and many other "brothers" and "sisters") had no incentive to look towards the art[s] as a record of the history that had always eluded us. (MC, 1995 credential candidate)

Unfortunately, only one or two students from each of the three main ethnic groups in California (Latino, African American, and Asian American) usually participate in our program. Because these students often feel like "tokens," they experience a certain amount of alienation during their professional preparation. Thus, ethnically identified students are more likely than other students to know from their lived experience the dire need for well-prepared teachers who are knowledgeable and effective with students from ethnic communities.

COMMUNITY-BASED IMMERSION EXPERIENCES AND SELF-NARRATIVE INQUIRY

SCU credential candidates' first reflective learning experience begins in the Immersion Experience course. When this course was initiated in 1988, as a one-week orientation retreat, student teams were assigned to conduct ethnographic observations in selected communities.

The Original Immersion Experience

Each team, equipped with a map, drove around a given community, stopped at assigned locations (e.g., a "mom and pop" ethnic store or a gas station), and made notes of what they saw. In most cases the candidates conducted their community observations in the neighborhoods where they would eventually student teach.

Despite a culminating debriefing session that included reflective group discussion of their observations, candidates emphasized negative aspects of the communities they "visited" during this experience. Their observations distanced them from the people who actually lived there. For instance, students described ethnic markets as unkempt and disorganized, and identified economically linked conditions, such as a large number of liquor stores in a given community, wrecked cars parked in driveways and poor yard maintenance, few public parks, and high unemployment, without any understanding of the circumstances that create these phenomena. These reactions demonstrate the need for a more effective method of teaching students about diversity and ethnic and economically impoverished communities—one that dispels rather than reinforces cultural deficit interpretations of ethnic communities.

Although this experience was designed to begin reflection and inquiry from a critical standpoint, the Immersion Experience was not followed up throughout the year. Candidates needed opportunities for critical reflection grounded in a developmental process model of inquiry that aids the recovery of identity and the discovery of community agency—a more naturalistic learning process that develops a deeper understanding of cultural difference (King, 1994, 1995). Consequently, we now place more emphasis on cognitive reflection through self-narrative inquiry that is systematically integrated into the overall teaching and learning process of the credential program.

The Revised Immersion Experience

In 1994 we reorganized the Immersion Experience into a comprehensive, structured, field-based course that provides a basis for continual self-reflection and community-based experiential learning. This three-unit course is ongoing throughout the academic year and provides opportunities for cognitive and critical reflection through a variety of group experiences and self-narrative inquiry assignments. By examining their own growth and development concerning issues related to their observations, field assignments, and student teaching, candidates see and experience connections between the academic world and the real world. Immersion assignments include observations, participation in school restructuring, and community involvement. For example, candidates participate in interagency collaboration; teach in nontraditional education settings like juvenile court school tutoring programs; assist in employment training centers; and work in soup kitchens, in homeless shelters, and on crisis lines.

Through self-narrative inquiry assignments (directed observations and journal writing) and reflective group processes in courses and field experiences (guided discussion and systematic debriefing), candidates examine their initial perceptions in required practicums and gauge the change in their perceptions, cultural knowledge and awareness, and teaching practices in relation to ethnic "others." The self-narrative inquiry assignments, which require candidates to form personal, academic, and professional goals, inform this relation between theory and practice. For instance, at the beginning and end of the school year, in a group reflective activity, candidates generate a metaphor to describe the change in their perceptions and feelings during the school year. The ultimate goal of self-narrative inquiry is transformation of perceptions and practice through the development of cultural knowledge.

The Immersion Experience provides valuable opportunities to learn about and experience theory–practice linkages such as cultural agency in ethnic communities. We reiterate this concept throughout the year to help candidates recognize community cultural constants and the dynamics of change—how cultural constants sustain and change cultural identities, for example, and maintain and transmute culture through historical processes. In sum, faculty also encourage candidates to appreciate the need to develop flexibility in their life-long learning process and to view themselves as agents of change in their own lives, in society, and in history.

COLLABORATION AND INQUIRY
IN TWO FOUNDATIONS COURSES

In a recent report on the Internet's *Report Card* (May 22, 1995), Ann Lieberman, a professor at Teachers College, Columbia University, discussed the need for a "radical rethinking" of teacher development. Lieberman posits that "most educators agree that American students need a wide array of learning opportunities that engage students in experiencing, creating and solving real problems, using their own experiences, and working with others." Yet, according to Lieberman, these opportunities are denied teachers when they shift to a learner role. Inquiry-based models tend to emphasize analysis within learning environments rather than analysis of one's own learning (Zeichner, 1983).

The problem begins with the conditioned learning process to which preservice teachers are subjected as undergraduate students. Students enter credential programs with constructions and schemata already formed about teaching and learning. To overcome years of didactic methods, these learners need to develop the ability to recognize their own learning processes through exploration, experimentation, and discovery (Cannella & Reiff, 1994). Instead, by the time they enroll in graduate study at SCU, the majority of credential candidates expect to be lectured to in classes; they expect to be told what and how to think!

Critical reflection begins with an examination of how students are conditioned to think in traditional, competitive environments that engender limited opportunities for understanding their own cognitive development and for life-long learning to occur. Ultimately, the goal is to develop cognitive mapping skills, by synthesizing difficult concepts, making associations among concepts, and developing practical knowledge that constitutes a strong, holistic foundation for teaching and learning.

I teach two foundations courses: Psychological Foundations of Education and Second and First Language Acquisition Theory. Both courses deal with a critical examination of learning theories, especially as they pertain to linguistically and culturally diverse learners. I use the *Learning Thru Discussion* (LTD) format (Hill, 1977), which requires students to be prepared to discuss the issues presented in the readings in small discussion groups in a structured manner with an assigned group leader. Rules for group behavior are determined by the students. For instance, group members who are not prepared for discussion take notes and present a summation at the end of the session. The students are expected to define difficult concepts and discuss their individual comprehension of the readings assigned for a given day.

The discussion leader usually provides an outline of the readings and formulates probing questions to guide the conversation. The leader's most important responsibility is to generate discussion and guide it from one topic to another. Every student gets an opportunity to lead a discussion. This format provides learners with a guide for critically exploring the issues presented in the lecture and the concepts presented in the readings.

Students maintain a reflective narrative journal of their thinking to document the process of making associations among concepts presented in class. In this journal they are asked to examine their perceptions of issues in relation to what they observe in their field experience and how their culture, whether identified in terms of their identified ethnicity or as mainstream American culture, has contributed to their perceptions of teaching and learning. Students share their journal entries with the entire class. These narratives usually exemplify a process of growth in learning about issues such as ethnic identity, controversial sociopolitical issues related to cognition and linguistic policy, their personal dilemmas, fears, and insecurities about teaching. A myriad of unexpected perceptions usually emerge in these narratives, especially as related to controversial issues like the "English-only initiative," testing and achievement, and ability grouping. Usually, through constant examination of their preconceived notions of learning, from course readings, discussion, and narrative and reflective inquiry, the majority of students change their initial perceptions.

Preservice teachers conduct a case study of a student in the classroom where they observe or student teach. They are required to use the theories presented in class by systematically observing a situation in which they can identify a practice that reflects their comprehension of a given theory. For instance, when working with bilingual students, the use of code switching from one language to another and the context of the switch are examined based on the sociolinguistic theories discussed in class that address the learning environment and the perceptions held by the teacher with regard to language use in the classroom. The final project is a team assignment in which preservice teachers present interpretations based on the knowledge they gained by participating in class activities. Each team member prepares a paper that contributes to an assigned theme. In the Second and First Language Acquisition Theory course, preservice teachers are expected to develop working units that are guided theoretically by at least one of the Crosscultural, Language and Academic Development (CLAD) domains in the California credentialing emphasis requirement. (See Chapter 15, this volume, for a description of these requirements.) The selected domains—second language acquisition, ESL methods, or cross-cultural diversity—have to be articulated, substantiated, and supported based on assigned readings.

Preservice teachers are encouraged to exceed their *zone of proximal development*, according to Vygotskian principles (Moll, 1993). By the end of the course, students will have acquired a foundation for reflective learning by reading and participating in class discussions and by examining, through narrative inquiry, their own learning process. Applying their growing knowledge of teaching through experiential case studies and group project assignments provides them with additional experience as reflective thinkers, researchers, and classroom teachers. These experiences build a foundation for their life-long professional learning.

THE NARRATIVE VOICE OF PROSPECTIVE TEACHERS

Three student teachers working in the same school district collaboratively prepared lessons to teach about culture through music. One of the students, who has a genuine love for jazz music, traced the Harlem Renaissance through the evolution of jazz artists and motivated the students by connecting the evolution of jazz to artistic rap and then to the historical contributions of African Americans in literature. Langston Hughes's poetry and other forms of literature and popular culture were used to develop the literacy skills of the culturally diverse high school students. This exemplifies the effective use of critical reflection on the human condition through historical, political, and artistic devices for teaching. These candidates were transformed through this collaborative process of cognitive and critical reflective inquiry.

The following excerpt illustrates how the preservice teachers viewed the concept of cultural constants:

> One cultural constant has been the legacy of communalism that defines . . . African American life: "one is not a human being except as he [or she] is part of a social order" (King, 1994). Through the art of the Harlem Renaissance, students would find that the values they have are not without a history—a foundation. . . . With so much civil unrest in certain African American neighborhoods, it would be good if the children could take home the concept of shared perceptions, values, and behaviors, being motivated to incorporate them into their own structures of family and friends. (Team Project Final Report)

Grounded in a theoretical understanding of African American culture that eschews cultural deficit interpretations (King, 1994), the report discusses how teachers can incorporate such cultural constants into their pedagogy: "The teacher of this unit would do good to make use of this time-honored tradition [communalism] by providing opportunities for pupils to engage in cooperative group activities."

In an attempt to capture the final thoughts of candidates concerning their experiences during the credential process and their feelings about becoming teachers, we asked for a closing self-narrative inquiry. The underlying purpose of this activity was to see whether candidates discussed cultural knowledge with regard to teacher preparation. (Most of them did address this concept.) Narrative theory predicts "disorderly" experiences, especially when catalyzing experiences fundamentally change subjects' political consciousness (Kohler-Riessman, 1994). In theoretical terms, narratives do not mirror a world "out there." They are constructed, creatively authored, rhetorical, interpretive, and replete with assumptions (Kohler-Riessman, 1994). As Richert (1992) observes, teachers can

> draw on what they know and believe as they enter the world of schools. Similarly, they can prepare themselves for responsible work that is responsive to the increasingly complex demands of teaching in the twenty-first century. Preparing teachers to exercise their voices prepares them to act with agency in their own lives. (p. 197)

If this process of preservice teacher development through self-narrative inquiry is continued into the first year of teaching, perhaps new teachers will continue to grow in ways that will make a difference in the quality of schooling for all students, including culturally and linguistically diverse learners.

CONCLUSION

The SCU teacher education program is constantly changing in order to better prepare teachers who are responsive to the needs of all learners. In California the notion that teachers should have a strong foundation of cultural knowledge concerning the students in their classrooms, who mostly come from cultures different from the teachers', is not new. Teacher educators must be able to determine whether prospective teachers are sufficiently sensitive to cultural difference to be effective teachers in diverse settings. We must understand how teachers acquire and use cultural knowledge as a basis for constructing learning environments that are responsive to cultural dimensions of learning. We must determine how undergraduate ethnic studies courses and community-based learning can contribute to the knowledge and experiences teachers need. Furthermore, we must assess teachers' sensitivity to the multiplicity of meanings or "intertextual" cultural expressions through which lived experiences affect learning (Hoffer Gosselin, 1978). Culture changes and transmutes our cultural identities in complex ways that require constant awareness of the process of social change. Ricoeur (1992) states that the task of the changing Self requires "living well with and for others in just institutions." Teacher development and growth is a complex and dynamic process that warrants further investigation in this direction.

11

"Thank You for Opening Our Minds"
On Praxis, Transmutation, and Black Studies in Teacher Development

JOYCE E. KING

A schema is "a mental codification of experience that includes a particular organized way of perceiving cognitively and responding to a complex situation or set of stimuli" (*Webster's New Collegiate Dictionary*). Santa Clara University (SCU) teacher education program graduates often describe the intellectual, professional, and personal development they experience during the program as "opening" their minds. This aptly describes the focus of my teaching in a foundations course sequence and student teaching seminars (from 1982 to 1994) on enabling credential candidates to change the cognitive and affective schemata that limit their understanding of and commitment to the possibilities of transformative teaching. This chapter illustrates modes of narrative inquiry and self-reflective, experiential learning processes that constitute a praxis of transmutation of cognitive and affective schemata.

This praxis, or "practical-critical activity" (Kilminster, 1979, p. 20), in my courses is designed to bring about changes in the intellectual, emotional, social, and professional development of teacher candidates.[1] The term *praxis* denotes more self-consciously reflexive teaching processes and learning experiences than the term *practice* suggests (p. 17). A reflexive process changes as the knowledge, thinking, and abilities of the students change (Carr & Kemmis, 1986) and thus has the capacity to enable new forms of competence. The grounding of this praxis in a Black Studies theoretical perspective also is discussed.

"Black Studies is critical and corrective of the inadequacies, omissions and distortions of traditional white studies" (Karenga, 1993, p. 18). The discipline's theoretical perspective consists of an epistemological critique of school knowledge and practices that transcends multicultural approaches. Wynter's (1995) application of this conceptual paradigm deciphers the cultural rules governing the "symbolic representational systems" and the "conceptual-cognitive categories" (p. 13) of the social order that govern (and limit) our thought and behavior. This includes the roles of conceptual "blackness" and "whiteness" in our society (King, 1995; Morrison, 1992). Thus, Wynter's (1992) "deciphering practice" of Black Studies aims to advance human freedom from the "specific perceptual-cognitive processes by which we know our reality" (Wynter, 1995, p. 13).

INTERROGATING IDEOLOGY AND IDENTITY SCHEMATA

Student teachers usually begin the program without any critical comprehension of societal injustice (King, 1991) or awareness of the constitutive role of teachers, schooling, and school knowledge in the production of school failure and the reproduction of inequity. Teacher candidates usually have not recognized or reflected critically upon the ideological quality of their knowledge and their own miseducation and alienation from the struggle for justice; they have no concrete understanding of or commitment to teaching for change (King, 1991).

Social Foundations of Education and Interpersonal/Cross-Cultural Communications—courses taught fall and winter quarters, respectively—address the educational ideology and identity schemata of credential candidates that often include the beliefs that

1. They are either "conservative" (or "liberal") and that "liberalism" (or "conservatism") is suspect; there are no viable alternatives to these positions; and their particular outlook is the result of their own choosing.
2. "Whiteness" is not itself a conceptual category but is normative and is tantamount to "We the people," that is, being an American; being an American means being "just like us" (them); and assimilation is an unquestioned aspiration of diverse (non-white and non-middle class or affluent) "others" and is the normal goal of teachers.
3. Schools are benevolent and beneficent institutions; schools are the way elementary credential candidates remembered them when they "played school" as children; their own schooling experience is typical, so schools must, therefore, provide access to the "good life" for all.
4. "The American Dream" is a reality and continuing possibility for all individuals who work hard enough; education is the route to a good job;

the poor, hungry, homeless, imprisoned, or jobless have merely to put forth the right kind of effort to benefit from the meritocracy.

5. The children they will teach love teachers who "love children" as they do; or adolescents will love their subjects as secondary teachers do.

6. Emphasizing cultural dimensions of learning and recognizing students' racial and ethnic identities constitute acts of prejudice; and racism and prejudice are characteristic of "human nature," so teachers should avoid enacting such prejudice.

7. An African American teacher education professor who teaches about "white privilege" (McIntosh, 1989) and distinguishes between prejudice and racism as "power plus prejudice" (Rothenberg, 1988, p. 6), for instance, or a Mexican American professor who teaches about the benefits of bilingual education and community agency are anti-white, biased, self-interested, and possibly anti-American.

8. Teachers (including teacher education professors) who question any of these beliefs are necessarily indoctrinating students.

Not every student holds these beliefs, or holds them to the same extent; nor do all respond to the courses in the same way or change their beliefs. The praxis that I developed while teaching at SCU addresses the limited cognitive-perceptual ability of credential candidates to question basic assumptions about self, society, and cultural difference, as well as their willingness to engage in socially transforming teaching. Informal interviews with practitioners and graduates, and exit interviews affirm the significance of the pedagogical praxis demonstrated here.

A PEDAGOGICAL RESPONSE TO MISEDUCATION AND DYSCONSCIOUSNESS

Biased and distorted knowledge in the academic disciplines and school texts that reflects the "representational or cultural system" (Wynter, 1995) of the social order contributes to the miseducation of the relatively privileged class (King, 1991). Elsewhere (King, 1991) I have defined the "limited and distorted understandings my students have about inequity and cultural diversity" (p. 134) as *dysconsciousness*. This term refers to "an uncritical habit of mind (including perceptions, attitudes, assumptions, and beliefs) that justifies inequity and exploitation by accepting the existing order of things as given" (p. 134). Dysconsciousness, therefore, "involves a subjective identification with an ideological viewpoint that admits no fundamentally alternative vision" (p. 135) of either self, teaching, or society. It is a form of thought that not only reflects a lack of critical judgment against society and schooling as well as a lack of "social ethics" (Cox, 1974) but also is closely tied to self-identities and emergent professional identities that include emotionally aberrant responses to cultural diversity.

The praxis described in this chapter is a pedagogical response to miseducation and dysconsciousness that enables me to model consciously the relevance of culture for learning. My approach avoids dogmatism and disrespect for students, especially those who have had little opportunity to analyze the cultural system in which they have been socialized, to experience the strengths of diversity, or to question their own miseducation and cultural encapsulation. For example, SCU credential candidates often view themselves as homogeneously "white" (or "white-identified" culturally) and middle class, if not affluent. Writing on critical pedagogy that focuses on liberating the "oppressed" does not address the needs of these students. However, "reading the word" and the "world" in my courses involves students in examining their own knowledge, assumptions, life experiences, educational ideology, and teaching philosophy. This praxis facilitates recognition that the school/academic knowledge as well as the personal and cultural knowledge that students bring into the classroom, including their ethnic, racial, and gender identity, and so forth, can and should inform teachers' judgment about what needs to be taught and how, what students need to learn and why. This pedagogical response to dysconsciousness and miseducation is grounded in a Black Studies theoretical perspective.

USING A BLACK STUDIES THEORETICAL PERSPECTIVE

Black Studies recognizes a dialectical link between intellectual and sociopolitical emancipation and is ethically committed to knowledge for human freedom from the social domination of ideas as well as institutional structures. Thus, Black Studies "challenges the interests the dominant ideology conceals in myths about 'we the people'" (King, 1992, p. 321). The Social Foundations of Education course embodies the Black Studies theoretical approach to knowledge and social change by focusing on the practical-critical comprehension of society and alternatives to the complicity of educators in the reproduction of societal injustice (Cagan, 1978; Kozol, 1975; MacLeod, 1992; Weiler, 1988). Credential candidates analyze certain cognitive-perceptual categories, such as their understanding of "ideology," the "American Dream," the social interests of school knowledge, the social purposes of education, and so on. Candidates are assessed in terms of their ability to reflect critically upon perceptions and beliefs about social and educational inequality and to articulate their own philosophy of education taking this self-reflective analysis into account in their teaching practice.

In Interpersonal/Cross-Cultural Communications credential candidates further examine and extend their awareness of self and society in relation to teaching (e.g., beliefs and assumptions about racism, sexism, and culture). The focus is on the relevance of culture and cultural competence for effective classroom communication, using community resources, selecting instructional content, and goals for students' cognitive and affective development, particularly in diverse classrooms. Candidates are assessed in terms of their ability to develop and demonstrate *informed empathy*, that is, an understanding of the effects of white supremacy/racism *on themselves* as well on diverse "others."

Theory–Practice Linkages

Course assignments in field placements in contrasting wealthy, suburban, and predominantly white versus racially, socioeconomically, and linguistically diverse schools complement the theoretical perspectives presented and student learning in the foundations courses. For example, at a middle school for "newcomers" Mexican American junior high students challenged a Mexican American student teacher to accept his own identity before they were willing to accept him and learn from him. In fact, his "crew cut" made him appear to be Asian American. In a class project on cross-cultural communication, he incorporated this experience and his understanding of the difference between his experience growing up as "the only one" in an affluent white community and their "newcomer" experience of becoming the (unwanted, if not despised) "majority" in an English-only political climate. The theoretical focus on understanding the "black–white" dynamic in society and how the racial hierarchy affects other groups was also a factor in his ability to address these issues and to understand their relevance to student learning and development (including his own).

Modes of (Self) Narrative Inquiry

We use narrative inquiry as a mode of student learning that engages credential candidates in thinking critically about their cognitive and affective schemata in relation to their teaching practice. These schemata include narratives or stories that shape and are shaped by the way they perceive self, society, and others, and often are based on their lived experience under white supremacy/racism. Various modes of narrative inquiry (film analysis, reading fiction, writing personal essays, and guided reflective journal writing/dialogues with me, etc.) help them to recognize unacknowledged societal contradictions (Cagan, 1978, p. 244) and societal myths, and to decipher the narratives they carry in their minds and bodies.[2] For example, students have revealed traumas and crises of identity—which are apparently personal but have a social basis—that influence their idea of teaching, their responses to diversity, and in some cases their resistance to the SCU program's emphasis. One white woman student shared painful memories of being called "Nigger Coon" as a child because she had "frizzy" blond hair (before she "discovered mousse"). After reading the novel *Donald Duk* (Chin, 1991), about a Chinese American boy who hated being Chinese until he learned to value his heritage, another credential candidate developed lessons to help students affirm their ethnic and racial identity—an approach he initially opposed. In guided journal reflections on the novel, the student teacher discussed how he, like the character Donald Duk, grew up hating his Italian name and feeling ashamed because his immigrant parents spoke only Italian. That his experience and aspiration to assimilate were not exactly the same as Donald Duk's, however, because of the way racism works in our society, was a significant realization. Still another student, who also criticized the focus in my courses, eventually admitted that she harbored a deep fear of black students after attending inner-city schools on the east coast where she grew up. The following are examples of generative concepts, themes, and practical-critical learning experiences in the two foundations courses that extend narrative inquiry and self-reflection toward cognitive and affective cross-cultural competence and teaching skills.

GENERATIVE CONCEPTS AND COURSE THEMES

The praxis of transmutation is an ethically imperative pedagogical process. Generative concepts, themes, and questions used to guide critical reflection and analyses model social justice teaching for change (Center for Economic Conversion, 1992; Wolf-Wasserman & Hutchinson, 1978). A central generative theme in Social Foundations of Education that reflects the Black Studies theoretical perspective is drawn from Kozol's (1975) passionate declaration of the ethical obligations of teachers: "Education is not . . . neutral" (p. 108). Other concepts elaborate this theme and focus analytical attention on the social purposes of schooling, educational ideologies and philosophies, and the hidden curriculum (Vallence, 1977); school indoctrination (Anyon, 1979; Kozol, 1975); the "IQ myth," teacher expectations (Rist, 1970), and teacher socialization; organizational change and school reform; and the social interests of the curriculum and economic exploitation. Films, such as *The Business of America*, illustrate unacknowledged contradictions in the notion of "meritocracy," for instance. Such course material juxtaposes the reality of economic exploitation with the ideal of the "American Dream" and its limits, even for white Americans who have become victims of de-industrialization. Reading Kozol's *Savage Inequalities* (1991) provides what for some students is shocking evidence of the reality of societal injustice.

Individualism versus Collectivism

Cagan's (1978) essay "Individualism, Collectivism, and Radical Educational Reform" is a pivotal course reading in Social Foundations of Education that explores connections between social justice and education. Contrasting socialism and capitalism, it suggests that socialist education and the value of cooperation and altruism are needed alternatives to competitive individualism and the U.S. value system. Cagan argues that true freedom and individuality are possible only through participation in a human community. The author also critiques the cycles of radical and liberal school reform in the 1960s and 1970s that "failed to consider that education under capitalism has an essentially undemocratic function—the perpetuation of social inequities and the ideologies that rationalize them" (p. 244). Cagan suggests that radical school reformers must define their work as part of a larger political movement that seeks to change society as well as the schools. Reading and discussing this material introduce students to a critical conception of teaching for change that transcends the dualism of liberal versus conservative sociopolitical and educational approaches. Also, through observations and analyses of ethnographic research on school change, candidates examine changing rationales and social purposes of schooling and school reform. The course returns to the generative theme of teachers' responsibilities as change agents in greater depth in the work of Giroux and McLaren (1986), MacLeod (1992), and Weiler (1988).

Ideology, Hegemony, and School Knowledge

During the first Social Foundations of Education class, the concept of *ideology* is introduced to credential candidates in a way that permits them to re-experience consciously not only what ideology means but what it does (to them), both cognitively and affectively. Not surprisingly, when I ask them to describe how they *feel* about the word, not what they think it means, many say the word makes them feel "uncomfortable." During the discussion, I explain that they are conflating ideology and indoctrination. This practical-critical learning experience demonstrates that "ideas have consequences": Ideas influence students' cognitions as well as their actions and affective responses to the world. Students also read empirical research on ideological curriculum bias at work in U.S. history textbooks and school knowledge (Anyon, 1979), against the backdrop of Kozol's (1975, 1981) ethical exhortations against societal injustice and examples of "hidden" social justice struggles, such as a graphic account of working people's exploitation and resistance in a biographical sketch of labor organizer Mother Jones (Nies, 1977). Three educational documentary films about inequity and injustice in different historical periods, *Labor Comes of Age, Hunger in America,* and *The Business of America,* narrate ideological positions about the unemployed, the poor, the hungry, and the labor movement.

By comparing the explanations of working people's lives, struggles, and economic exploitation in these films with the historical information in the biographical sketch of Mother Jones and in Anyon's research, and their own knowledge, candidates deconstruct the social class interests in these "educational" resources. In one film, poor Mexican American children are said to be hungry "because they [sic] daddies just won't work." In another, a poor white man, who blames himself because his wife and children are malnourished, says: "I don't need no hand-out from the government . . . that's for bums." Such lessons contribute to the historical knowledge of credential candidates and also demonstrate that ideological positions can be sincerely *believed* by the people who have been induced to accept these worldviews.

As credential candidates examine empirical examples of how hegemony and ideology work—that schooling fosters certain ideas and forms of knowledge and not others, often in accord with the social class and racial backgrounds of students (Anyon, 1981; Kozol, 1991)—they also begin to wonder whether teachers (like me) who want to challenge what students know and believe, can avoid indoctrination. Making my praxis explicit and linking it with analyses of critical pedagogy (McLaren, 1989; MacLeod, 1992) as a response to ideology, miseducation, and hegemony are helpful in addressing this concern.

"White Is a State of Mind; It's Even a Moral Choice."

The African American author James Baldwin made the above statement in a public speech entitled "The View from Here," which students hear and respond to in discussions and journals in Interpersonal/Cross-Cultural Communications (National Press Club Library, December 10, 1986). "Conceptual whiteness" is a generative theme of the course. Understanding the concept—about which many of our students are and prefer to remain oblivious—is elemental to interrogating the celebratory narrative of (white) American identity. The following are examples of concepts and competence developed in this course through readings and learning activities designed to explicate and transmute this cognitive-perceptual category. These include novels (see Note 2), films (*Racism 101* and *In the Eye of the Storm*), reflective group discussion, journal writing exercises, and community-based assignments that require the students to interact with community people of diverse backgrounds.

Informed empathy versus sympathy is a type of competence that reflects knowledge of how societal cognitive-perceptual categories shape our perceptions and beliefs; it requires reflective self-knowledge of one's own experiences as well as those of others with whom one interacts or whom one teaches. The course materials, activities, and my lectures emphasize that such *self-knowledge*—a foundation for informed empathy—requires *accurate* knowledge of the culture and society as a basis for awareness of how one's relations with others are affected by race, culture, and other forms of difference. This includes understanding the difference between the immigrant experiences of European Americans and the particular experiences of people of color. The course begins with readings on America's development from the perspective of diverse "others" in books like Zinn's *A People's History of the United States* (1980).

Worldview encompasses the way a culture group perceives people and events and the way culture shapes perceptions, beliefs, attitudes, assumptions, and self-perceptions. Particular emphasis is placed on racism, prejudice, alienation, and assimilation. In addition to Baldwin's taped lecture, which is a sharp historical critique of the dominant U.S. worldview, students are exposed to other literature, such as the autobiographical book of essays by the Native American artist Jamake Highwater. In *The Primal Mind*, Highwater (1981) embraces his identity and describes his alienation from the dominant society's value system as a "precious gift": Being acculturated in two cultures allows people to discover their common humanity (e.g., "a cherished alienation"). Through such material, students not only explore their own cognitive and affective responses to racism, prejudice, alienation, and assimilation; in addition, they encounter culture-centered perspectives that oppose their own worldviews regarding diversity, difference, and their idea of American and being American.

Each year some students indicate that they are very uncomfortable with the "facts" of American history that Zinn, Highwater, and Baldwin, for example, present, that is, with those authors' perspectives—and my point of view as well. Some express their resistance in these terms, when invited to comment on the course.

- "History cannot be changed, so why not live for tomorrow instead of hanging on yesterday?"
- "Why do we have to *see* color? Aren't we all the same?"
- "I feel like I should apologize for being born into the upper white middle class. I don't think I should be made to feel this way!!"

- "I'm being accused of crimes I didn't commit."
- "I feel as if I'm being indoctrinated. Is that the intention of this course?"

Presenting such reactions (without names) to the class for discussion acknowledges these perspectives while also providing another reflexive teaching moment.

Specific journal writing assignments permit me to be responsive to student development through ongoing dialogue with students as they work through issues that challenge their self-definitions, knowledge, and perspectives; assess changes in their perceptions and competence; and, when necessary, respond critically to their resistance. I pose provocative questions like, "What can white Americans be proud of?" (given the Black Studies critique of knowledge and "hidden" facts of American history). My method of teaching tests students' ability to recognize and transcend the predominant worldview and to embrace a personal and professional identity not grounded in the assumptions and beliefs of white supremacy/racism or the goal of assimilation. Personalizing the course by including additional readings further facilitates clarifying dialogue.

American cultural patterns, such as racism, social class, and gender oppression are presented not as aberrations but as forms of inequity that have characterized the development of the nation since its inception. In recent years, I have found it necessary to provide students with basic definitions of racism and prejudice so that they can distinguish between these terms. Even students who majored in history and ethnic studies conflate racism and prejudice or argue that "racism is just part of human nature." The implication that I challenge is that, "therefore we can't do anything about it."

Both courses, but particularly Interpersonal/Cross-Cultural Communication, also challenge the dualistic discourse of multiculturalism: that people of color who do not embrace an identity based on the notion that "we are all the same" because "we are all multicultural" are therefore espousing separation and segregation (in popular parlance), a view that supposedly reflects an "essentialized and narrow politics of ethnic identity" (in the language of scholars). The Black Studies theoretical perspective transcends this simplistic duality.

REFLECTIONS OF PARTICIPANTS

Interviews with several practitioners who have participated in the program and graduates as well as the exit interviews of credential candidates indicate the effectiveness of the praxis described here. Selected examples of their reflections follow. (Pseudonyms are used in each case.)

Reflections of a Practitioner

Mr. Brown is a bilingual central office administrator in a school district in which 93% of the students are not white. His district has hired a number of SCU graduates. Mr. Brown emphasized how well prepared SCU graduates are in his district and that they are "just more able to deal with all the changes that are going on" because they have a "sound methodology for teaching." He has been involved in the SCU program for a number of years as a supervisor, and he also has taught Interpersonal/Cross-Cultural Communications with me and on his own. Mr. Brown stressed how important it was that "this was not a multicultural class, giving student teachers rules about how to relate to the Vietnamese, for example." Mr. Brown continued:

> Ninety percent of them [credential candidates] did not have experiences with diversity. The class made them confront certain feelings. I met some of them after the class—for pizza—they were more open with me outside of class. They admitted that they didn't like some of the course—that it was difficult for them because of their background. They hadn't been exposed to that. What hit them was *Racism 101* [a documentary film]. That was something that they couldn't deny. It was there; it made them think. Even though some of them didn't change, it made them think. But some of them changed in the sense of how they approached certain situations.

Mr. Brown commented on the course materials and, without naming it, affirmed the relevance and effectiveness of the Black Studies theoretical perspective.

> The selection of materials—novels and films—was outstanding, a good mixture. It gave them a lot of things they needed to think about. . . . We served them the real stuff . . . because the black/white [dynamic] is much more realistic . . . it's what they grew up with. The foreigners (immigrants) come and that is easier for them to deal with. It's exotic and is not as threatening . . . I think words like "multicultural" and "diversity" are thrown around because they're easier to use—they're nice.

Mr. Brown also observed that my course design was appropriate for the students' background. He said, "Exposing them to this material was very interesting and more challenging because . . . these students . . . were more willing to say that you (the professor) are biased. But you had to do it."

Reflections of a Graduate

One program graduate vividly recalled specific learning experiences, including metaphors that I used, that he said enabled him to recognize, re-think, and change certain beliefs, attitudes, and practices—changes that made him more "open-minded." Paul, a white male graduate of the sec-ondary credential program, whom I recently interviewed, said: "I often go back to the Onion—that each person is multilayered and the levels of the onion make up the identity of the student." (I used this metaphor to de-scribe students' multilayered, complex levels of thought and behavior in contrast to the way credential candidates identified themselves noncomplexly and one-dimensionally as being "a conservative," for example.)

Paul has been teaching English for 10 years in the same racially and linguistically diverse and less than affluent high school where he completed his student teaching. Sixty-two languages are spoken at his school and he is the director of a Teaching Academy that is preparing high school students to become teachers. He explained that his initial "idea of teaching" changed through the "provocative stuff" we read and "all the processing that we did" in the foundations courses and the student teaching seminar. When I que-ried Paul about whether and how these courses specifically influenced his teaching, he said:

> . . . I was going to recreate myself—create small versions of myself—
> a really arrogant point of view. The program got me to understand
> that the students come to school already with their characters
> intact—that my job as a teacher is to take who they are and help
> them to define themselves culturally and personally and to develop
> their gifts and give that to the world. . . . [In your classes] you would,
> without any fear, challenge people's ideas—politely but strongly—
> and get us to support our ideas, get us to reconsider what we be-
> lieved. I ended the year being more open-minded than I started, and
> I took my job as a teacher more seriously. I also realized that I had
> more to learn, as much as the students.[3]

The personal and professional journey from arrogance to informed empa-thy, in some cases, or self-doubt to increasing confidence, and greater cul-tural, critical, and self-awareness, often involves supporting the development of credential candidates by provoking their discomfort.

Reflections of Credential Candidates

In (audiotaped) self-narrative exit interviews two students recalled tra-jectories of personal and professional growth that indicate that they entered and completed the program at different stages of development. While their commitments also diverge, their emphasis on the affective and cognitive needs of students is consistent with the praxis in my courses. Both had student teaching experiences in culturally diverse, urban high schools. Alex, a 22-year-old white male student, shares his ambivalence about teaching.

> It was like a step into adulthood. I was blown away by the enormity of it. . . . Because you're not just doing the subject. . . . Gosh! You're dealing with people's lives. There was one girl this year who had sex for the first time. She got pregnant, she lost the baby, and now she's going out with this guy who's in jail. Good heavens! But what we've learned, Dr. King said it perfectly: "Every student comes in with a big suitcase full of their previous education experiences but also their lives and they plop that big suitcase up on the desk and you just have to address it." . . . My ideal was to be this dynamic person—you know, do it all. [But] I don't know if teaching is for me. It's just so much work and there's not a lot of glory in it. There is and there isn't. . . . When I think about writing screenplays for Star Trek, there's glory there, that's tangible. The pay [for teaching] isn't that bad, it's working for an audience that really doesn't care if you're there or not. It's frustrating . . . I come in with my lesson plan and I think: Don't they know they should be enjoying this? But teaching is about being fulfilled with your best effort, I suppose. It's kind of like boot camp. If you survive it, you can survive anything.

Fran, a "re-entry" student, had a successful 12-year career in a health profession before entering the teacher education program. She was more confident and certain of her decision to become a high school science teacher. Also, she was not dismayed about the need to support students' academic and affective development.

> There was really no other place that I'd rather be. This was a startling realization, that maybe I was on the right path, doing some good. . . . The other day—as I was presenting some information on decision making and about talking to their peers and boy/girl friends about issues related to reproduction—a girl said, "I wish someone had given me this information a year ago." Maybe I am having an impact. . . . I guess I really love interacting with my students. . . . Half the time I feel like I'm teaching social skills, and that's OK, all the better. Then they'll feel better and come back more ready to learn, and we can spend more time on our science subjects. And what's really great is when they get really involved and ask more questions. . . . That's the purpose of it all, to get them thinking.

CONCLUSION

Despite apparent differences in age, sex, race, or previous experience, most of the students we have taught at SCU share cognitive dominant culture schemata that limit their knowledge and consciousness of themselves, society, diverse "others," or teaching for change. Credential candidates are required to infuse in their lessons the cultural knowledge and awareness they gain in the program and in my courses. I introduce them to the praxis of teaching for change or transmutation experientially in a way that includes conceptualizing not only the realities of racism, poverty, and so on, but a role for themselves in the struggle against this reality. This praxis of transmutation is guided by epistemological and ethical considerations grounded in a Black Studies theoretical perspective that aims to move credential candidates beyond arrogance and alienation toward teaching for change. One student acknowledged this in her exit interview by saying, simply, "Thank you for opening our minds."

NOTES

1. According to Jane Fried (1993), university faculty need pedagogical methods that "connect emotion and intellect" (p. 123) when the curriculum discourse emphasizes "illuminating the dynamics of power in society" (p. 124) because "discussion of cultural, gender and class differences" that often challenges the cognitive understandings and personal constructs of "culturally encapsulated Anglo-Americans" (p. 123) also evokes strong feelings. In response to the "culturally reproductive function of education" that contributes to such encapsulation, Kenneth A. Sirotnick (1990) calls for a "process of *critical* socialization" that is a "deliberatively educative experience grounded in ethics of inquiry, knowledge, competence, caring, and social justice" (p. 309).

2. The novels used in this course present accurate historical information about the experiences of particular groups that fills in gaps in student knowledge; these readings also present the culture-centered perspectives (King, 1995) of diverse groups (e.g., *Beloved, Donald Duk, Love Medicine, Pocho, Rain of Gold*).

3. Paul is a 1985 graduate of the SCU program. He teaches English and is head of both the Gifted and Talented Program and a Teaching Academy, which he helped to establish, at his urban high school. In the latter program, high school students return to middle and elementary schools as tutor/mentors.

PART IV

Responding to the Challenge: Field-Based and Community-Based Models

The chapters in Part IV provide insight into the planning of teacher preparation programs and the implementation of new credentialing standards that are responsive to the diversity of learners presently in public school classrooms. Each program differs in the planning process and approach to teacher development.

In Chapter 12, "Harambee: Building a Community of Learners," Nedra A. Crow, her colleagues, and students present a multiple-voiced narrative account of the redesign of the field-based experience of the preservice program for secondary teacher candidates at the University of Utah. In this unique approach, university professors model student-centered instruction, reflective practice, and guided inquiry as they redesign the program in collaboration with preservice teachers. The idea of creating a community of learners is central to the approach employed in this redesign effort. Knowledge of teaching and learning is constructed and reconstructed simultaneously by members of the learning community as the candidates examine the relationship of diverse life experiences to classroom learning. Such approaches facilitate responsiveness to human diversity.

Next, Chapter 13, "Redesigning Field Experiences: From Exposure to Engagement," by Della Peretti, illustrates the way the faculty at the University of California at Berkeley redesigned the teacher preparation program in response to the dean's desire to initiate a credential program with an urban/multicultural emphasis. Peretti explains the basic premise of the Developmental Teacher Education (DTE) Program: "Instruction is most effective when teachers understand the complexities of child development and

171

when children have guided opportunities to construct their own knowledge." A major change the faculty implemented involves an informal collaborative approach with the principal and teachers at a year-round, urban elementary school where six to eight student teachers are assigned.

In Chapter 14, "A Community-Based Model Recruitment Process for Teacher Preparation," Anne Bouie presents Project Interface, a program for preparing community college student mentor/tutors to facilitate urban middle school students' academic learning in math and science and their social development. This church-based program provides direct educational services to youth who are underserved by public schools; it is also a vehicle for recruiting ethnic minorities into teaching as a career. The students form study teams, which become support groups that share more than improved academic success: They learn to share the responsibility for helping each other cope with the problems of daily life and for giving each other hope. This program builds a community of learners and helps prospective teachers understand how to help youth living in adverse conditions to build survival networks.

Chapter 15, by Priscilla H. Walton and Robert E. Carlson, the concluding chapter, is entitled "Responding to Social Change: California's New Standards for Teacher Credentialing." The authors describe the recently developed and implemented standards of the California Commission on Teacher Credentialing (CTC) for the preparation and credentialing of teachers for limited-English-proficient students. Several preceding chapters in this volume refer to these new teacher preparation standards. (See chapters by Garcia, Peretti, and Quintanar-Sarellana, for example.) Central to California's new approach is redesigning teacher preparation programs to include specific knowledge about language acquisition and related instructional methodologies that will enable teachers to better facilitate learning for limited-English-proficient students. In accomplishing this goal, CTC engaged in a lengthy process involving a diversity of people to develop the "Crosscultural, Language and Academic Development" (CLAD) credential and the "Bilingual, Crosscultural, Language and Academic Development" (BCLAD) credential. The CLAD/BCLAD credentials and certification examinations address six domains of knowledge and skill: (1) language structure and development; (2) methodology of bilingual, English language development, and content instruction; (3) culture and cultural diversity; (4) primary-language instruction methodology; (5) the culture of emphasis, and (6) the language of emphasis.

The teacher preparation programs and new certification requirements described in Part IV share the goal of avoiding replication of traditional practices and promoting increased responsiveness to diversity. Each of the programs described is unique and provides particular insight into approaches to redesigning teacher preparation programs.

12

Harambee: Building a Community of Learners

NEDRA A. CROW
WITH CHRISTINE WAHLQUIST, MARIANNE BENSON-SEARE,
JAMES GORDON, SHARON GRETHER, BRYAN HUNT,
DIANA LEBARON, ANGELA PARKIN, TARA STAUFFER,
RICHARD STATLER, PAMELA LARSEN, AND TERRI TAYLOR

The Swahili language allows communication among African peoples who speak different languages. The word "harambee" in Swahili refers to the concept of "each one, teach one." John Peregoy (personal communication, 1994), a Flathead Indian, explains "harambee" in this way: " . . . as a reflective human being, we become aware of our broad range of knowledge and wisdom, and we then teach others, and in that teaching we share with others and learn from others." John's wisdom speaks to the experiences a cohort of undergraduate students and professors created and shared in a University of Utah teacher preparation program. This "harambee" cohort included nine teacher candidates and three clinical professors who participated in a new secondary education program together for one year.

This chapter describes the "harambee" experiences that altered our beliefs about ourselves, our teaching, our students, our community, our schools, and our profession. In the process, we began the conversation about meeting the challenge of diversity encountered in our classrooms of teachers. First, we will outline the University of Utah's program for secondary education teacher candidates. The remainder of the chapter is a narrative case study written from the alternating points of views of the clinical professors (cohort leaders) and their students (teacher candidates).

A BRIEF HISTORY OF THE SECONDARY
EDUCATION PROGRAM

From 1978 through 1994, the University of Utah's teacher education system for secondary preservice teachers culminated in a "cohort" program comprising three academic quarters (autumn through spring). The first quarter included a 4-hour curriculum development course, and the second quarter housed the instructional methods course. Each course was tied to field experiences in the same school in which full-time student teaching occurred during the third quarter. Twenty-five preservice teachers or teacher candidates worked with university instructors and teaching assistants in two to three geographically close schools. Although the program was successful, in the academic tradition of constant improvement, the secondary education faculty decided to redesign the teacher education curriculum and create a new program.

THE NEW COHORT PROGRAM

The new cohort program comprises four quarters, beginning with combined curriculum and instructional courses in field activity schools in the spring quarter of the first year. In mid-August, the public schools' calendar begins, and teacher candidates return to their assigned school sites to co-plan and co-teach activities with their Site Teacher Educators (STEs), or cooperating teachers. During the autumn and winter quarters, candidates carry a half-day teaching load and plan lessons and observe other teachers and cohort peers for the remainder of the day. This constitutes a full-time student teaching load. The candidates also take two classes, Student Teaching Seminar and Action Research, in the evenings during the autumn and winter quarters. Finally, two additional courses, Transition to Teaching and Teachers and Teachers' Work, are completed during the second spring quarter.

The Plan

Once the new program had been designed and approved, we devised a transition plan so that one cohort per year for 3 years would move from the old to the new program structure. Nedra Crow (clinical faculty member), Dick Statler (teaching assistant), and Christine Wahlquist (district–university liaison) led the first cohort into the new program. We had two quarters prior to the first spring quarter in which to incorporate the planned curriculum into the lives of 25 teacher candidates in three secondary "cohort" schools.

Using the general goals and activities the secondary education faculty created for each course, the cohort instructors planned the curriculum. Our guiding curricular belief was that the candidates brought with them powerful images of being a teacher assembled from years of being students and constructed from selective remembrances of schools, classrooms, students, and teaching. The image of self as teacher was strong, and we designed a curriculum to challenge these images and remembrances while helping candidates build strong professional roles capable of positively influencing their own students' learning. First, the candidates' beliefs would be best challenged and shaped through vibrant experiences in the schools, coupled with inquiry into their associative beliefs, knowledge, and skills along with those of their peers and professionals in the school system. Second, the curriculum was designed to be authentic, following the Mountain School District's calendar. The first spring quarter would be sensitive to the end of the school year events. Our candidates would begin student teaching when the public school year began and teach with the STEs throughout the December holidays.

Student teaching was scheduled to end in the middle of January, when public schools finished their first semester. During the 5-week period between the end of the public school semester and the end of the university's winter quarter, candidates could create their own learning projects to further their professional development, without the imposition of specific boundaries. The activities were open, the evaluation criteria were unknown, and the syllabi were yet to be developed. This undefined experience was known as "?". Once the autumn quarter was underway, the instructors could better design "?" based on the candidates' experiences.

HARAMBEE: SO WHAT HAPPENED?

The following sections of the chapter highlight the significant program structures that created "harambee"; portray the difficulty in establishing a community of learners; illustrate some of the ways we turned candidates' attention to diversity issues among learners; and illuminate the knowledge and wisdom gained within our community of learners.

First Spring Quarter

The Instructors' Story. Spring quarter went well considering that we had a brand-new program, new cohort leaders, and new schools. During most weeks we spent two 4-hour days at the university and two 4-hour days in our cohort schools. During one week, the candidates taught two or three classes each day in a self-selected teacher's classroom (the "short course").

The syllabus included flex time and activities in order to accommodate the needs of the candidates and to take advantage of unanticipated "teaching moments." This meant working with the candidates to develop an evaluation system that included individual interviews that allowed them to demonstrate their professional development.

The candidates' images and remembrances were used to construct solutions to classroom management case studies. For instance, we examined eight models of classroom management (Charles, 1992) by comparing the model's principles with the candidates' beliefs and life experiences. Each candidate developed and used her own classroom observation instrument based on the eight models and her own beliefs, observations, teaching experiences, and unanswered questions, as well as the educational literature. Once developed, the management systems were evaluated by peers.

Believing that the candidates had strong images about effective and ineffective teaching, the instructors designed a series of lessons to teach the candidates about lesson planning. To form principles for designing their own classroom lesson plans, we derived generalizations from their experiences. Then, candidates used their lesson plan formats as observation instruments in the cohort schools. They discussed their formats with their STEs and refined the design to suit their own patterns of thinking about teaching and planning. Finally, they used the formats during the "short course" teaching experience.

By the end of the spring quarter, candidates began to re-evaluate their beliefs and practices as well as those of the schools. Each candidate presented a portfolio of evidence illustrating professional growth and understanding in the areas of classroom management, curriculum development, instructional strategies, lesson design, evaluation activities, and reflective skills. During the final exam interviews, we probed each candidate's knowledge using hypothetical situations, role-plays, and questions. The candidates appeared to have developed the skills and understandings necessary to begin to become reflective professionals. We looked forward to the start of the public school year and to our candidates' student teaching experiences.

A Candidate's Story—Angela Parkin. In retrospect, perhaps the most beneficial and memorable experiences during the first spring quarter that prepared us as a cohort for the upcoming year involved revising our course syllabus, observing and teaching in the schools, working on a classroom management plan, and being interviewed by Dick and Nedra, our cohort leaders. All of these activities made us feel stronger because they allowed us continually to rethink our roles as prospective teachers.

A powerful learning experience that served as a model for our student teaching was restructuring the course syllabus. Consistently responsive to our ideas, our instructors revised the syllabus to reflect the needs and concerns of the entire group. The new syllabus incorporated many activities that proved instrumental in our success as student teachers and in obtaining jobs. These activities included creating portfolios, classroom management plans, and individual lesson plans, and conducting mock interviews. Nedra's and Dick's flexibility and willingness to allow us to participate in structuring the class served as a powerful model to carry into our teaching careers. They demonstrated that collaboration between students and instructors is vital if we want our students to be motivated intrinsically and to take ownership in their own learning.

Observing classrooms and teaching short courses in our future school sites prepared us for student teaching. The purpose of our observations was threefold. They allowed us to become more familiar with the faculty and administration at the schools where we would be working; examine and evaluate different teaching styles and teacher–student relationships; and choose an STE who would be most compatible with our own developing teaching ideologies, allowing us to take over, make mistakes, and create our own curriculum and management plans.

Teaching a short course in our future schools provided an authentic environment for interacting with teachers and students and solving management problems, gauging how realistic our lesson plans were in secondary classrooms, and planning collaboratively with our STEs. Developing lesson plans for the short course was a lengthy process. We began by sharing the best and worst lessons we had observed as students and examining what made them engaging or lifeless. These memories, coupled with our evaluations from lessons we observed in the schools, influenced our short course lesson plans. Throughout this planning process we received feedback from our STEs, Nedra and Dick, and our fellow cohort members, who encouraged us to think continually of alternative ways of hooking the students and reaching those with various learning styles.

Our final interview with Dick and Nedra was a simulated job interview that required us to demonstrate our competence as future teachers. We brought in portfolios, lesson plans, management plans, and anything else that effectively revealed our growth. In addition, we were required to evaluate ourselves in terms of our improvement over the quarter and to provide our interviewers with a written rationale for a letter grade. During the interview many of us showed videotapes of our student teaching. Initially the videotape enabled us to analyze privately our style of teaching and to delete little quirks that diminish effectiveness. It proved to be a magical tool for seeing ourselves just as the students do. The videotape also became useful for demonstrating our progress in managing the classroom, engaging the students, and creating effective communication with them.

Autumn Quarter

The Instructors' Story. Candidates usually began the school year by teaching one course, and co-planning or co-teaching three additional courses with their STE. By the end of September, the candidates increased their student teaching loads, picking up full-time teaching duties in their three co-taught courses. However, the beginning of the school year did not go as smoothly as planned. Two students dropped out of the teacher preparation program and the main cohort leader, Nedra Crow, was hired full-time into the dean's office. However, Nedra felt a strong tie to the cohort group and a need to provide continuity in piloting the new secondary education program for the department. Of the change, Nedra commented that "it felt like leaving your family halfway through a trip." So Nedra commuted academically, spending most of the day in the dean's office and teaching the student teaching seminar one evening each week.

The weekly seminar the instructors planned and taught together was structured so that principles of inquiry and the candidates' experiences formed the foundation for the class. Each seminar used the candidates' weekly experiences along with the supervisors' observations to launch discussions of classroom management, lesson planning, and instructional design. The student teachers wrote a case study based on their experiences in the classrooms. From the supervisors' observations, it became clear that the candidates were reflecting less and less upon their own and their STEs' practices and relying more and more on fitting into the "status quo" of the public schools. As cohort instructors, we were alarmed. We challenged the novice teachers to move beyond the "getting-through-the-chapter" mentality of teacher-centered lessons and to use more student-centered activities.

Rather than being reflective, the candidates seemed defensive and protective of their practices and those of their STEs. The candidates, along with some of their STEs, accused the cohort instructors of living too long in the "ivory tower" and out of the "real world." We refused to back down from our observations and feedback. Yet, we were depressed and in despair at the prospect that our bright, reflective teacher candidates were becoming absorbed into the status quo of the public schools. We were at our emotional, professional, and academic wits end as to how to stop the deterioration of cohort principles. At the end of the autumn quarter, the candidates' feedback was that the autumn quarter seminar had been a disaster that was designed too loosely, the outcomes about the case study assignment were vague, and expectations regarding student teaching standards were ambiguous.

A Candidate's Story—Sharon Grether. On August 23 the teacher candidates joined their STEs for the preschool week at their respective schools. I think we all felt a little excited, anxious, nervous, and eager.

I looked forward to working with my STE because I knew her teaching style well. I knew she would let me experiment in the classroom, and I was excited. I opened up the musty classroom that had been unused for 3 months and began my student teaching. Before the first day of school, my agenda included meeting with my STE to develop lesson plans, establish a classroom management system, design disclosure forms, and decorate the room.

As student teaching progressed, many of us felt as if we were losing contact with our cohort instructors and losing a sense of community developed during spring quarter. This occurred because the supervision assignments were confused, and once organized, we saw the instructors only once a week for classroom observations. When our university supervisor observed us, many of us did not know what to expect and were unsure about the supervisor's evaluations.

During the two evening classes from 5:30 until 9:00 p.m., everyone was usually tired, hungry, and worried about the next day's lesson plans. The stress was overwhelming. Many of us came 15 minutes early to gripe over whatever was happening in our classroom or in our personal lives. This was a much deserved time to get together and talk.

Our assignments during the seminar included writing a case study, grading ourselves, and conducting peer evaluations. I kept wondering what this case study had to do with teaching. My entire thoughts were on teaching—not a case study whose purpose I did not understand.

There was never time off from observations made by our university professors. When our supervisors entered our classrooms, heart rates went up, adrenaline rushed, and butterflies fluttered in our stomachs. We believed we were under attack from the university personnel, yet were receiving praise from our STEs. I felt I was in a verbal tug-of-war. Whom do we listen to? The internal struggle was challenging and emotionally exhausting. By the end of the student teaching experience many of us felt burned out; we wanted time for our families and for ourselves.

The student teaching experience left many of us with questions. How could we have gotten more out of our teaching experience? What would we do differently as first-year teachers? Did we fulfill those early personal philosophies we discussed in spring quarter? There were so many unanswered questions.

The End of Student Teaching and a Short Debriefing Period

The Instructors' Story. During January, the tension within the cohort group was high. First, the cohort program was new and we were in new cohort schools. Second, the STEs had not received any substantial staff development on supervision, mentoring, and evaluation. Although we had an STE Handbook and frequent meetings, there was still initial mistrust of the university, the personnel, and the program. We were always viewed as the "ivory tower," even though all the cohort leaders were recent public school teachers. Third, three of the four university supervisors were new to the university system, the cohort program, and supervisory duties. Finally, the autumn quarter consisted of two new courses, Student Teaching Seminar and Action Research, another layer of trial and error.

The cohort feelings, interactions, and structure had to change. To begin with, Nedra worked out an arrangement in which she would spend more time with the cohort during the winter quarter. The cohort leaders came together in December to design the "?" experience into a meaningful and educational package. We decided to allow the group to come together during the first few days at the end of the official student teaching activity for debriefing. Next, we outlined a one-week activity in which each candidate would design and implement an individual inquiry project related to classroom management, curriculum, students, or instruction. Then we planned a one-week activity in an elementary school, after which there would be several days for single topics like finding a job and first-aid in the schools. We then planned a cooperative learning activity, group inquiry, followed by an inquiry project about topics outside of the classroom but inside the educational system. In all, we wanted to give the candidates freedom and flexibility to explore their own beliefs and experiences. Yet, we learned from the case study assignment that the candidates needed guidelines for time management, evaluation criteria, and goal setting. The 5-week "?" experience became known as "Community Inquiry Activities" (CIA), and we called the syllabi the instruction manuals.

When we introduced the CIA syllabi and experiences in January—as student teaching wound up—the candidates were stunned that the break would be delayed for 5 weeks. They were surprised that the instructors were not going to lecture on cooperative learning and they could not take it easy during this period. Instead, candidates were expected to explore questions they had about any aspect of teaching, learning, the system, or themselves. They were responsible for their learning. We would facilitate their inquiry. It was not a popular idea.

We used the debriefing days to talk about their personal and professional experiences and feelings. The candidates spent the next 4 days completing their inquiry projects in the community and schools. On the fifth day of the inquiry experience, we came together again as a group to share what the candidates had learned. They did a great job in "showing us, not telling us" about their projects. During the lively discussion that day, people seemed to be enjoying each other more—the cohort spirit began to return. Yet, by the end of the day, tensions were high again. The candidates seemed uneasy about something. After a pointed discussion, the candidates decided they wanted time alone to talk about "their issues."

While the tension was painful, we had to allow the candidates the opportunity to express their voices in their chosen way. It was a strange feeling to be a struggling community of learners searching for balance and meaning. But, such was the case, and all the instructors could hope for was that all of us would learn to be a community.

A Candidate's Story—Tara Stauffer. As student teaching came to an end, the group was in a state of emotional disarray. We had many things to accomplish and we were quite tired. The gamut of emotions included fatigue, excitement, anticipation, confusion, and anxiety. The tensions that existed in the seminar during the autumn quarter were not resolved over the December vacation. We were all waiting for our student teaching experience in the schools to end.

As we embarked upon the beginning of the inquiry projects, many of us were dealing with hurt, confusion, and concern. However, the first set of inquiry projects lifted our spirits. Each of the candidates shared vibrant experiences. The rationale behind the syllabi that had come as such a shock was beginning to shine brightly. Now with the additional day of debriefing among the candidates, we seemed more ready to get on with the remaining 3½ weeks of work, beginning with the assignment in the elementary school. The combination of 5-week experiences and activities allowed us to dissolve our conflicts and proceed with new vigor. Both teacher candidates and instructors proceeded into the remainder of the activities with a new vision, a new understanding of what it meant to be a community of learners.

Community Inquiry Activities—Elementary School

The Instructors' Story. The elementary school experience was designed to challenge the candidates' thinking about curriculum, teacher–student interactions, and the culture of teachers, learning, and students. The instructors hoped to rattle teaching practices submerged in teacher-centered instructional strategies, fragmented curriculum dominated by single-subject teaching, and preoccupation with the teacher's content knowledge rather than the learner's background.

Working in conjunction with our elementary education cohort instructors, we placed secondary education candidates at Wright Elementary School, and elementary education candidates moved to our secondary education cohort schools. The secondary education teacher candidates observed and/or taught in an assigned elementary school classroom each day, spending most of the day with the same teacher and changing teachers and grade levels twice throughout the 4-day experience. At the end of each day candidates and cohort instructors debriefed the day's experiences.

At the end of the first day, we sat together in a kindergarten classroom and discussed our experiences. The candidates reflected on how excited elementary pupils were about learning and about how teachers and students were involved in interactions that were positive, meaningful, and real. They realized that while they had valued being student-centered teachers, in reality, they had become teacher-centered. With these realizations came further reflections.

As instructors, we could see the light turn on in the candidates' eyes. Each day's discussion period produced more thoughtful reflections about the candidates' student teaching experiences and beliefs developed during the previous 5 months. The teacher candidates were challenging themselves and each other about the aims of education, teacher-centered curriculum, and teacher-directed instruction. More than ever before in our cohort year, we were all together and "on the same page." We began to help each other understand what it meant to be a teacher within our own particular circumstance.

A Candidate's Story—Marianne Benson-Seare. The first official activity in our 10-page syllabus was the "Elementary School Experience." The purpose of the experience was to illustrate the differences and similarities between elementary and secondary environments. Initially, the cohort members protested this activity. We were secondary teachers; what could we learn in an elementary school? The first day at Wright Elementary transformed the skeptics into believers. I observed a fifth-grade class where the environment alone was a drastic variation from that in the secondary school. The small desks and chairs, the colorful wall hangings, and the sporadic energy of the children were strange yet refreshing. Hands would enthusiastically shoot up in response to the teacher's questions. The youngsters were eager to demonstrate an answer on the chalkboard and would race to complete the daily story problem. They approached new concepts with interest. This fifth-grade class really enjoyed learning.

Our cohort met in a vacant kindergarten room to debrief at the end of the day. Nedra, chalk in hand, asked us to share what we had seen in the elementary classrooms. She could barely keep up with our responses as we yelled: "Fun!" "Enthusiasm!" "Student-centered!" "Variety!" "Eagerness to learn!" "Positive!" "Cooperation!" "Hands on!" "Respect!" and "Integration!" We felt both energized and depressed. We were inspired, yet we thought we had missed something in our own teaching practice. We realized how wrong we were to assume that the elementary school had nothing to teach us.

Day two was even more eye-opening. As I entered the classroom I was greeted by three young students. Instantly, they wrapped their arms around me and said, "We're so glad that you're back. Are you going to teach us today?" With these simple words of praise, these three students had enlivened my day. This recognition and warmth from students rarely occur at the secondary level. Through interviews with both faculty and students, I discovered the formulas that made learning both engaging and fun. The teachers believed in student-centered classrooms, hands-on teaching, and integrated curriculum use. This integration is rarely seen in the secondary school, where most teachers practice only one method. Using hands-on learning, implementing integrated curriculum, and being student-centered, the elementary school sets a precedent for all other learning institutions. Going back to the early years of education helped us see education as it should be seen through the eyes of a student. During our student teaching at the secondary level, we were too focused on ourselves as teachers. Spending time in the elementary school taught us more about education than we thought possible.

Community Inquiry Activities—Individual Projects

The Instructors' Story. The individual inquiry projects were grounded in beliefs that learners need to construct their own knowledge through inquiry into areas in which they are passionately interested. Therefore, we structured the curriculum so that each candidate would be driven to investigate her own pressing professional questions outside her "normal" frame of knowledge using innovative strategies. We wanted the teacher candidates to use the entire community (educational, social, cultural, and academic) in our area, state, nation, and planet to answer their posed questions.

To provide some guidance and structure, we asked each candidate to develop a plan around a question of interest and create daily goals and activities. We used our connections in the community and professional understandings to motivate the candidates to search and explore the community in exciting ways. At the end of the week's activity, we wanted the group to come together for the purpose of teaching each other about their questions, answers, and musings.

Harambee! The discussions and questions raised during those teaching sessions were some of the richest, most exciting, and most academically challenging conversations we have ever had as teachers and professional educators. The excitement of learning from each other about our own teaching practice was a celebration of learning and community. Throughout the CIA time period, all of the cohort members began to wonder aloud about what was going on in terms of curriculum and instructional strategies. We knew it was unique, powerful, and authentic. The 5-week experience turned into 6 weeks and then 7 weeks. We didn't want the learning to end.

Two Candidates' Stories—Bryan Hunt and James Gordon.

According to the class syllabus the first CIA was to deal with curriculum, instruction, and/or classroom management—matters *in* the classroom. The second CIA was to deal with law, school administration and governance, and/or support services—matters *outside* the classroom. The entire group—instructors and candidates—demonstrated a great deal of flexibility throughout the CIA experience. In one instance, the instructors decided to change the evaluation process from the previous quarter. The instructors were responsible for the entire evaluation, which allowed the teacher candidates, who were not teaching, to participate fully in the learning activities, rather than worrying about how to evaluate each other. Second, switching to mastery grading removed the ambiguity: Either we met the criteria and moved on, or we had the opportunity to try until we did. This ensured the opportunity for the success of all.

Another example of flexibility stemming from our experiences of the previous quarter and initial CIAs was that we decided to allow more time for discussion. Everyone saw the benefits of allowing deeper group exploration of the issues. It allowed the teacher candidates more freedom in the use of instructional techniques. In the end, we added several days to the original schedule.

Although the expectations and criteria set forth to receive credit that quarter appeared very structured, we had a great deal of freedom in selecting individual topics, the procedures we would use to gather information, and the methods we would use to present our findings to our peers. This freedom made the projects more personally relevant and allowed the group to learn about more topics and to explore them in greater depth than we would have done otherwise.

For Sharon and Pam this meant following up on personal experiences they had while student teaching. When a student was killed in an accident, Sharon was angered at the administration's reaction. She inquired into district programs organized for crisis intervention, spoke with educators and students, and collected numerous pamphlets and guides to create a resource file for our use as future educators. She drew us into the experience with role playing and small-group discussions focusing on traumatic experiences others had as students and teachers. She then ended her report with information on the professional support that exists to help in these situations.

Pam received a note from the mother of one of her students telling her not to expect much from him academically because he had an attention deficit disorder (ADD). Pam talked to teachers and counselors to find out how they generally would respond. She collected information about ADD, ADHD (Attention Deficit Hyperactivity Disorder), instructional methods, and testing from psychologists—at the university and the school—and from alternative school teachers. In Pam's teaching session, we completed an ADHD inventory; it was surprising to find that two teacher candidates would have qualified for further evaluation. Then we formulated strategies for effectively managing a classroom with ADHD students.

Diana investigated students who had difficulties with the usual classroom structure and instruction: students in Youth-in-Custody programs, Youth Services, and a Juvenile Detention Center school. She interviewed students ranging in age from 9 to 17 and found anger, hurt, and a need for acceptance among these youth. She also heard complaints about teachers who did not believe in them and parents who did not care. In trying to communicate this to the group in her teaching activity, Diana "handcuffed" each teacher candidate, had them guess what crime they had committed, and took them to "Juvenile Detention." We realized both the importance of seeing the students as individuals with personal histories and the need to adjust our instruction and classroom environment to incorporate these students better.

Similar issues arose in James's investigation of types of and reasons for alternative schools. He observed classes in several alternative schools in different districts; interviewed administrators, teachers, and students; and examined research on related literature and reform proposals. To teach the group about his inquiry, James first used induction to create generalities about a school "system," identifying both positive and negative aspects, and he presented a summary of different programs and the "alternatives" they offer. We role played two types of alternative classrooms and concluded that one size does not fit all in education, and "alternative" schools often are not all that alternative.

Bryan selected a topic from his own high school experience—that he had concentrated too heavily on academics to the detriment of extracurricular experiences for learning. Bryan worked with a broad scope of extracurricular activities but focused his inquiry specifically on sports. He interviewed coaches, students, and representatives of the state high school activities association; he researched correlations between extracurricular involvement and success in higher education; and he attended sports activities. Bryan used the "Family Feud" game to convey the excitement of extracurricular activities in secondary education. We recognized that the team competition between the groups also created teamwork, positive support, and sharing— all objectives in extracurricular activities that he wanted to explore.

The diversity within the cohort was an essential strength. Through this diversity, different subject areas, teaching styles, backgrounds, and personalities were brought together. We were able to learn not only about a subject but also about *each other* in new and different ways. These projects also represent the process of "harambee" we all have come to appreciate. We were bringing individual knowledge to a group setting, learning as a group, sharing our own views and "selves," and walking forward together with a common bond of experiences and better understanding of each other and education. It was while we were teaching each other, learning from each other, and supporting each other that we grew the most, individually and collectively.

Community Inquiry Activities—Group Projects

The Instructors' Stories. Throughout the cohort year, the instructors believed the candidates needed to consider the learners in their classrooms as real people who brought with them various cultures, learning styles, levels of learning, interests, emotional needs, physical challenges, and disabilities. Particularly during student teaching, we watched as many of our candidates constantly used lectures, worksheets, and discussions, while overlooking individual students' needs and seeing only the monolith called "the class." While we understood that novice teachers' professional development often moved through stages, we still wanted to challenge the candidates' teaching beliefs and practices. Therefore, we decided to use the group inquiry projects as an opportunity to turn the candidates' attention to diversity issues among learners.

When we introduced diversity topics, we realized that the candidates were not excited with our decisions. We held firm in our beliefs that the candidates had not experienced diversity of learners in meaningful ways, and we wanted them to explore their thinking, the schools, and communities. We divided the nine candidates into two groups and presented them with a choice of two project topics to investigate: multicultural education and learning/interests/styles/abilities ("lisa").

We required an approved plan for these group projects that directed the candidates' time and energy toward answering questions they designed. Discussing the plans allowed us to help the groups focus their questions and create rich community-based methods of inquiry. It also became clear that the candidates needed to think about diversity in more human terms. This wasn't just another topic in an educational textbook; it was life. The meetings with the candidates proved to be lively, honest, probing, and reflective.

The candidates did exceptionally well learning to work together in designing their inquiry projects, collecting data, and analyzing the findings. The discussions were intensive, sophisticated, and complex; we all wanted to talk about learners, learning, and teaching. Harambee was on the move.

The CIA structure was flexible enough to allow for group consented diversion. For instance, during one CIA session, we learned that the Graduate School of Education was having a colloquium meeting on "Diversity." We attended, and the students contributed to the discussion. Our undergraduate cohort students had gained knowledge and confidence born out of inquiry within the community. The candidates' understandings were real and authentic, and in a humble way they knew it, were beginning to enjoy it, wanted to share it, and desired to learn more. During the colloquium one of the cohort instructors acknowledged that she had learned that understanding the nature of instruction and diversity among learners begins in one's own classroom by inquiring into one's own teaching practice and beliefs.

A Candidate's Story—Diana LeBaron. Throughout the student teaching experience, I felt isolated from other cohort members. We were looking for something beyond individual inquiry projects and colorful discussions to connect our disjointed community. The group CIA gave us the impetus and growth for which we were searching as developing teacher candidates, friends, and colleagues.

"Diversity of Learners" was the theme around which we designed the group projects. We were required to create objectives and learning activities commensurate with inquiry topics assigned to our groups. My group took the topic of multicultural education. We all felt overwhelmed by the tasks before us. We realized that addressing group dynamics was as important as researching our designated themes. We were not merely observing diversity within the community and schools; we were exploring the cohort's unity within our individual diversity.

To form the plans needed for the inquiry project, both groups created strategic game plans. Nedra evaluated our project proposals and rationales, asking about specific objectives. We communicated our intent to take a community-based approach while examining multicultural issues. She pointed out the inconsistency of approaching our inquiry with lists of resources, many of which remained within administrative offices and school rooms. My group's plans changed as we discussed new ideas with Nedra. We were learning about the importance of mutual support and reflection, and the result was the impetus to direct our research outside our comfort zones and familiarity and focus our projects on community-based activities.

Each group explored their questions using very different methods. The "lisa" group administered learning preference tests to junior and senior high school classes taught by our cohort interns. After thoughtful analysis, the group members explained the test results with students in our interns' classes.

For our multicultural group, Sharon and I attended a myriad of religious services, talked with multicultural counselors, and listened to parent suggestions. Pam and Terri visited social services, the NAACP, and schools with ethnically mixed populations.

After hours of data collection, interviews, and reading, both inquiry groups faced the difficult task of incorporating what they had learned into concise and meaningful lessons. All of us were advised by our cohort leaders to show what we learned, rather than tell about it. Throughout the group CIA project, we learned about each other through discovery and hands-on experiences. We wanted our lessons to reflect similar processes.

The "lisa" group struggled to transform their findings into a meaningful concept referent. Finally, the group was inspired by food, no less! At the university their lesson came to life as candidates and instructors clapped their hands, stomped their feet, and sang, "Peanut Butter, Peanut Butter, Jelly, Jelly." Angie, with her dramatic interpretation and vibrant voice, entertained auditory learners with a picture book story about peanut butter sandwiches. What is so significant about peanut butter? The lesson was less about peanut butter, and more about the celebration of our unique learning preferences. The lesson was a time for our groups to share with and learn from each other.

At the beginning of the "lisa" lesson, Nedra asked James and Tara to clarify their purpose in asking a particular question. The group spent several minutes explaining their rationale, yet Nedra pushed them to clarify further and reflect. I wanted to wave my magic wand and make the group's discomfort disappear. Instead, the group worked through the challenge, not alone, but with each other. It was uncomfortable to see them struggle, but the end result was truly magnificent! We rose to a greater level of learning and community.

The multicultural education lesson began with student portraits: Student cohort members were asked to describe their personal cultures. We traced the heritage of James, Nedra, and Marianne on a giant map of the world. In order to generate discussion about misjudgment and stereotypes, we attempted to sort and label cohort members. As we did this, the discussion took on new dimensions. I was pleasantly reminded that my agenda is enhanced by others, even when its course changes entirely, and that we work better with each other than alone. Our group CIA projects contributed to the cohesive unit we found ourselves in at the end of a week-long process.

CONCLUSION

During one of the last days of winter, we met with the intern candidates who had been meeting together during the winter quarter with their university supervisor in their own student teaching seminar. We felt like a family returning from a trip. Yet, something was different among the interns, teacher candidates, and instructors. All of us believed that "something" wonderful had happened between January and mid-March among the teacher candidates and cohort instructors. The interns told the nine teacher candidates that they experienced professional and personal growth well beyond the norm of novice teachers. The interns believed that the candidates had become true professional educators who understood more than the interns about being reflective, working in the educational system, teaching students, developing curriculum, and improving the schools. The nine teacher candidates and cohort leaders smiled and looked at each other with admiration. Indeed, the nine teacher candidates and cohort instructors had grown into a community of learners dedicated to being students of teaching. As the quarter came to a close, one day the cohort instructors asked the candidates what they wanted to do about their experience. The discussion was uncharacteristically short: The cohort wanted to continue learning together as a community throughout the remainder of the university school year and on into the next years of their lives. At that point we understood "harambee."

13

Redesigning Field Experiences
From Exposure to Engagement

DELLA PERETTI

In addition to techniques for responding to unprecedented ethnic and linguistic heterogeneity in their classrooms and in the communities where they live and work, teachers need skills to address the specific needs of children whose families struggle for economic survival. Economically segregated schools continue to prevail. The National Commission on Children estimates that approximately 25% of U.S. children live below the poverty line and that number is growing. Any preparation for meeting the challenge of diversity in teacher education must include an understanding of the range of economic circumstances in which our nation's children grow up. Requiring student teaching placements in two or more contrasting settings provides *exposure* to diversity, but teacher preparation programs must go beyond this to foster more enduring *engagement*.

THE EVOLUTION OF THE PROGRAM

The Developmental Teacher Education (DTE) Program at the University of California at Berkeley is a 2-year sequence of study leading to the Multiple Subject Credential and an M.A. in educational psychology. It was founded in 1980 on the premise that instruction is most effective when teachers understand the complexities of child development and when children have guided opportunities to construct their own knowledge. We provide five student teaching placements, assigned to maximize diversity of field experiences. Initially, "diversity" was narrowly construed to mean placements in five grade levels in constructivist classrooms in several school districts.

This generally meant that our graduates gained *exposure* to a variety of cultural and economic settings, while we attempted to keep the pedagogical approach consistently developmental. Although we felt successful in finding a range of placements, by 1989 we recognized a need to increase the level of *engagement* in understanding cultural, linguistic, and socioeconomic differences. In 1990 we began altering the field experience and developing new criteria for selection by broadening opportunities for engagement in urban, multilingual classrooms, in neighborhoods where children lived in poverty.

RATIONALE FOR CHANGE

The organizational impetus for change came in November 1990, when the dean expressed a strong desire to initiate a credential program with an urban/multicultural emphasis. Despite the fact that all members of the Teacher Education Committee supported the idea, there were inadequate resources to launch a completely new credential program at that time. However, within our existing DTE program, there was room for improvement in our treatment of diversity. We were complying with Standard 31 of the California Commission on Teacher Credentialing (CTC). (Chapter 15 presents a fuller discussion of CTC standards.) Standard 31 states:

> *Capacity to Teach Diverse Students*: Each candidate demonstrates compatibility with, and ability to teach students who are different from the candidate. The differences between students and the candidate should include ethnic, cultural, racial, gender, linguistic and socioeconomic differences.

We were dutifully providing field experiences in classrooms where students' backgrounds differed from those of the candidates. Our reliance on exposure to "do the job," however, did not automatically lead candidates to acquire the abilities and understandings necessary to design and teach developmental lessons that are adapted to the broader life circumstances of children from different economic, ethnic, and linguistic backgrounds.

In considering the options for change, I reflected upon the experiences of Kenya and Kiyomi, two candidates of color from diametrically opposed economic backgrounds, who were placed at Manuel Alvarez Year Round School in one of the most culturally and linguistically diverse and economically depressed neighborhoods of Oakland. Both women were attempting to implement developmental curriculum and management techniques while trying to (1) understand a year-round school calendar; (2) familiarize themselves with a campus that had over 100 employees, 1,200 students, and countless special programs; (3) increase their understanding of general cross-cultural issues while also learning about specific groups; (4) foster positive interactions among ethnic groups with long histories of hostility to one another; (5) acquire theoretical and practical knowledge regarding second language instruction and bilingual education; (6) learn about characteristics of specific languages in order to provide appropriate lessons; (7) devise strategies for communication with families with whom they shared no common language; and (8) comprehend the perspective of families who were struggling to escape the grasp of poverty.

For Kenya and Kiyomi, the *letter* of the state standard was being met but the *intent* of preparing them to teach in such a setting actually was being undermined. Although they were full of pedagogical information, good will, and robust energy, they felt isolated, overwhelmed, and demoralized. They were expected to master the same range of teaching skills as their peers, many of whom were in monolingual, well-funded schools with stable populations. It was difficult for the two student teachers at Alvarez to discuss their experiences with peers who were unable to imagine the many layers of complexity at Alvarez.

Kenya and Kiyomi were not gaining an understanding of how to teach in a school like Alvarez because their placements there were treated identically to the others. The concerns were curriculum design, assessment, management, balancing the needs of individuals and the group, and relations with cooperating teachers. Issues germane to teaching in a culturally diverse and economically depressed neighborhood were subordinated to more generic classroom concerns in applying developmental theory. The result was that both students lost confidence in their ability to become fine teachers.

To improve this situation we considered increasing the number of placements in schools like Alvarez. Merely increasing the amount of time without implementing structural modifications did not seem promising, however. Another perceived barrier to multiple placements in linguistically or ethnically diverse or economically depressed neighborhoods was our commitment to selecting cooperating teachers who exemplified a constructivist perspective in keeping with DTE's theoretical base. The placements we found that fit this description were often (but not always) in homogeneous, middle-class neighborhoods. We cycled all our candidates through the same small pool of developmentally oriented cooperating teachers. With only a small portion of our candidates simultaneously placed in heterogeneous schools or in impoverished areas at once, seminar time was filled with "culture-free" dialogue that suffered from the erroneous underlying assumption that white, middle-class behavior was normative.

The situation was critical enough for us to restructure our field placements and to override the stricture that all of our cooperating teachers espouse a constructivist perspective. There was a pressing need for our students to supplement their coursework on multicultural, multilingual issues with direct input from children, families, and teachers who possess relevant knowledge and experience. Our students also needed their field placements to be supported with sustained, frank, and open seminar discussions about privilege, bias, culture, racism, and the implications of poverty, multilingualism, and multiculturalism. An explicit curriculum was needed to serve as scaffolding for the restructured field placements and to keep attention focused on these issues.

REDESIGNING THE FIELD EXPERIENCE

In conjunction with four other field placements, the school population at Alvarez seemed ideally suited to a diversity agenda. At that time (1990) there were 1,077 students: Asian (37.4%); Hispanic (36.8%); African American (24.2%), and others (1.6%). By 1991, there were 1,220 students, of whom 953 (78.1%) were officially classified as limited English speaking (LEP). These included speakers of Spanish (32%); Mien (15.9%); Cantonese (11.4%); Cambodian (11.4%); Vietnamese (5.2%), and Lao, Tagalog, Tongan, and Arabic (less than 2% each). The principal footnoted this information with the observation that virtually all of the 267 children classified as fluent English proficient (FEP) spoke nonstandard variants of English (e.g., African American English or Ebonics).

Despite the attractiveness of the ethnic and linguistic mix, there seemed to be insurmountable impediments to forming a collaboration with Alvarez. A lack of developmental teaching, a confusing year-round calendar, a distracting open-classroom architecture, the overwhelming size of the student body, and the disappointing experiences of Kiyomi and Kenya caused me to question the value of using Alvarez as a viable site for new teacher development. Joseph Dicrescenzo, the Alvarez principal, encouraged me to reconsider ways to overcome these objections. His ardent desire to forge a partnership with DTE led us to re-examine the structure of our program. He helped me to see an opportunity to reconfigure placements to achieve the desired results for our candidates, while simultaneously rendering valuable assistance to Alvarez's teachers and children. Mr. Dicrescenzo showed me how all the elements that I had considered to be impediments to preservice teachers' growth were potential learning opportunities for our students.

DTE students complete their 10-day solo teaching requirement in the third semester of the program. In the fourth and final semester they write their M.A. papers while carrying a reduced student teaching load (2 days per week). This last placement originally was conceptualized as an opportunity to fine tune skills at a new grade level (most students already had experience in four different grades) and/or with a curricular or management focus that had not been explored fully in prior placements. This placement sometimes seems like a step backwards for confident candidates who only weeks before had been in full charge of their "takeover" classrooms. Therefore, the final placement is an ideal time to broaden our students' repertoire of skills for teaching in culturally and linguistically diverse settings. This approach also eliminates the persistent concern about exploiting poor children for the purpose of training new teachers for diverse classrooms. As the saying goes, "If you travel to find good ideas, you must take good ideas with you." Our post-takeover students had well-developed classroom skills and were qualified to contribute to the education of Alvarez's children. At no additional cost, with strategic modifications to the fifth placement and contemporaneous support from innovations in academic coursework, we were able to redesign our field experiences.

The Revised Field-Based Experience for First-Year Students

In the initial semester of the program, students have two short participant-observer placements, the first in a primary and the second in an intermediate grade. These two placements are now made at opposite ends of the economic spectrum, which usually leads to culturally dissimilar first and second placements as well, due to the nature of housing patterns in the San Francisco–Oakland Bay Area. For many candidates, this is the first concrete recognition of the vastly divergent opportunities for children based on the economic status of their families. Discussions in supervisory groups become grounded in a broader concern for equity for children, and candidates begin to question the nature of normative behavior.

As a further impetus to keep the discussion focused on diversity issues, we recently have begun to divide the cohort into thirds and assign each group to a different school—one suburban K–6 school in an affluent bedroom community (80% white); one urban K–5 school with a population that lives at or below the poverty line (49% African American); and one K–3 school that is economically and racially integrated through busing (47.1% African American and 44.1% white). Supervisors consent to go to all three schools, in spite of the added travel time, because they see the value of having representation from each of the schools in their group. Their supervision groups represent all three of the schools, and discussions inevitably include a variety of perspectives. This ensures a focus on teaching strategies for diverse populations.

Another change in the first-year program is a journal assignment requiring an investigation of family involvement. This sets the stage for a more extensive community project in the second-year restructured placement. It also makes it clear that we expect our candidates to learn techniques for familiarizing themselves with any neighborhood in which they may teach, not just poor or non-white communities.

The Revised Field-Based Experience for Second-Year Students

In the fall of their second year, our students participate in their most intensive placement, in a classroom that most closely approximates the setting in which they expect to teach upon graduation. This includes a 10-day solo teaching experience. We restructured our field-based experience for the following spring semester, with the goal of engaging our candidates in issues of diversity. Six to nine student teachers elect to go to Alvarez as a mutually supportive group with a shared interest in learning about poverty and urban diversity as the focus of their final placement. Because the candidates have already completed their solo teaching, their cooperating teachers are able to count on them to capably teach individuals, small groups, or the whole class. They are ready to concentrate on the multiple layers of complexity at Alvarez. We emphasize getting to know the community and working with individuals or small groups of children who seem to be "falling through the cracks."

The first logistical problem we faced in assigning eight student teachers to Alvarez was the year-round calendar. Since Alvarez is on a 12-week cycle, it initially seemed to make sense to have a 12-week placement, confined to the cycle that best matched the university calendar and placing all student teachers on that cycle. However, since cycles are determined by linguistic group, it defeats our purpose in selecting a school with a diverse population to limit ourselves to one cycle. Also, some of the cooperating teachers who are excited about working with us are on Cycles B, C, and D and would be on vacation for 4 of the 12 weeks.

Rather than attempting to fit candidates into a single 12-week cycle, Mr. Dicrescenzo suggested a two-part placement for each student. Within this format, it is possible to have one 8-week regular classroom placement and another 4-week specialty placement in an area of interest. This flexibility provides far greater advantages than anticipated. The expected value of the 4-week miniplacement was that it would give candidates an opportunity to work with prep-period classes (music, physical education, computer lab), to become involved with a second linguistic/cultural group and/or grade level, or to work with the nurse in health education. Table 13.1 illustrates the diversity of experiences that this allows.

Table 13.1. Typical Placement Configuration for Alvarez Cohort

Student Teacher	First Four Weeks	Second Four Weeks	Third Four Weeks
Student 1	5–6 Spanish	1 Mien	
Student 2	1–2 Cantonese	4 English	1–2 Cantonese
Student 3	AM K Spanish PM K Spanish	3 Mien	
Student 4	3–4 Cantonese	AM K Cambodian PM K Mien	
Student 5	4–6 Vietnamese Newcomer Center	2 Mien	
Student 6	2 Spanish		4–6 Vietnamese Newcomer Center
Student 7		AM K Spanish	
	PM K Spanish	PE Prep—1–6	
Student 8	4–5 English		Nurse
Student 9	AM K Cantonese PM Dean of Students		

Changed Relationships

We did not predict that the flexible flow between the 4-week and the 8-week segments of the placement would create such a strong sense of interconnectedness with the entire school. This contributes to genuine engagement in the educational life of the community, changing the relationships among the various players.

Student Teachers' Relations with One Another. Placing six to eight student teachers at Alvarez simultaneously encourages spontaneous collaboration and a sense of personal engagement. For instance, discussions during carpooling lead to reciprocal classroom visits for observation or, more frequently, for team teaching. This facilitates interactions with children across language groups and grade levels.

Student Teacher/Supervisor Relations. In lieu of scheduling formal observations, university supervisors are available for consultation at Alvarez all day every Tuesday. A considerable proportion of supervision time is devoted to conversations during the extended noon hour. In general, discussions are pedagogically productive; include Alvarez faculty and staff; and belie negative stereotypes about teachers' lunchroom gossip. Although discussions are informal, they offer compelling opportunities for colleagues to seek answers together. University supervisors participate in a collaborative mode rather than presenting themselves as expert higher authorities.

Cooperating Teacher/Student Teacher Relations. Our students often are invited into classrooms where they are not officially assigned. They assist with lessons, field trips, or special projects. With our new, less restrictive criteria for selecting cooperating educators, we are able to include some beginning teachers who previously had not been considered for supervisory responsibilities. It is a good fit because our candidates easily identify with induction year issues. There is a commonality of interest and a sense of shared innovation in designing curriculum. Cooperating teachers take a personal interest in our group of candidates and often enrich our seminars as speakers on topics such as the Standard English Program, resource specialists' duties, bilingual education, or ESL instruction. Holding seminars in the classrooms of the presenters is a major improvement over having visitors come to the university to speak. Children's work, technology, materials, and texts are all readily available for demonstration. Since student teachers are regularly on site, they can return to see the techniques in action.

Student Teacher/Children Relations. Student teachers frequently select or are assigned individuals or groups with special needs for remediation or enrichment. The challenge is to create developmentally appropriate lessons that are sensitive to each child's linguistic and cultural background. For example, Jonah noticed that the Mien children talked about going fishing with their families, so he began to teach math concepts using a fishing game that he created. Not only were the children more motivated to participate but their achievement increased as well, as documented by his M.A. research. The children of Alvarez soon became familiar with the distinctive constructivist approach of DTE student teachers. A fifth-grade boy asked one of our student teachers if she knew Mr. Serra, another DTE student. "Sure," she replied, "but why do you ask?" The boy grinned. "I just knew it. You both teach the *same* way."

Student Teacher/Community Relations. Since this placement is so interwoven in the fabric of the school, credential candidates and supervisors come to know community members who work at Alvarez. Instructional assistants, secretaries, campus supervisors, and the library assistant are recognized as repositories of valuable knowledge. All are most generous in interpreting their life experience for our candidates and supervisors. Student teachers also complete an extensive community assignment and present it to the group. For example, two of our candidates collaborated with members of the Mien community to have them record audiotapes, in Mien, of stories remembered from their villages in Laos. The parents made picture books to accompany the recordings, which became very popular in the classrooms. Since Mien is not a written language, this was a needed provision of literacy development in the children's first language. The project also has value in helping to preserve a culture that is imperiled by dilution through cultural assimilation. The community research project is one of the most valuable aspects of the Alvarez placement.

THE REVISED COURSE

We saw how the initial steps in transforming the fifth placement depended on opening our minds to a totally different way of conceptualizing the placement process and the roles of the players. We moved away from a traditional view of incremental increases in student teachers' responsibilities to focus primarily on the "zoom" (individual children) and the "wide angle" (the surrounding community). The middle range (whole-class instruction) had been substantially addressed in the four previous placements.

Students are expected to "zoom in" on individual students in a way that will no longer be possible once they assume full responsibility for their own class of 30 children. One candidate, Molly, was placed in an upper-grade, special day class. She wanted to communicate with a parent about perceptions of special education for bilingual children, so she worked intensively with a pupil, Luis, for several days and phoned his home. His mother was happy to talk about her son's academic difficulties as well as his strengths in sports and interpersonal relations. She explained her ongoing efforts to move Luis from school to school in search of teachers qualified to work with him in Spanish. This opportunity to concentrate deeply on the needs of one student is rarely possible in more traditional student teaching placements. Having had the experience, it is likely that Molly will feel comfortable calling parents when she begins teaching her own class.

For the "wide angle" view, students spend time getting to know the full range of programs within the school. Students must familiarize themselves with 10 programs, selected from a list of approximately 30 options, and reflect upon their experiences in their journals. One of the options is to sit in the main office for 20 minutes and describe what takes place there. There are fascinating journal entries about the sheer volume of business that is conducted in a profusion of languages. The experiences of families who come to enroll their children, but have no language in common with any of the office staff, make a big impression on our candidates and lead them to contemplate ways in which they can make the initial school contact more welcoming.

The community awareness assignment pushes students beyond the walls of the classroom and the school. This experience breaks down preconceived notions about life in a neighborhood that is continually maligned in the media as a "high crime" district. Each student selects one facet of the surrounding community for in-depth study, which requires an illustrated written report as well as an oral presentation. Topics are chosen with an eye to guiding candidates to personalize their conceptualization of the lives of the families of the children in their classes. "Community life," "food," "commerce," "extracurricular educational opportunities," "health," "governmental agencies," "media access," "linguistic diversity," "homelessness," "violence," and "historical demographics" are some of the topics selected for study. It is expected that students will (1) examine and reduce invidious assumptions about race, class, and national origin; (2) increase their capacity to take the perspective of families of diverse cultural and linguistic backgrounds; (3) come to understand that people do not elect to be poor out of a desire to avoid work; (4) learn how governmental agencies place constraints on individual liberties of poor people; and (5) develop transferable techniques for integrating themselves into communities wherever they teach. We expect students to use their knowledge to improve the relevance of instruction by incorporating children's life experiences into their classroom practice.

One candidate, Rebecca, immigrated to this country from Ireland as a child. Her topic was "governmental agencies." She attempted to negotiate the voice mail system of the Immigration and Naturalization Service (INS), taking the perspective of a limited-English-speaking immigrant parent. She called me at home one night, outraged, "How do you expect me to complete my assignment when after 45 minutes of pushing buttons, I can't even get to a human being on the INS phone maze?" Suddenly she realized, "That's just what you wanted me to experience, isn't it? Oh, my goodness, and English is *my* native language!" She returned to the phone tree (which she described as cross between Kafka and Alice in Wonderland) with renewed vigor and made a dramatic seminar presentation on the degrading and demoralizing experience that awaits noncitizens when they try to contact the INS.

Melanie, whose topic was "historical demographics," went to the Oakland History room of the public library and found photographs of Alvarez dating back to 1894. The photos show that in 1933, classes composed entirely of Caucasian children received their instruction in rows of desks bolted to the floor. A 1952 class photo shows four African American faces and three Asian Americans among the Caucasians. A 1954 class photo displays seven

African Americans and seven Asian Americans. Forty years later, the school is populated exclusively by children of color. Melanie followed up by interviewing the Alvarez school librarian, who has lived in the neighborhood for 38 years and worked at the school since 1972. Her report gave a vivid picture of a changing neighborhood and put her students' interactions into a dynamic historical context.

Molly, an Asian American candidate who speaks Spanish and remembers a small number of Chinese characters from her lost childhood language, selected "linguistic diversity" as her topic. She researched characteristics of all the languages at Alvarez and made practical suggestions for teaching children from each linguistic background. Many Asian languages, for example, do not have plural nouns, so the existence of English plurals must be made explicit to native speakers of those tongues. Spanish-speaking children, on the other hand, do not need to learn how to form English plurals because they do it the same way in their language. Molly also explained how each language conceptualizes personal names and the order in which family and given names generally are written. This is important for respectful personal interactions with students and families. Molly taught us to recognize the alphabets of all the languages in the school, an essential skill for teachers who must be sure that notes to families are in the proper home language. Finally, she shared proverbs from several cultures to illustrate differences in their value systems. She then created a lesson for the children in her class based on proverbs and riddles.

Emily selected "food" for her project, adding the idea of having several of her sixth-grade students serve as guides to neighborhood stores and restaurants. She secured permission for them to take her on a walking tour. Afterwards, they helped her order "Pho" (Vietnamese noodle soup) at a restaurant of their choice, where she treated them to lunch. The young guides brought Emily well beyond the requirements of her original assignment by explaining the uses for religious items on sale at the local grocery store. For her oral presentation, Emily brought in necessities for traditional spiritual practices, such as joss sticks and paper money used in rituals to honor deceased ancestors. The following year, Joan took another approach to this assignment by having her students prepare a guide to local restaurants, which was distributed in the community.

In the future, children's participation in the community research project will be recommended as a matter of course. This provides an excellent opportunity to instill a sense of community pride in children who assume the role of neighborhood guides and cultural interpreters. It also serves to allay the discomfort of students like Lisa, a European American who plans to become a Spanish bilingual teacher, who sometimes felt like an outsider "spying" on the neighborhood. It will be important for her to shed her feelings of alienation if she is to connect with the Spanish-speaking community in which she eventually will teach.

As a developmental program, we respect the readiness levels of our students and offer them support in progressing along a continuum toward fuller understanding of diversity. Meeting the challenge of diversity in teacher education includes requiring students to assess their own starting points and providing a realistic, individualized curriculum to move to ever higher levels of consciousness. Our candidates become so immersed in the realization that there are vibrant, exciting cultures at Alvarez about which they know nothing, that they begin to seek out information and to share it with one another. Beyond the required assignments, they circulate audio- and videotapes and books about Mien, Cambodian, Vietnamese, Latino, and African American cultures.

The candidates attend the Refugee Educators' Network Annual Southeast Asia Faire in Sacramento, sponsored by the Refugee Educators' Network, where almost all of them have presented highly rated multicultural curriculum workshops to hundreds of veteran teachers. Most of their workshops draw from multiple cultures and include information on cross-cultural issues as well as "hands-on" activities (e.g., Chinese chops, math games, candle making, heritage dolls, Chinese dragons, mask making, and batik). At the presenters' banquet on the eve of the Faire, DTE students are thrilled to find themselves seated at the table with some of the authors and film makers whose works they have encountered in their research on the cultures in the Alvarez community.

Potential for Preparing Teachers for Diversity

The DTE Program operates from the perspective that human development theory informs teaching practice across languages, cultures, and economic conditions. People learn most effectively when they construct their own knowledge, starting at an appropriate point and proceeding along a continuum. Social interaction is crucial in developing new understandings. This perspective underpins our approach to preparing teacher candidates as well as forming the basis for their interactions with children in their classes. After our students gain a grounding in constructivist theory and ample practice in field applications, the Alvarez placement provides a structure for expanding their understandings in a complex multilingual, multicultural social setting. We are convinced that the participatory group experience at Alvarez, in conjunction with the four previous placements, provides an invaluable opportunity for understanding issues of diversity.

Suggestions for Replication

For a 2-year M.A./Credential sequence of study, replicating our innovations does not pose much difficulty if the teacher preparation program is situated in a diverse geographical area.

Selecting the School and Cooperating Teachers. It is necessary to take risks in selecting the school site and the cooperating teachers. Schools must be selected for diversity of the student population and the presence of an enthusiastic principal. The qualifications of cooperating teachers must be assessed in a new light. The first criterion should be openness to thinking about issues in new ways rather than competence in doing things the old way.

Student Teacher Characteristics. Also, placements in impoverished areas must not exploit children for the purpose of assisting student teachers to learn how to teach them. It is important that our candidates have something to offer in return for the information they take away from this community. We send our best-prepared student teachers to the most demanding placements, those who have already acquired a strong repertoire of skills by successfully completing their solo teaching experience. We assign a group of volunteers who are excited and challenged by the prospect of learning together about teaching in a multicultural setting.

Group Functioning. Having a cohort of students placed simultaneously in a school for an intensive multicultural experience creates opportunities for collaboration and social construction of knowledge. Planning and teaching lessons jointly and reflecting collaboratively upon issues of diversity reduce the sense of isolation that student teachers feel when confronted with seemingly insoluble problems. By allowing that there are few "right answers" our work as a group becomes an opportunity to come up with good questions and to devise strategies for improvement. The supervisors become a part of the group, foregoing structured observations in favor of informal collaboration in the classroom and weekly on-site meetings for ongoing discussion as issues arise. Including school faculty and community members as participants sets a professional tone. Weekly journals with timely responses from peers and supervisors bring the collaboration into a more formal and reflective plane.

Progression of the Field Placements. We begin the first year with exposure to the disparity of educational opportunity for wealthy and poor children. This informs all that we do subsequently. In the second year, making individual children and the community the highest priorities permits a deeper focus on issues of diversity than more traditional placements with emphasis on the whole-class level. This frees the supervisor to be present on a consultative basis without the need to schedule artificial observations of "safe" lessons. Each candidate is assigned one cooperating teacher, who is responsible for supervisory tasks and paperwork, but the candidate is encouraged to work with all teachers in the school based on shared needs and skills. This does not exclude beginning teachers. In a large, year-round school with multiple programs, it is of paramount importance to model flexibility and cheerful resourcefulness by seeing opportunities in unexpected last-minute changes.

Modifications for a One-Year Program

In a one-year program this kind of immersion would still take place after student teachers successfully completed the solo teaching sequence so that they would be confident of their ability and possess professional skills to contribute to the school. This could mean moving the solo teaching 8 weeks earlier and reserving the final 8 weeks for an intensive "zoom to wide angle" multicultural experience. Or student teaching could be extended into the summer, taking advantage of schools with year-round schedules. Increasing unit totals for student teaching should be avoided by decreasing the number of hours in the summer program (e.g., 4 days a week instead of 5, or 3 instead of 4) except during the 2-week solo experience. In the DTE Program, we have found that a 5-day student teaching week is not necessary because students make excellent progress when they have time to reflect upon their practice between assigned days.

CONCLUSION

At the time we began redesigning the field component of DTE, our candidates were almost all white, middle-class women. Selecting a school populated with poor children of color leaves us open to charges of mandated "cultural voyeurism." We are ever cognizant of the imperative to guard against giving the impression that such children and their neighborhoods are objects of study set apart from "regular" children in "regular" communities (where "regular" is equated with "white" and "middle class"). We have begun to address this issue by also requiring community research across the racial and socioeconomic spectrum in the first year of DTE.

As our candidates come closer to representing the ethnic and economic diversity of California, the standards require us to assign candidates from poor and working class backgrounds to placements in affluent neighborhoods. There is potential benefit to all of our candidates in learning about the lives of children with backgrounds different from their own. However, placing candidates of color from working-class or poor backgrounds in affluent, white schools is not analogous to sending "mainstream" candidates to poor neighborhoods with high concentrations of children of color. People who look white have the luxury throughout their lives of choosing whether to acknowledge the existence of other cultures, races, and ethnicities, while minority students perpetually must live within the boundaries of "mainstream" norms. So in the first case, a cross-cultural placement may open the eyes of teacher candidates to the unexamined effects of white privilege; in the second case, the placement may magnify the all too familiar sense of oppression that has permeated their lives. In both situations, candidates may become uncomfortable, but the discomfort is valuable only to the extent that it raises consciousness to inform classroom practice.

Early on we saw that mere *exposure* to diversity was insufficient, so we restructured our placements to produce student *engagement*. As our faculty and candidates learn from one another, we collectively realize that passing from exposure through engagement to transformation will be a life-long process for us all.

14

A Community-Based Model Recruitment Process for Teacher Preparation

ANNE BOUIE

Well-designed, after-school programs provide opportunities to supplement the education children receive in school, provide safe places for children until parents return home, support prosocial conduct and behavior, and often become a part of the extended family in the care and nurture of children. These programs also can provide a setting for recruiting and training prospective teachers.

This chapter discusses the inception, design, and implementation of a community-based academic enrichment program designed to serve two client groups. The first is high-potential, yet underachieving urban middle school students. The second is the college students who, as study group leaders (SGLs), serve as role models and teachers to the younger students while learning pedagogy, curriculum development, and effective work with parents and community members.

THE PROGRAM'S INCEPTION

Project Interface began in 1982 as a collaborative effort between the Allen Temple Baptist Church and a black professional society, the Northern California Council of Black Professional Engineers (NCCBPE). The pastor of Allen Temple was contacted by a former colleague who shared with him the existence of a small fund designed to launch innovative math and science programs. Members of the two organizations collaborated on a proposal. Upon funding of the project, I was hired as director and began work to get the program up and running in late August 1982.

Allen Temple Baptist Church became the program's home. The church is located in the midst of the city's most challenged neighborhood, the Elmhurst district of Oakland, California. The majority of our students are from two "flatland" schools, located in the Elmhurst area, and one "hill school" in a middle-class community adjacent to the district. As the program matured, students who attend schools throughout the city under the district's open enrollment program, but who actually live in the Elmhurst neighborhood, also began to attend. As word of the program's effectiveness spread, many middle-class families, who had avoided the program's location, began to brave the flatlands to enroll their children. The resulting mix of social classes has led to interesting dynamics and opportunities for mutual support in a racially homogeneous program.

Characteristics of the Middle School Students

The program is designed to work with middle school students who exhibit one or more of the following characteristics:

1. Belief in one's inability to do school work successfully and that intelligence, not effort, is the key to academic success
2. Gaps in learning that hinder grasping new material
3. Lack of intentional support at home and school to learn the discipline and study habits needed for success in school
4. Low standards and expectations for student performance and achievement at school and lack of contact with the home
5. Lack of exposure to math and science professionals
6. Lack of information about the academic preparation needed for access to college and careers
7. Lack of effective, culturally consistent pedagogy
8. Lack of monitoring of student performance and progress
9. Low connection to community infrastructure that could counter antisocial elements in poor communities

Many of these characteristics are not personal but circumstantial and can be successfully countered. We have sought seventh- and eighth-grade students currently enrolled in general math and ninth graders enrolled in pre-algebra. These students usually do not enroll in the college preparatory courses needed to pursue academic careers in math and science. Another group of students often seeks us. They are enrolled in the appropriate courses for their grade level but are in jeopardy of failing. Too often the consequence is removal from the college prep class and placement in a general math class.

We find, without romanticizing the students or their circumstances, that they exhibit an impressive array of strengths that frequently are not acknowledged. That is:

1. They are bright and curious.
2. They are sensitive and aware of how they are perceived.
3. They struggle with issues around ethnicity, race, and gender.
4. They respond to support and exhortations to improve.
5. Many assume tremendous responsibilities in their families and church communities, which causes them to be more adult-like than many adults expect or are comfortable with. (These responsibilities are powerful tools that perceptive adults use to acknowledge their skills and competencies.)
6. They have high aspirations and want well-paying jobs; they do not know the instrumental steps to reach their goals.
7. They are loyal, care about what significant others think of them, and do not want to disappoint these people.
8. They respond to discipline, structure, and consistency.
9. They respond to caring, firm, friendly adults whom they trust and respect and who they feel care for and respect them.
10. They work when what they are doing has meaning in their daily lives and will help them achieve a goal or a dream.
11. They learn and achieve when taught as if this is expected.
12. Their parents and extended family are concerned and will use suggestions, and respond to coaching, from staff.
13. Their parents and extended families are proud when they do well and will support their effort and achievement.

Characteristics of the College Students

Recruiting and hiring the college student staff who serve as SGLs requires close work with the placement offices of the community college district. We identify essential characteristics of college students who will be effective.

Positive Perceptions of Urban Middle School Students. The college students who are most effective believe in their own ability to work with middle school youth. The SGLs demonstrate a certain affinity and are "simpatico" with their students; this helps them sense "where they [the students] were coming from," so that they are able to explain the work in ways that makes it matter to children. The work and fellowship come to matter so much that youngsters will ride public transportation across town, or walk several blocks after school, with their books, to work on math and science for 2 hours, 4 days a week, for the entire year.

In their study groups of four to eight middle school students, and working together as a staff, the SGLs and their students create what Noddings (1988) refers to as caring communities where "teachers and students live together, talk with each other, and take delight in each others' company." Noddings (1988) further states that caring is not an intellectual panacea.

> Hard work and great pedagogical skill will still be required. But I think it is obvious that children will work harder and do things—even odd things like adding fractions—for people they love and trust. (p. 32)

The SGLs do not view their students as "culturally deprived," "at risk," or so traumatized by life in an urban setting that they cannot learn. Many, though not all, of the SGLs have grown up in that same community and have even attended the same schools as youngsters. Those who have not are imbued with a sense of insight and hope that enables them to focus on strengths and potential as opposed to poverty and lack.

The program's conception of young people as resources to be developed rather than as problems to be managed means that their views and opinions are sought and respected even when not acted upon or agreed with. The program's components and activities intentionally address the youngsters' basic developmental needs for structure, support, challenge, caring, connection, respect, belonging, and meaningful involvement (Bernard, 1994).

Special Connectedness with Students. We find that effective SGLs either understand or are willing to learn how to grasp and use the "complex set of behaviors" Foster (1994) refers to when she notes that "effective black teachers [who] take on the role of kin" are able to administer "appropriate doses of firmness and nurture" (p. 232). These SGLs assume responsibility for student behavior and learning and are willing to do whatever it takes to ensure achievement. They become intentional and determined in creating lessons and activities that capture the attention of students so that the students want to learn. They see how their own experiences can be directly applied in helping students want to learn.

Self-Reflective. We want SGLs who assess themselves and their effectiveness. One of our SGLs, from an African nation, was an excellent math and science instructor who was quite structured in his approach. He came to me one day and said, "I cannot work with these seventh graders. They are driving me crazy. They move too much and talk too much. They are bad for my ulcer. I am not good with them. Please give me a ninth-grade group. I like them because they are more stable, and I can work with them better." We presented the situation to the staff, and another staff member agreed to change study groups. Students and parents were informed and notified that a change would be occurring at the upcoming grading period. The SGL's ninth-grade algebra group blossomed. His students left each year entering geometry as sophomores in high school. He worked with them to implement excellent physical science experiments. He had the courage to confront his ineffectiveness and ask for change.

A Sense of Their Own Growth and Career Path. We seek junior college students intent on transferring to a four-year college in a reasonable time period. Intent, good grades, and actual transfer are requirements to maintain the job. Their own progress serves as an example for the younger students. Acceptance to four-year colleges and scholarships are occasions for acknowledgment and praise.

Subject Matter Competence. The college students working with our students are competent in their subject matter. All of them teach math along with the science in which they are majoring. We find that high self-esteem and self-confidence are not based on simply telling students they are "okay," but on their discovery that they are competent and can do the work asked of them. This requires effort on their part that increases as they see their competence increase.

PROGRAM PLAN

Project Interface was designed to create an educational environment where bright, committed college students could be nurtured, taught, and groomed to provide quality services to younger students. This requires structure and support, infused with high expectations for students and staff alike, and invigorated with challenging and engaging academic content. This environment is the result of staff collaboration on content and process issues, with an emphasis on student achievement and matriculation into college preparatory math and science classes.

Program Goals and Objectives

The program's goals for middle school students are to

1. Provide students with the necessary skills and competencies for success in college preparatory math and science classes

2. Create learning and provide support activities that help students adopt attitudes and behaviors for success in school and positive coping strategies for adverse circumstances
3. Expose students to people, options, and instrumental steps to careers in math and science
4. Monitor student progress in school and at home to work with parents and teachers as partners
5. Ensure completion of math and science courses for matriculation into and success in college preparatory classes

Our goals for the college students are similar. We wish to

1. Ensure transfer to four-year colleges
2. Provide exposure to personal and professional role models and mentors
3. Provide learning opportunities that teach skills for teaching, public service, and math and science careers

Program Operation and Orientation

Project Interface operates 2 hours daily, Monday through Thursday from late September through June. An intense 4–6-week, 4-hour-a-day summer session is held in August as well. A mandatory parent–student orientation launches the program. In cases where parents simply are not available, we acknowledge and work closely with existing kin networks (Billingsley, 1992; Foster, 1994) by welcoming the caring adult who assumes parental responsibilities in the child's life. This person may be a relative or fictive kin. Our primary concern is a face-to-face connection and discussion with a caring adult who has assumed parental responsibilities in the child's life.

An orientation is provided that establishes community and common ground among the program staff, children, and parents. It is designed to instill pride in the academic achievements of the SGLs and the returning students. It inspires and motivates incoming students and assures parents that they are our strongest allies. The orientation provides an opportunity for everyone to hear the expectations held for student and parental behavior and achievement. We are explicit regarding what we expect from students and give specific suggestions to parents on what to do at home.

CURRICULUM CONTENT

The program consists of several content and process components aimed at affective or cognitive goals in mathematics and science.

Mathematics

We request students' most recent report card and Comprehensive Test of Basic Skill (CTBS) scores. We administer our own diagnostic test to determine strengths and weaknesses. These are scored by the SGLs as a part of the orientation week preparation and training activities and for student placement in heterogeneous math study groups. The SGLs are told that the grades and test scores indicate present *competency* but tell us nothing about student *capacity* to learn and achieve at higher levels. The program's rules and reward structures are designed to help students learn to change behaviors that get in their own way. The SGLs also are asked to think about the three spheres of material they continually have to cover: (1) review previously covered material; (2) ensure mastery of current work; and (3) introduce new material students will encounter.

The SGLs write lessons on activity sheets to break the work session into four 28-minute blocks, allowing 10 minutes for the daily break. The director reviews these math activity grids and provides comments and feedback. The activities are designed so that students alternately work individually, in pairs, in teams of three or more, or in competition against other teams. The SGLs lecture, lead discussions, conduct demonstrations, prepare hands-on activities, and coach as a student introduces the lesson or illustrates a problem at the board. The SGLs develop math worksheets, used for collective work by students, that contain a range of problems, from one or two that everyone in the group could get correct, to one or two that no one in the group would be able to do. The problems include some current homework problems; in this way, students receive help on their homework without it becoming the major focus of the program. Students often are told: "That's why they call it *homework*, because it is done at *home*." This enhances our approach as one of acceleration and enrichment, not remediation or mere tutoring.

We tell students that the math study group has three major tasks to accomplish. The first task—to identify gaps in previous learning—is essential in mastering the second: mastery of their current material. Finally, since they are bound for college prep classes, they have to be introduced to new material that will be taught later in their current grade or material they will encounter in an actual college prep class. The SGLs show how these three streams of work are interrelated, and they are coaches and monitors of sessions where students work on the activity sheets in a group and do board work to demonstrate how they get the answers. The SGLs help the students work through problems in order to apply the concepts presented.

The unplanned outcomes of heterogeneous grouping are delightful to observe. Often, a student who is not as far along as one of his peers grasps a new, more difficult concept more quickly than his more advanced peers.

This provides some needed humility for the advanced student and needed self-confidence for the struggling student. High-competency students are afforded opportunities to help low-competency students; the fact that most of the math competitions are between groups and not individuals means that students have a vested interest in helping fellow group members do their best. This equalizing effect contributes to the esprit and mutual support among students.

Science

Students are taught the three core sciences using the California State Curriculum Frameworks as the foundation for interdisciplinary units. A team of four SGLs develops and teaches science activities to a group of 15 to 20 students. Science, like math, is taught 2 days each week. The science strands incorporate a number of critical process variables: (1) lessons consider a variety of learning styles; (2) learning activities apply concepts to the students' own environment; (3) activities stress cooperation and mutual support; and (4) activities use interdisciplinary approaches.

The SGLs structure science sessions so that students learn to take notes and keep a science notebook; conduct experiments and record the results; and present reports to sharpen their oral language skills. The objectives of the lessons are to (1) teach underlying thinking processes along with skills, so that students are not just solving problems but understand what they are learning, doing, and why; (2) gradually turn over responsibility for the learning process to students; (3) vary the pace, mode, and configuration of learning activities within instructional units; (4) encourage cooperative and team-learning arrangements; and (5) facilitate SGL–student and student–student discussions about mathematical and scientific ideas and skills and their application to real-life situations.

Science speakers visit the science study groups once each month to present lectures, give demonstrations, and involve students in hands-on activities. They share information about their careers and academic work, and their struggles and setbacks, with the students. The speakers are living proof that people who look like them are actually scientists and enjoy it. Many of these speakers are members of one of three African American professional societies who work closely with the project. Along with the engineers, the National Organization of Black Chemists and Chemical Engineers (NOBCCE) and the Sinkler Miller Society contribute science speakers on a regular basis.

It is inspiring to see young college students in a huge church fellowship hall engaging middle school students thoroughly in activities like baking bread from scratch using math and science, dissecting fetal pigs, and preparing lab reports, or researching the ingredients of the "junk" food they love to consume—so that they learn how chemicals and additives are packaged for their consumption. This affirms our belief that expensive equipment and elaborate settings are not the only or even the most important factors in generating learning and enthusiasm.

Career Exploration

To expose students to real-world work sites, we work with three companies at Harbor Bay Business Park that are engaged in state-of-the-art scientific research and development. The companies make their facilities available for field trips and company staff lead the tours. These on-site visits are structured learning activities that break the routine and add a sense of realism and purpose to the program. Students are allowed to touch, ask questions, wear the goggles real scientists wear, and talk with them about their work. In addition, the scientists are able to talk about the need for eighth-grade pre-algebra and share with students their own experiences of middle school. One scientist shared her work on cancer; another on sickle cell anemia, a topic of direct interest to our students, one of whom shared that a family member had the disease. The relevance of the topic and demonstration was obvious. Finally, the companies donate equipment for our activities.

STRATEGIC PROGRAM COMPONENTS

Parents and mentors provide strategic support; counseling, opportunities for structured dialogue about their lived realities, and recognition of the students' efforts and success are other important strategic components of the program.

Parental Involvement and Support

Contact with parents is structured and frequent, and parents and students sign contracts committing themselves to the program's goals at the beginning of each year. Before the orientation, each SGL makes a welcome call to introduce him- or herself and extend a personal invitation to parents. This is the first step in a deliberate process of earning the parents' active partnership in working with us. It also ensures at least an open ear, if the occasion to call with a problem arises.

Parents and students receive explicit academic and career counseling about the math and science courses required each year during middle and high school. Absences and tardiness are reported to monitor attendance, and parents receive monthly written feedback on student behavior and performance. The weekly call to touch base reports good news and updates parents on student progress and program events. Conferences are scheduled as needed regarding effort and misbehavior.

Role Model/Mentor Involvement

The professional scientists and mathematicians and people in math and science-based careers who speak to the students twice a month are also role models and mentors. They share their experience, strength, and hope with students who show particular interest in their topic. Students perk up when a speaker shares that she has grown up poor, or has parents who are divorced, died, or from whom they have been separated. They sigh when speakers confess to flunking classes in school and recommend that the students study hard rather than drop out. Second, students want to know how the speakers got where they are—how they "got over." Finally, students always ask—in spite of being told not to—how much money the speaker makes.

Students and SGLs alike are bombarded with supportive, realistic messages about their aspirations and what it takes to become the person and professional they wish to become. They listen to the guest speakers, who reinforce messages from parents, teachers, and the program. Hearing a well-dressed, polished professional or experienced journeyperson say the same things about schoolwork and effort as one's parents, teacher, or SGL, has a profound impact on students and helps to ease the inherent tension parents and children experience during adolescence. Role models are invaluable in their repetition of the themes of excellence, effort, and perseverance. In addition to the core academic components, other key program components consist of a complement of support processes.

Academic and Career Counseling

Contrary to the perceptions of many practitioners and researchers, we find that our students have high aspirations. They speak of desires to become doctors, lawyers, engineers, car mechanics, and other careers that require math and science courses and postsecondary schooling. What they do not have is the instrumental knowledge of how to make those dreams become reality—no sense of the courses they need to take in high school, of how to apply to college, or where "college" is. Information and coaching are lacking; desire and dreams are not. A component of the program is the provision of this information. We tell students it is not too early to begin thinking about college; in just a few years they will be graduating from school and ready to enter college.

Informally Structured Dialogue

Life in East Oakland presents many "teachable moments" around the vicissitudes of gender, social class, ethnicity, and race. Local events provide material to discuss with students individually and in large-group "fireside chats." Students assemble at the close of each day for a 5- to 10-minute "chat" with the director. The theme is usually the discussion of an idea, the meaning of a word, or a current event that has captured the students' attention. Students are asked to share their own definitions and perceptions of events. The director elaborates on themes students raise and engages them in dialogue about their hopes and aspirations.

SGLs are encouraged to bring student concerns about unfair treatment at school to the director. Students sometimes complain that "the teacher is a racist," or "she doesn't like me because I'm black." We probe to learn the basis of these student perceptions. We often hear of students being removed from a pre-algebra class and placed in a general math class because the student received a "D" on the report card; or a student says, "I raise my hand to answer the question and she never calls on me." Students also share experiences of differential treatment for the same offense; of negative remarks about African American students; and of good work not being acknowledged.

We use these as opportunities to talk of the reality of prejudice and how to handle it so that they do not end up in the principal's office for "willful disobedience." We often find that students have legitimate concerns but express anger and disagreement in such a way as to land in the principal's office with a referral or a suspension. Often, adults choose to focus on the child's behavior to the exclusion of the circumstances or the adult behavior that might have provoked it. The legitimate concern is ignored and, while the student's behavior is addressed, that of the adult involved is ignored. We encourage students to tell their parents and we suggest that they reflect on their contribution to the situation as well. We apprise parents of these incidents and encourage them to investigate further.

Incentive Awards

The monthly Incentive Award ceremony acknowledges outstanding students in four areas: attendance, scholarship, effort, and citizenship. Students who receive all four ribbons also receive a fifth, for overall excellence. The ceremony is held on a day when a role model has been invited to address the students. It is a special reward to be acknowledged for achievement when a guest is present. Students look forward to the ceremony and are proud of the ribbons they receive. Parents say that students display the ribbons in their rooms.

Program Outcomes

Each year we gather student scores on the Comprehensive Test of Basic Skills (CTBS). Middle school students are expected to show at least 10 months academic growth and a 3- to 5-point increase in their percentile ranking. They also are expected to matriculate into the appropriate college preparatory math and science classes. The college students are expected to be in good standing at a two- or four-year institution and, if they are in a two-year college, to have a definite plan and date to transfer to a four-year institution.

For the past 10 years, two-thirds to three-fourths of the students enrolled in Project Interface have matriculated to college-prep-level math and science classes in junior and senior high school. Students enrolled in public schools throughout the city also perform on standardized tests in an exemplary manner, consistently averaging increases of 3 to 7 points in their percentile ranking and a minimum 12 months' growth per academic year. The benefits of higher achievement in math and science also affect students' performance in other classes and after they have graduated from the program. Students in high school continue in math and science classes and maintain solid grade point averages.

Implications for Teacher Preparation

Over time, staff recruitment has aimed at identifying students who wish to become teachers and who wish to pursue careers as scientists and engineers. It is clear that the college students need training to be effective with the younger students. They receive 3 hours of academic credit through the Peralta Community College District for attending and participating in a weekly 3-hour training session, taught by the program director, each year before the program begins. Also, they are on board for a week at the end of the year to close up and to complete year-end assessments; they work one week before and after the beginning of the summer session. Thus, they participate in ten 8-hour days of training and preparation that focus on the four key areas. Each of these areas has lessons for preparing effective teachers for urban schools.

Ensuring High Expectations

All SGLs know the content of the mathematics curriculum from sixth-grade general math through geometry. While specialization and preferences are accommodated, they are expected to teach at any of these levels. Senior SGLs use state and district grade-level expectations to research and present to the project staff the skills, scope, and content sequence at each grade level. An

SGL is able to plan lessons using the content and skills required in the previous, current, and upcoming grades. This knowledge establishes the Senior SGLs as competent resources for fellow staff. The staff as a whole is more competent and confident as a result of the depth and breath of their preparation.

Ensuring a Culturally Compatible, Orderly Learning Environment

Teaching SGLs how to build positive working relationships with their groups in ways that are culturally compatible is essential. SGL training demonstrates ways to initiate students' first encounter with the study group. They participate in role-plays, taking turns at being the SGL and a member of a study group. These scenarios are critiqued and debriefed until the entire staff of 12 to 15 SGLs feels they can build upon the cultural mores of how leadership and authority are established and maintained in the African American community.

The project also acknowledges and adheres to traditional African American cultural norms regarding dress for professional roles. The dress code that SGLs adhere to disallows shirts with no collars, jeans with holes, shorts, and the like. In the words of one math teacher at an East Oakland high school:

> My students ask me why so-and-so comes to school dressed as if she/ he were going to the beach or a picnic. They don't like their teachers dressing like students or looking like they don't care about coming to work. It makes them feel disrespected and as if they don't care about their work. I always wear a tie, or a sports jacket, or a sweater.

Students at Project Interface are required to follow seven explicit rules developed with their input along with parents and the program's staff. SGLs are trained to implement these rules, which prohibit

1. Engaging in forms of verbal jousting, e.g., "playing the dozens," "sounding," "capping," etc.
2. Eating food during the project activities
3. Horseplay on the premises, e.g., running, hitting, wrestling, taking others' belongings, screaming, and not returning to the study group promptly after break
4. Pencil sharpening or going to the restroom except during the break

In addition, students are expected to

5. Bring the necessary math and science books and materials to the project each day—even when no homework has been assigned

6. Be respectful of fellow students, parents, and other adults
7. Be diligent and consistent in studying outside of class and take care of personal business during the free time before project activities begin or during the break

These rules complement the "series of consequences" that are presented as a natural consequence of behavior and attitudes that are not constructive. At the first incidence, the SGL talks with the student and shares the remaining steps in the series. At the second incident, the student's parent is telephoned. At the third occurrence the parent and child are asked to a conference with the SGL and the director.

SGLs receive explicit training in how to talk to parents to create a mutually supportive relationship. This is important because most of them balked at calling parents and telling them anything negative about their child. They said, "We don't have any children, and the parents are older than we are." We explain that parents are very concerned about what their children are learning and how they are progressing. Parents want their children to do well in school and are pleased and proud when they do. Second, parents want to know when their children are misbehaving or not trying in school. In most instances, once a parent has been informed, an immediate change in the student's behavior and attitude can be observed. Once the student understands that parents endorse and support the program's staff, good behavior and solid effort usually can be expected. Parents are strong allies in helping students feel good about achieving in school and being a part of their community as well. Finally, parents very much want to hear that their children are doing well in school. Parents often share that a phone call reporting progress and success makes their day.

SGLs are often surprised at the depth of parents' concern for their children, given all that they have heard or been taught about poor parents who are thought not to care about the education of their children. It is important to note that this endorsement is consciously sought and earned and is rendered by parents who feel that staff genuinely care for the students as if they were their own children. Parents who feel that staff do not care about their children are formidable in their children's defense and are difficult to win as allies.

Supporting and Encouraging Proactive Behavior

SGLs need training to help students become "bicultural" and allow themselves to feel self-esteem based on doing well in school. Discussions on the history and struggle of African Americans help them understand that excellence and achievement are not "white" but are valued by African Americans as well and that doing well in school can co-exist comfortably with being an African American. The fact that the black SGLs are achieving in school is a statement to that effect. SGLs receive explicit coaching to counter student resistance to higher expectations of them for quality and quantity of work. They are taught how to use praise effectively to motivate and challenge students and how to use students' ethnic history and heritage as inspirational tools.

Creating Challenging Content and Engaging Instructional Strategies

SGLs are coached by the director, with support from the Oakland Museum, the Lawrence Hall of Science, and Stanford University. They receive guidelines and support in learning instructional practices to teach math and science in ways that are related to the students' real-life experiences, and they are provided with systematic instruction on how to solve problems. These guidelines include processes that use a variety of group configurations that build upon student interests, aptitudes, strengths, and needs, while exposing them to new material that requires the use of new skills. These skills are integrated with existing ones and provide safe, structured opportunities for learning until mastery is achieved. SGLs also participate in monthly Professional Development Seminars where scientists or other professionals tailor their presentations directly to the needs of college students aspiring to four-year colleges, graduate school, and eventual professional careers.

CONCLUSION

Project Interface illustrates the potential of community-based organizations to accomplish multiple, complementary goals. The primary goals are the creation of a structured, supportive learning community that provides high-quality educational services to underachieving youngsters. Second, promising college students learn the attitudes, behaviors, and pedagogical skills to become effective service providers and gain a sense of their competence as young professionals.

15

Responding to Social Change
California's New Standards for Teacher Credentialing

PRISCILLA H. WALTON AND ROBERT E. CARLSON

The California Commission on Teacher Credentialing (CTC), in collaboration with its Bilingual Crosscultural Advisory Panel and others, recently developed and implemented a new system for the preparation and credentialing of teachers for limited-English-proficient (LEP) students.[1] The new system encompasses teacher preparation programs and coursework, teacher credentialing examinations, and teaching credentials and certificates that authorize the teaching of LEP students. In this chapter we describe components of the new system, including (1) a description of linguistic and cultural diversity in California; (2) the specialized knowledge and skills needed by teachers of LEP students; (3) the new system; (4) the participants in the reform effort; (5) the impact of the new system; and (6) recommendations for replication of the system in other states.

THE NEED FOR CHANGE: LINGUISTIC AND CULTURAL DIVERSITY IN CALIFORNIA

California's K–12 student population has changed dramatically over the past 2 decades. It is becoming more diverse, and increasing numbers of students come to school with primary languages other than English. In 1990, California had the largest number of LEP students of any state in the nation, accounting for 42% of all LEP students (Office of Bilingual Education and Minority Languages Affairs, 1991). In the spring of 1994, there were over 1.2

Preparing Teachers for Cultural Diversity. Copyright © 1997 by Teachers College, Columbia University. All rights reserved. ISBN 0-8077-3605-8 (pbk.), ISBN 0-8077-3606-6 (cloth). Prior to photocopying items for classroom use, please contact the Copyright Clearance Center, Customer Service, 222 Rosewood Dr., Danvers, MA 01923, USA, tel. (508) 750-8400.

million LEP students in California in grades K–12. Of the 20 school districts in the United States with the largest numbers of LEP students in 1993–94, 12 were in California (Green, 1993; LA & NYC have largest LEP #s, 1995).

Another important feature of the current school population in California is that the composition of schools and communities is continually changing. Many of California's communities are ports of entry for immigrants (Cornelius, 1991; Portes & Rumbaut, 1990). These neighborhoods have high mobility rates among families and children. Thus, many of the schools serving LEP students have high transiency and low attendance rates. Teachers continually must find ways to integrate new students, representing a wide variety of languages and cultures, into their classrooms (Berman et al., 1992; Olsen, 1988). Even bilingual classrooms are increasingly characterized by cultural diversity. For example, many Spanish/English bilingual classrooms include students from a variety of countries, each with its own cultural characteristics (e.g., El Salvador, Guatemala, Mexico, and Nicaragua).

Previous policies for the preparation and credentialing of teachers for LEP students were ineffective in meeting the needs of California's evolving LEP student population. The prior policies did not provide an entry-level route for monolingual English teachers to work with LEP students. The focus on the needs of Spanish-speaking students made it difficult to develop programs and examinations to prepare and credential teachers for LEP students who speak other languages. Finally, inadequate emphasis was given to specially designed academic instruction delivered in English (SDAIE) and to general cultural competencies. Thus, the prior policies were not a consciously designed, integrated response to a variety of diverse language and cultural needs (Work Group, 1993).

Specialized Knowledge and Skills Teachers of LEP Students Need

The instructional needs of LEP students fall into two primary areas: English language development (ELD)—also known as English as a second language—and access to the subject matter curriculum. Teachers of LEP students must have the skills and knowledge necessary to deliver appropriate instructional services in these areas. In addition to instructional competencies, teachers of LEP students must be knowledgeable about culture and its role in education. The two areas of instructional needs and the importance of cultural knowledge are discussed below.

English Language Development

A primary goal of all programs for LEP students is to help them acquire English as soon as possible through the provision of instruction for

English language development. Teachers who provide such instruction must be specially trained. They must be knowledgeable about language structure, language use, and theories and factors in first and second language development. They also need to be competent in specific instructional methodologies designed to facilitate LEP students' acquisition of English, including techniques for infusing subject matter, or content information, into language instruction. In addition, teachers who provide instruction for ELD must be knowledgeable about procedures and instruments used in the assessment of language.

The Subject Matter Curriculum

There are two ways that LEP students can be given opportunities to learn the subject matter curriculum: (1) through content instruction delivered in the students' primary language and (2) through SDAIE.

Primary-Language Instruction. California state law requires that, when necessary for equal educational opportunity, LEP students be given content instruction delivered in their primary language. In this way, the students' academic achievement is not delayed while they are learning English. In fact, the knowledge gained through the study of academic subjects in the primary language assists in the acquisition of English (Krashen, 1991; Krashen & Biber, 1988). Allowing students to learn in their primary language also encourages multiculturalism, accommodation, and additive acculturation. It is based on the view that English proficiency is an additional set of skills and not a replacement of the home language and culture (Gibson & Ogbu, 1991). The opportunity to learn in their primary language and the incorporation of their cultures into the curriculum enable students to take pride in the personal resources they bring to the educational setting, enhancing their self-esteem. It helps them to function in both their home culture and mainstream society, rather than forcing them to choose between the language and culture of the home and those of the mainstream culture (Banks, 1988a, 1989; Cummins, 1989; Gibson, 1988; Grant & Sleeter, 1989; Nieto, 1992).

Teachers who teach LEP students in their primary language need to be proficient in all four skill areas of that language (i.e., listening, speaking, reading, and writing). They need to have a repertoire of instructional methodologies for providing content instruction in bilingual settings. They must be able to locate, review, develop, and adapt instructional materials in the primary language. Bilingual teachers also need knowledge about the culture of the students with whom they work.

Academic Instruction in English. Limited-English-proficient students who are at an intermediate level of English proficiency or higher can receive access to the core curriculum through SDAIE. This type of instruction involves the use of specific instructional techniques and strategies to make grade-level content instruction comprehensible to students with sufficient proficiency in English to benefit from such instruction, but whose proficiency in English would not allow them to benefit from mainstream instruction. SDAIE involves strategies based on an understanding of language development and the important role of culture in education. Many of the techniques are drawn from the literature on effective instruction but are given more prominence, in terms of frequency and intensity, than in mainstream instruction because of the students' language abilities.

SDAIE is an important instructional component of bilingual programs. Once students achieve an intermediate level of English proficiency, they can begin to learn elements of the subject matter curriculum in English. Because their English proficiency is not at the level required for mainstream instruction, however, these students need specially designed instruction that takes into account their developing proficiency in English. Subjects such as mathematics and science are often the first to be taught using SDAIE because they are less language-dependent than other subjects. As English language proficiency increases, subjects that involve more abstract use of language can be taught with this approach.

Unfortunately, due to the shortage of bilingual teachers, LEP students below the intermediate level of English proficiency frequently do not have the opportunity to receive content instruction delivered in their primary language. Only about 40% of the students in California who need academic instruction in their primary language are receiving it (California Association for Bilingual Education, 1991). In such cases, SDAIE is often the only alternative. Although not designed for LEP students with low levels of English proficiency, it is better than mainstream instruction, where no modifications are used to make content comprehensible to LEP students.

SDAIE requires a teacher who understands and can implement the specific techniques and strategies for making content instruction comprehensible to LEP students. These techniques include, among others, contextualizing the content information presented, using conceptual scaffolding, appropriately using paraphrase and repetition, checking for comprehension, and making learning strategies explicit for students.

Knowledge About Culture

Policies of assimilation have predominated in the education of LEP students. These policies are based on the unfounded assumption that LEP students must give up their home languages and cultures to be successful in school. In reality, however, assimilation-based policies frequently have undermined the very qualities that enable LEP students to excel in school. Case studies of a number of successful immigrant students have found that these students succeed in school because they have strong home cultures and languages and a strong, positive sense of their ethnic identity (Gibson, 1988; Gibson & Ogbu, 1991; Nieto, 1992). Students' home languages and cultures are important resources for success and should be allowed to flourish rather than be eradicated.

Teachers need information about their students' cultures in order to appropriately apply the methodologies discussed in this chapter (i.e., culturally responsive pedagogy) and to earn the respect and trust of students and their parents. Because of the often rapid demographic changes in school populations, and because of the limited time available in teacher preparation programs, teachers are not expected to have in-depth knowledge about all of the cultures they might encounter. Instead, they need to know and be able to apply basic social science skills, such as classroom ethnography, in order to acquire cultural information about their students. This information should serve as a basis for the development of curriculum and the selection of appropriate pedagogical practices. Teachers also need a general understanding of the interplay between culture and language in the school and in the community (Banks, 1988b, 1989; Cummins, 1986, 1989; Díaz, Moll, & Mehan, 1986; Heath, 1986).

In response to the need to provide teachers with the competencies necessary for teaching LEP students, CTC, in collaboration with educators throughout California, developed and implemented a new system for the preparation and credentialing of teachers for LEP students.

THE NEW SYSTEM FOR TEACHER PREPARATION AND CREDENTIALING

The new system for the preparation and credentialing of teachers for LEP students consists of two primary parts. One part addresses the preparation and training of teachers to provide instruction in English to LEP students. This aspect of the system is referred to as "Crosscultural, Language and Academic Development" or "CLAD." The second part addresses the preparation and training of bilingual teachers and is referred to as "Bilingual, Crosscultural, Language and Academic Development" or "BCLAD." The system as a whole is known as the CLAD/BCLAD system. The CLAD in both parts of the system reflects the common core of knowledge and skills needed by all teachers of LEP students.

The CLAD/BCLAD system is presented graphically in Figure 15.1. It includes the following elements: (1) CLAD/BCLAD Examinations, (2) CLAD/BCLAD Emphasis Credentials, (3) CLAD/BCLAD Certificates, and

Figure 15.1. The CLAD/BCLAD System for the Preparation and Credentialing of Teachers for LEP Students

CLAD and BCLAD Emphasis Credentials and Certificates

The CLAD/BCLAD Domains of Knowledge and Skill

1. Language Structure and First and Second Language Development

2. Methodology of Bilingual, English Language Development, and Content Instruction

3. Culture and Cultural Diversity

4. Methodology for Primary Language Instruction

5. The Culture of Emphasis

6. The Language of Emphasis

CLAD	**BCLAD**
(Domains 1–3 and experience learning a second language)	(Domains 1–6)
Prospective teachers:	Prospective teachers:
Emphasis Program	Emphasis Program
(Emphasis Credential)	(Emphasis Credential)
Credentialed teachers:	Credentialed teachers:
College Coursework or	Examinations 1–6 or
Examinations 1–3	CLAD & Examinations 4–6
(Certificate)	(Certificate)

CLAD and BCLAD Specialist Credentials

Available through CLAD/BCLAD Specialist Credential Programs
Prerequisite: CLAD or BCLAD authorization or the equivalent Program focuses on:

(1) assessment and evaluation of students

(2) program development and evaluation

(3) staff development

(4) curriculum development

(5) parents, school, and community

(6) research

(4) CLAD/BCLAD Specialist Credentials. Figure 15.2 presents the types of instructional services to LEP students authorized by CLAD and BCLAD Emphasis Credentials and Certificates. The CLAD and BCLAD Emphasis Credentials, Certificates, and Examinations are all based on the same domains of knowledge and skill. A description of these domains of knowledge and skill is given below. This is followed by descriptions of the CLAD/BCLAD Emphasis Credentials and Certificates, the CLAD/BCLAD Examinations, and the CLAD/BCLAD Specialist Credentials.

The CLAD/BCLAD Domains of Knowledge and Skill

The top box in Figure 15.1 lists the six domains of knowledge and skill that are the foundation for all of the elements in the CLAD/BCLAD system.

Domain 1: Language Structure and Language Development. Domain 1 includes two primary areas. The first is language structure and use, including universals and differences among languages and the structure of English. The second area includes theories and models of language development as well as psychological, sociocultural, political, and pedagogical factors affecting first and second language development.

Domain 2: Methodology. Three areas are included in Domain 2. The first covers theories and methods of bilingual education at a level needed by all teachers of LEP students (not just bilingual teachers). This first area in-

Figure 15.2. Types of Instruction to Limited-English-Proficient Students Authorized by the CLAD and BCLAD Emphasis Credentials and Certificates

Credential or Certificate	Type of Instruction		
	Instruction for English Language Development[1]	Specially Designed Academic Instruction Delivered in English[2]	Instruction for Primary-Language Development and Content Instruction Delivered in Primary Language[3]
CLAD	Yes	Yes	No
BCLAD	Yes	Yes	Yes

[1] Preschool, K–12, and adults, with some exceptions.
[2] In subjects and grade levels authorized by the prerequisite credential or permit.
[3] Content instruction delivered in the primary language in subjects and grade levels authorized by the prerequisite credential or permit. Instruction for primary-language development at preschool, K–12, and adults, with some exceptions.

cludes the foundations of bilingual education, program models, and instructional strategies. The second area covers theories and methods for instruction in and through English, including approaches with a focus on English language development, approaches with a focus on content area instruction (including SDAIE), and working with paraprofessionals. The third area in this domain consists of the knowledge and skills needed to appropriately assess students' language abilities and subject matter achievement.

Domain 3: Culture and Cultural Diversity. Domain 3 includes three areas. The first area, culture and cultural interactions, includes the nature of culture (e.g., definitions of culture, intragroup and intergroup differences), the content of culture (e.g., values and beliefs, roles and status), and cross-cultural contact and interactions (e.g., acculturation, pluralism, prejudice). The second area, cultural diversity in the United States and California, includes historical perspectives, historical and contemporary demography, migration, and immigration. The third area includes issues related to the provision of culturally responsive instruction, such as classroom organization and interactions, curriculum, instructional strategies, and the roles of families and community resources. This domain does not focus on any specific cultural group but on culture in general and its role in education.

Domain 4: Methodology for Primary-Language Instruction. Domain 4 also includes three areas. First is instructional delivery in a bilingual classroom, including topics such as organizational and instructional strategies for teaching content in English and a student's primary language and for teaching language arts, transferring language and literacy skills, and primary-language support. The second area deals with language and content assessment in a student's primary language. The third area focuses on the evaluation and use of primary-language materials for instruction and assessment. It includes criteria for selection and strategies for augmenting existing resources.

Domain 5: The Culture of Emphasis. Domain 5 consists of knowledge and skills related to the culture associated with a bilingual teacher's language of emphasis and is divided into two areas. The first area includes the origins and characteristics of the culture of emphasis, that is, the commonalities of the culture of emphasis in the country or countries of origin. Topics include major historical periods and events, values and beliefs, communication systems, demographics, family structure, and the arts. The second area includes the experiences of the people of the culture of emphasis in both the United States in general and California specifically. This area includes topics such as major historical periods and events, demography, migration and immigration, cultural contributions, and intragroup and intergroup relations.

Domain 6: The Language of Emphasis. Domain 6 includes proficiency in the language in which the teacher wishes to be authorized to provide primary-language instruction (the language of emphasis). Proficiency is expected in the language of emphasis in the areas of speaking, listening, reading, and writing.

These six domains of knowledge and skill are the heart of the new CLAD/BCLAD system. The requirements for the CLAD and BCLAD Emphasis Credentials and Certificates are based on these domains, and a CLAD or a BCLAD Emphasis Credential or Certificate is a prerequisite for the CLAD or BCLAD Specialist Credential.

CLAD/BCLAD Emphasis Credentials and Certificates

As shown in Figure 15.1, the CLAD/BCLAD system includes both CLAD and BCLAD Emphasis Credentials and Certificates and CLAD and BCLAD Specialist Credentials. Opportunities to earn CLAD and BCLAD Emphasis Credentials and Certificates are available to preservice and inservice teachers who have not already earned a credential authorizing instruction to LEP students.

A Common Core. Central to the CLAD/BCLAD system is the recognition of a common core of knowledge and skills needed by all teachers of LEP students. A CLAD/BCLAD Emphasis Credential Program is a single program with a core curriculum focusing on the first three domains of knowledge and skill. This core constitutes the basic training needed by all teachers who work with LEP students. Candidates who successfully complete this core of studies receive a CLAD Emphasis Credential. Candidates who also receive training or show competence in Domains 4 through 6 receive a BCLAD Emphasis Credential. By definition, a BCLAD Emphasis Credential Program incorporates the CLAD core curriculum. Institutions may develop a CLAD Emphasis Credential Program first, however, and add the BCLAD component at a later date. If this occurs, the BCLAD Emphasis Credential Program must incorporate the CLAD core curriculum.

Standards of Program Quality. The Commission's Standards of Program Quality and Effectiveness for Professional Teacher Preparation Programs for Multiple and Single Subject Teaching Credentials with a (Bilingual) Cross-cultural, Language and Academic Development (CLAD/BCLAD) Emphasis (Commission on Teacher Credentialing, 1992) shape the CLAD/BCLAD Emphasis Credential Programs at California colleges and universities. A "standard" is a statement of program quality that must be fulfilled for approval of a professional preparation program by CTC. The Commission determines whether a program satisfies a standard on the basis of consideration, by a trained evaluation team, of all available information related to the standard. The standards generally describe the quality that CTC expects to find in programs of professional preparation.

The standards for all professional teacher preparation programs approved by CTC are organized into the following five categories: Institutional Resources and Coordination, Admission and Student Services, Curriculum, Field Experiences, and Candidate Competence and Performance. Standards consist of three parts: a statement of the standard, a rationale for the standard, and a set of factors to be considered by the evaluation team when judging whether the standard has been fulfilled. An example of a standard from the Candidate Competence and Performance Category is presented in Figure 15.3. This particular standard is not only in the CLAD/BCLAD Emphasis Credential Program standards, but in the standards for all other professional preparation programs as well.

Credentialed Teachers: The CLAD/BCLAD Certificates

The CLAD/BCLAD Emphasis Credential Programs described above are for prospective teachers, individuals who have not yet earned a teaching credential. Teachers who already have a teaching credential can earn CLAD and BCLAD Certificates through college coursework and/or examinations.

The CLAD Certificate. A teacher who already holds a credential can earn a CLAD Certificate by meeting the same general requirements that a prospective teacher must satisfy to earn a CLAD Emphasis Credential: demonstrating competence in Domains 1 through 3 and having experience learning a second language. There are two ways of demonstrating competence in Domains 1 through 3. One way is by completing 12 upper-division or graduate semester units of coursework. The coursework must be applicable toward a bachelor's degree or higher at a regionally accredited college or university. All of the coursework must be in Domains 1 through 3, and all three of the domains must be covered in the set of coursework used to satisfy the requirement. An alternative way to demonstrate competence in Domains 1 through 3 is to pass Tests 1, 2, and 3 of the CLAD/BCLAD Examinations, described below.

A teacher seeking a CLAD Certificate must verify experience learning a second language. This could be satisfied by having six semester units of college coursework in a language other than English, or in one of a dozen other ways, including completion of Peace Corps language training; passage of an examination that assesses language proficiency; and growing up,

Figure 15.3. An Example of a Program Standard

Category V: Candidate Competence and Performance

Standard 31
Capacity to Teach Diverse Students

Each candidate demonstrates compatibility with, and ability to teach, students different from the candidate. The differences between students and the candidate should include cultural, linguistic, racial, ethnic, gender, and socio-economic differences.

Rationale

A California teaching credential authorizes a person to teach in any public school throughout a state that is culturally, ethnically, linguistically, racially, and socio-economically diverse. A teacher whose preparation occurs exclusively among pupils who are similar to the teacher is not well prepared to teach in California.

Factors to Consider

• Each candidate fulfills Standards 23 through 31 [other standards in the Candidate Competence and Performance category] while teaching students who are different from the candidate in culture, language, race, gender, and socio-economic background.

• Each candidate exhibits understanding, appreciation, and sensitivity toward the cultural heritage, community values, and individual aspirations of diverse students.

• Each candidate encourages respect for human diversity through planned lessons and through personal interaction with students, parents, and community.

• Each candidate understands prejudice and is able to implement strategies to prevent and/or reduce it.

• The program meets other factors related to this standard of quality brought to the attention of the team by the institution.

---

or living as an adult, in a country in which a language other than English is the primary language. The holder of a CLAD Certificate has the same authorization as the holder of a CLAD Emphasis Credential (see Figure 15.2).

The BCLAD Certificate. To earn a BCLAD Certificate, an already credentialed teacher must demonstrate competence in Domains 1 through 6. As described above, demonstrating competence in Domains 1 through 3 can be accomplished through college coursework or by passing Tests 1, 2, and 3 of the CLAD/BCLAD Examinations. Passing CLAD/BCLAD Tests 4 through 6 is how already credentialed teachers can demonstrate competence in Domains 4 through 6.[2] The holder of a BCLAD Certificate has the same authorization as the holder of a BCLAD Emphasis Credential (see Figure 15.2).

The CLAD/BCLAD Examinations. The CLAD/BCLAD Examinations, which teachers already holding credentials can take to earn CLAD and BCLAD Certificates, consist of six tests, one for each of the domains of knowledge and skill on which the CLAD/BCLAD system is based. For each test, CTC has adopted a set of knowledge and skill areas to be assessed. In addition, detailed content outlines for Tests 1 through 5 and detailed information about the format and content of Test 6 are available in study guides. These materials are a valuable source of information to both prospective examinees, who can use them in preparing for the exams, and teacher trainers in school districts, county offices of education, colleges, and universities, who can use them to design training programs. The CLAD/BCLAD Exams have replaced the earlier LDS and BCC Exams. Tests 1, 4, and 5 consist entirely of multiple-choice items. Tests 2 and 3 each have multiple-choice items and an essay assignment. Tests 1 through 4 are in English and appropriate for all prospective CLAD/BCLAD teachers regardless of their language(s) of emphasis. There are multiple Test 5s, each focusing on a different culture of emphasis, and one in English. Test 6, assessing proficiency in the language of emphasis, has separate components for listening, speaking, reading, and writing. There are multiple Test 6s, each focusing on a different language.

The CLAD/BCLAD Specialist Credentials. The final element in the CLAD/BCLAD system is the CLAD and BCLAD Specialist Credentials (see the bottom box in Figure 15.1). The CLAD/BCLAD Specialist Credential requires the equivalent of one year of full-time study beyond the basic teaching credential at a Commission-approved professional preparation program at a college or university. A CLAD or BCLAD Emphasis Credential or Certificate (or an equivalent authorization) is a prerequisite. The specialist programs build on the six CLAD/BCLAD domains of knowledge and skill that are the basis of the emphasis credential programs and exams. To be approved by CTC, a CLAD/BCLAD Specialist Credential Program must meet the standards described in the Standards of Program Quality and Effectiveness for Professional Teacher Preparation Programs for the (Bilingual) Crosscultural, Language and Academic Development (CLAD/BCLAD) Specialist Credential (Commission on Teacher Credentialing, 1995). Each program focuses on the following six areas: assessment and evaluation of students; program development and evaluation; staff development; curriculum development; parents, school, and community; and research. Holders of the CLAD/BCLAD Specialist Credential are prepared to work with mainstream teachers, teachers of LEP students, other school and district staff, and parents and community members to design, implement, and evaluate effective programs for LEP students.

THE PARTICIPANTS IN DEVELOPING
THE CLAD/BCLAD SYSTEM

The development of the CLAD/BCLAD system for the preparation and credentialing of teachers for LEP students in California was initiated in 1990. The primary participants in the effort were the California Commission on Teacher Credentialing and its Bilingual Crosscultural Advisory Panel and BCLAD Language Sub-panels. In addition, many other California educators and two test development and administration companies played important roles. These groups and the process for developing the new system are described in this section.

The California Commission on Teacher Credentialing

The Commission on Teacher Credentialing, created in 1970, is an agency in the Executive Branch of the California state government. A primary purpose of the agency is to develop and implement standards for the professional preparation and credentialing of teachers and other educators in the state. CTC establishes policy for the approval of university and college teacher preparation programs. It licenses approximately 150,000 teachers and other educators each year, the majority of whom are prepared in California universities and colleges.

The Bilingual Crosscultural Advisory Panel

In 1987 CTC appointed an 18-member panel to advise the Commission on all matters related to the preparation and credentialing of teachers and other educational professionals who provide services to LEP students. Members of this Bilingual Crosscultural Advisory Panel (BCAP) were selected from nominations submitted by school districts, county offices of education, institutions of higher education, relevant professional organizations, the California Department of Education, and the California Legislature. From the nominations, members were picked so that the panel would be representative of the various constituents involved in the education of LEP students.

The BCLAD Language Sub-panels

As described earlier, the CLAD/BCLAD Examinations include culture and language tests (i.e., Tests 5 and 6) for multiple language groups. Based on recommendations from the BCAP and others, sub-panels of the BCAP were appointed by CTC staff to advise and assist them in the development of specific tests. These BCLAD Language Sub-panels were created for the following languages: Armenian, Cantonese/Mandarin, Hmong, Khmer, Korean, Pilipino, Spanish, and Vietnamese. Each sub-panel consists of educators and others who are proficient in the language and knowledgeable about the culture for which the sub-panel was created. The sub-panels for Cantonese/Mandarin, Hmong, Korean, Spanish, and Vietnamese also include one or more BCAP members who are proficient in one of those languages. The BCLAD Language Sub-panels met for the first time in August 1992. They designed and assisted in the development of various Test 6s of the CLAD/BCLAD Examinations and served as content experts in the development of the different Test 5s.

Other California Educators

Thousands of California educators participated in the development of the CLAD/BCLAD system by reviewing and responding to draft program standards for the CLAD/BCLAD Emphasis Credential Programs and CLAD/BCLAD Specialist Credential Programs, draft content outlines for the CLAD/BCLAD Examinations, proposed knowledge and skill areas for the CLAD/BCLAD Examinations, proposed state legislation and regulations pertaining to the CLAD/BCLAD Examinations and Certificates, and initial editions of study guides for the CLAD/BCLAD Examinations. In addition, numerous California educators wrote draft test questions for the CLAD/ BCLAD Examinations and provided both written and oral input about all aspects of the new system, at CTC meetings and at presentations by CTC staff at professional conferences and workshops throughout California.

Test Development and Administration Companies

Two test development and administration companies were involved in the development of the CLAD/BCLAD Examinations under contract with CTC. Cooperative Personnel Services of Sacramento, California, worked with CTC staff, the BCAP, and the BCLAD Language Sub-panels in the initial examination development work. National Evaluation Systems, Inc. (NES) of Amherst, Massachusetts, worked with the same groups to complete development of the exams. NES administers the CLAD/BCLAD Examinations for the Commission in multiple locations around California approximately every 3 months.

The Impact of the CLAD/BCLAD System

The new CLAD/BCLAD system for the preparation and credentialing of teachers for LEP students is affecting the field in many ways. For example, large numbers of prospective teachers are taking advantage of the new entry-level route (i.e., the CLAD Emphasis Credential). Many school districts have indicated to potential teachers and to teacher training institutions that they will give priority in hiring to teachers who have CLAD or BCLAD Emphasis Credentials. In response, a number of institutions have replaced their basic teaching credential program with a CLAD Emphasis Credential Program. This will have a significant impact on the shortage of teachers trained to serve LEP students. The new competencies in Domain 3 are providing CLAD and BCLAD teachers with the knowledge and skills needed to function in culturally diverse classrooms. With the new training in generic culture and basic social science skills, these teachers are prepared for future demographic changes. Bilingual teachers are gaining a deeper understanding of English language development. Monolingual teachers who serve LEP students are gaining a comprehensive understanding of the role of the primary language in the educational processes of LEP students.

The core competencies of the CLAD/BCLAD system (i.e., Domains 1 through 3) are helping to unify teacher training programs in universities and districts. A common understanding and mission for the education of LEP students is developing among faculty and teachers. There is a growing systemic commitment that all educators should be involved in the education of LEP students. The new system facilitates the development at teacher training institutions of programs for multiple languages. For the first time ever in the state, professional preparation programs for Cantonese, Hmong, Khmer, Lao, and Vietnamese bilingual teachers have been developed, approved, and implemented.

We are optimistic about the impact of the new CLAD/BCLAD system on the recruitment of underrepresented groups into teaching. In the CLAD/BCLAD Examinations, culture and language exams (Tests 5s and 6s) for nine language groups will be available statewide and all at the same time in the near future. This increases opportunities for native speakers of these languages to become certified bilingual teachers. Similarly, the range of languages for which teachers can earn bilingual teaching credentials has increased. This increased attention to multiple languages has a significant potential for diversifying the teaching force. In addition, CLAD Emphasis Credential Programs can be developed that deal with issues of dialect in English. One institution already offers a Commission-approved CLAD Emphasis Program with a concentration on African American English. The potential exists for the development of programs related to other dialects.

The attention the CLAD/BCLAD system gives to training teachers who have significant language development and cultural skills should, over time, create an educational environment in which cultural and linguistic diversity are more greatly valued and respected. This could lead to increased student self-esteem and academic success, and to greater success in recruiting a more diverse pool of teachers.

RECOMMENDATIONS FOR REPLICATION

The CLAD/BCLAD system for the preparation and credentialing of teachers for LEP students has great potential for application outside California. The CLAD competencies at the core of the system (i.e., CLAD/BCLAD Domains 1 through 3) are based on current theory and research in the field of language development and bilingual education and can be replicated anywhere. The CLAD core is applicable to any language group. The bilingual component (i.e., CLAD/BCLAD Domains 4 through 6) can be adapted to local language and cultural needs.

The system appeals to diverse factions (e.g., ESL vs. bilingual) and addresses many of the commonly encountered issues in the training of teachers for LEP students. It accommodates the philosophies of diverse groups whose main interest is the education of LEP students. It prepares teachers to provide students with both English language development and access to the subject matter curriculum. Because of its component nature, it can be adapted easily to any potential language needs that may be different from those in California. A major advantage of this system is that it makes it possible for teachers from a variety of language backgrounds to become certified as bilingual teachers.

States and other jurisdictions interested in replicating this model should first conduct an assessment of the linguistic and cultural diversity of their student population. Based on this assessment, a panel that represents the demographic profile of the student population could be created. The panel should represent the major languages that are identified in the demographic profile and should have expertise in the required domains of knowledge. State or local personnel with experience in the areas of language development, culture, and bilingual education should be assigned to coordinate the panel.

It is important that all affected constituencies be represented on the panel. Some of the same conflicts and issues that arose in California are likely to occur in other jurisdictions. All stakeholders need to be included. A continual process of dialogue needs to be maintained with all affected constituencies at all stages of development. Advisory panel members need to take a liaison role with their respective constituencies. Panel members must be prepared to take a leadership role in the field. Professional presentations as well as negotiation of the politically sensitive issues that arise with affected constituencies are expected panelist activities.

The core CLAD curriculum of the system is adaptable to any state. Once the state has determined its linguistic and cultural needs related to the BCLAD component, the content for the appropriate language and culture competencies for programs and examinations needs to be developed. The standards for programs of professional preparation and the examination specifications developed by CTC are applicable for all language and culture groups. The development of timelines for implementation that include time for affected groups to transition to the new system is critical. Also important is a process for field review in the initial stages of development as well as in the later stages of implementation. The first 2 years of implementation should be seen as formative. Feedback from the field should be used to review and revise the system as needed.[3]

CONCLUSION

The culturally and linguistically diverse student population in California made it clear that previous policies related to the preparation and credentialing of teachers for LEP students were inadequate. Working with its Bilingual Crosscultural Advisory Panel, the BCLAD Language Subpanels, and others, CTC pioneered an important set of reforms in this area. California educators have embraced the CLAD/BCLAD system enthusiastically. There is a strong belief that the new system will address the inadequacies of the previous policies and that LEP students will be better served in the future. It is hoped that the efforts undertaken in California will prove useful to other states and jurisdictions with cultural and linguistic diversity.

NOTES

1. The authors recognize the negative connotations associated with the phrase "limited-English-proficient students." We have chosen to use this phrase, however, because it is used in law and is commonly understood, and because no appropriate alternative has been widely adopted.

2. There are two situations in which a teacher can earn a BCLAD Certificate without having to pass Test 6. A teacher who holds a California Single Subject or Standard Secondary Teaching Credential with a major in a language other than English need not take Test 6. The same is true of a teacher who holds a three-year or higher degree from a college or university outside the United States in which all instruction is delivered in a language other than English. The college or university

must be equivalent in status to a regionally accredited institution of higher education in the United States.

3. The Commission is interested in exploring the possibility of other states and jurisdictions using or adapting the CLAD/BCLAD Examinations. Those interested should contact Robert Carlson at the Commission on Teacher Credentialing, 1812 Ninth Street, Sacramento, CA 95814–7000.

Afterword

The authors in this book clearly delineate the challenges faced by teacher educators in preparing classroom teachers for a culturally diverse society. Included among the most serious challenges are (1) teacher educators' and prospective teachers' beliefs and misunderstandings about the centrality of culture in human existence, in their own lives and the lives of others, and in schooling practices; (2) inadequacies in existing theory undergirding teacher preparation practices and in guidance for teacher candidates in developing personal pedagogical theory to guide individual practice; (3) providing direction and opportunities for teacher educators and teacher candidates to integrate, contextualize, and apply knowledge about culture and cultural knowledge in the "learning-to-teach" process; and (4) using existing research and models of best practice to advance the field and improve practices in teacher preparation.

Meeting the challenges involved in preparing teachers for a culturally diverse society requires collaboration and deliberation among a faculty well grounded in research and theory related to teaching culturally diverse populations; taking a holistic view of the teacher preparation process that is broader than individual courses and that addresses the selection and socialization of teacher candidates; developing and implementing a theoretically based conceptual framework; and deliberately applying knowledge about culture and cultural knowledge in designing a contextualized, inquiry-based program that facilitates teacher candidates' development of personal pedagogical theories that foster productive practices in culturally diverse classrooms.

The future of public schools and the society at large will be significantly influenced by our ability to change the teacher preparation process. Although the challenge is awesome, we have at our disposal more than adequate human and intellectual resources for the task. Our ability to collaborate and to engage in teamwork, focused inquiry, and reflective practice will be among our greatest assets.

References

AACTE. (1990). *Teacher education pipeline II: Schools, colleges, and departments of education enrollments by race and ethnicity.* Washington, DC: Author.

AACTE Commission on Multicultural Education. (1973). No one model American. *Journal of Teacher Education, 24*(4), 264–265.

AACTE Commission on Multicultural Education and Committee on Accreditation. (1992). *NCATE: In consideration of diversity.* Washington, DC: Author.

Adair, A. V. (1984). *Desegregation: The illusion of black progress.* New York: University Press of America.

Adams, D. W. (1988). Fundamental considerations: The deep meaning of Native American schooling, 1880–1900. *Harvard Educational Review, 58*(1), 1–28.

Adler, M. J. (1982). *The Paideia proposal: An educational manifesto.* New York: Collier.

Adler, N. (1981). Re-entry: Managing cross-cultural transitions. *Group and Organization Studies, 6,* 341–356.

Ahlquist, R. (1991, April). *Confronting dilemmas in the search for a critical approach to multicultural education.* Paper presented at the annual meeting of the American Educational Research Association, Chicago.

Ahlquist, R. (1992). Manifestations of inequality: Overcoming resistance in a multicultural foundations course. In C. A. Grant (Ed.), *Research and multicultural education: From the margins to the mainstream* (pp. 89–105). London: Falmer.

Alatorre Alva, S., & Padilla, A. M. (1988). *Factors influencing the academic performance of Mexican American students.* Unpublished manuscript, Stanford University, Stanford.

Albert, R. D., & Adamopoulos, J. (1980). An attributional approach to culture learning: The culture assimilator. In M. P. Hamnet & R. W. Brislin (Eds.), *Research in culture learning: Language and conceptual studies* (pp. 53–60). Honolulu: East–West Culture Learning Institute.

Allameh, J. (1986). *Learning among culturally different populations.* Paper presented at the Kentucky Foreign Language Conference, Lexington. (ERIC Document No. ED 273 137)

Allington, R. L. (1991). Effective literacy instruction for at-risk children. In M. S. Knapp & P. M. Shields (Eds.), *Better schooling for the children of poverty* (pp. 9–30). Berkeley, CA: McCutchan.

American Council on Education and the Education Commission of the States. (1988). *One-third of a nation: A report of the Commission on Minority Participation in Education and American Life.* Washington, DC: Author.

Anderson, J. G. (1969). *Teachers of minority groups: The origins of their attitudes and instructional practices.* Las Cruces, NM: Southwest Educational Development Corporation.

Anyon, J. (1979). Ideology and US history textbooks. *Harvard Educational Review, 49*(3), 361–386.

Anyon, J. (1980). Social class and the hidden curriculum of work. *Journal of Social Education, 162,* 1.

Anyon, J. (1981). Social class and school knowledge. *Curriculum Inquiry, 11*(1), 3–42.

Apple, M. W. (1979). *Ideology and curriculum.* London: Routledge & Kegan Paul.

Apple, M. W. (1988). *Teachers and texts: A political economy of class and gender relations in education.* New York: Routledge.

Aptheker, B. (1989). *Tapestries of life: Women's work, women's consciousness and the meaning of daily life.* Amherst: University of Massachusetts Press.

Armstrong, T. (1994). *Multicultural intelligences in the classroom.* Alexandria, VA: Association for Supervision and Curriculum Development.

Au, K. H., & Mason, J. M. (1981). Social organizational factors in learning to read: The balance of rights hypothesis. *Reading Research Quarterly, 17*(1), 115–152.

Baca, J. D. (1972). A comparative study of differences in perceptions of Mexican Americans between Anglo and Mexican American. (ERIC Document No. ED 065 218)

Baca de McNichols, P. (1977). *An assessment of perception of urban parents and school personnel toward bilingual bicultural education.* Unpublished doctoral dissertation, University of Houston, Houston.

Baines, A. (1987). Home thoughts of a broad. *Women in Management Review, 3,* 78–84.

Baker, G. C. (1974). Instructional priorities in a culturally pluralistic school. *Educational Leadership, 32*(3), 176–182.

Baldwin, J. (1985). *The price of the ticket: Collected nonfiction, 1948–1985.* New York: St. Martin's Press.

Baldwin, J. (1988). A talk to teachers. In R. Simonson & S. Walker (Eds.), *The Graywolf Annual Five: Multicultural literacy.* St. Paul, MN: Graywolf.

Baltes, P. B. (1973). Prototypical paradigms and questions in life-span research on development and aging. *Gerontologist, 13,* 458–467.

Baltes, P. B., Reese, H. W., & Lipsitt, L. P. (1980). Life-span developmental psychology. *Annual Review of Psychology, 31,* 65–110.

Baltes, P. B., & Willis, S. L. (1977). Toward psychological theories of aging and development. In J. E. Birren & K. W. Schaie (Eds.), *Handbook of the psychology of aging* (pp. 128–154). Belmont, CA: Wadsworth.

Bandura, A. (1977). *Social learning theory.* Englewood Cliffs, NJ: Prentice-Hall.

Banks, J. A. (1981). *Education in the 80's: Multiethnic education.* Washington, DC: National Education Association.

Banks, J. A. (1988a). Approaches to multicultural reform. *Multicultural Leader, 1*(2), 1–4.

Banks, J. A. (1988b). *Multiethnic education: Theory and practice* (2nd ed). Newton, MA: Allyn & Bacon.

Banks, J. A. (1989). *Multicultural education: Issues and perspectives.* Boston: Allyn & Bacon.

Banks, J. A. (1991a). A curriculum for empowerment, action and change. In C. E. Sleeter (Ed.), *Empowerment through multicultural education* (pp. 125–142). Albany: State University of New York Press.

Banks, J. A. (1991b). Social studies, ethnic diversity and social change. In C. V. Willie, A. M. Garibaldi, & W. L. Reed (Eds.), *The education of African-Americans* (pp. 129–147). New York: Auburn House.

Banks, J. A. (1991c). Teaching multicultural literacy to teachers. *Teaching Education*, 4(1), 135–144.

Banks, J. A. (1991/92). Multicultural education: For freedom's sake. *Educational Leadership*, 49(4), 32–36.

Banks, J. A. (1993). Multicultural education: Historical development, dimensions, and practice. In L. Darling-Hammond (Ed.), *Review of research in education* (Vol. 19, pp. 3–50). Washington, DC: American Educational Research Association.

Banks, J. A., & Banks, C. M. (Eds.). (1989). *Multicultural education: Theory and practice*. Boston: Allyn & Bacon.

Banks, J. A., & Banks, C. M. (Eds.). (1995). *Handbook of research on multicultural education*. New York: Macmillan.

Banks, J. A., Carlos, E. C., Garcia, R. L., Gay, G., & Ochoa, A. S. (1976). *Curriculum guidelines for multiethnic education*. Arlington, VA: National Council for the Social Studies.

Baptiste, H. P. (1979). *Multicultural education: A synopsis*. Lanham, MD: University Press of America.

Baptiste, H. P., & Baptiste, M. L. (1980). Competencies toward multiculturalism. In H. P. Baptiste, M. L. Baptiste, & D. M. Gollnick (Eds.), *Multicultural teacher education: Preparing educators to provide educational equity* (pp. 44–72). Washington, DC: AACTE Commission on Multicultural Education.

Baptiste, H. P., Baptiste, M. L., & Gollnick, D. M. (Eds.). (1980). *Multicultural teacher education: Preparing educators to provide educational equity*. Washington, DC: AACTE Commission on Multicultural Education.

Baratz, S. S., & Baratz, J. C. (1970). Early childhood intervention: The social science base of institutional racism. *Harvard Educational Review*, 40, 29–50.

Barker, N. C. (1986). *Cultural diversity: An expectation for teaching*. Paper presented at the Teaching for Potential Regional Conference on University Teaching, Las Cruces, NM. (ERIC Document No. ED 279 256)

Bateson, M. C. (1989). *Composing a life*. New York: Plume Books.

Befus, C. P. (1988). A multilevel treatment approach for culture shock experienced by sojourners. *International Journal of Intercultural Relations*, 12, 381–400.

Belenky, M. F., Clinchy, B. M., Goldberger, N. R., & Tarule, J. M. (1986). *Women's ways of knowing: The development of self, voice, and mind*. New York: Basic Books.

Bell, D. (1992). *Faces at the bottom of the well: The permanence of racism*. New York: Basic Books.

Bell, H. (1986). White teacher, black learner: The influence of the cross-cultural context on teaching practice. *Australian Journal of Adult Education*, 26, 29–32.

Bennett, C. I. (1990). *Comprehensive multicultural education: Theory and practice*. Boston: Allyn & Bacon.

Bennett, J. M. (1986). Modes of cross-cultural training: Conceptualizing cross-cultural training as education. *International Journal of Intercultural Relations, 10,* 117–134.

Berk, L. E. (1993). *Infants, children, and adolescents.* Boston: Allyn & Bacon.

Berman, J. (1982). *Preparing to teach in low-income area schools: A case study user's manual.* Cambridge, MA: American Institutes for Research in the Behavioral Sciences. (ERIC Document No. ED 212 578)

Berman, P., Chambers, I., Gándara, P., McLaughlin, B., Minicucci, C., Nelson, B., Olsen, L., & Parrish, T. (1992). *Meeting the challenge of language diversity: An evaluation of programs for pupils with limited proficiency in English* (Executive Summary CR-119/1). Berkeley, CA: B. W. Associates.

Bernard, B. (1994). *Applications of resilience: Possibilities and promise.* Paper prepared for the Conference on the Role of Resilience in Drug Abuse, Alcohol Abuse, and Mental Illness, Washington, DC.

Beyer, L. (1991). Teacher education, reflective inquiry and moral action. In B. R. Tabachnick & K. Zeichner (Eds.), *Issues and practices in inquiry-oriented teacher education* (pp. 113–129). Bristol, PA: Falmer.

Bickel, F. (1985). Classroom communication: An international problem. *The Clearing House, 58,* 222–224.

Billingsley, A. (1968). *Black families in white America.* Englewood Cliffs, NJ: Prentice-Hall.

Billingsley, A. (1992). *Climbing Jacob's ladder.* New York: Simon & Schuster.

Bishop, C. (1938). *The five Chinese brothers.* New York: Coward, McCann & Geoghegan.

Blau, P. M. (1964). *Exchange and power in social life.* New York: Wiley.

Bloom, A. (1987). *The closing of the American mind: How higher education has failed democracy and impoverished the souls of today's students.* New York: Simon & Schuster.

Bogardus, E. S. (1925). Measuring social distances. *Journal of Applied Sociology, 9,* 299–308.

Bogardus, E. S. (1933). A social distance scale. *Sociology and Social Research, 17,* 265–271.

Bok, D. (1986). *Higher learning.* Cambridge, MA: Harvard University Press.

Borko, H. (1989). Research on learning to teach: Implications for graduate teacher preparation. In A. Woolfolk (Ed.), *Research perspectives on the graduate preparation of teachers* (pp. 69–87). Englewood Cliffs, NJ: Prentice-Hall.

Bourdieu, P., & Passeron, J. C. (1977). *Reproduction in education, society and culture.* Beverly Hills, CA: Sage.

Bowen, D. N., & Bowen, E. A. (1992). Multicultural education: The learning style aspect. In C. A. Grant (Ed.), *Toward education that is multicultural: Proceedings of the first annual meeting of the National Association for Multicultural Education* (pp. 266–276). Morristown, NJ: Silver Burdett.

Bowles, S., & Gintis, H. (1976). *Schooling in capitalist America: Educational reform and the contradictions of economic life.* New York: Basic Books.

Boyd, W. L. (1991). What makes ghetto schools succeed or fail? *Teachers College Record, 92*(3), 331–362.

Boyer, J. (1983). *Multicultural education: From product to process.* Washington, DC: National Institute of Education. (ERIC Document No. ED 240 224)

Brameld, T. (1955). *Philosophies of education in cultural perspective.* New York: Dryden.

Bredo, E. (1988). Choice, constraint, and community. In W. L. Boyd & C. T. Kerchner (Eds.), *The politics of excellence and choice in education* (pp. 67–78). New York: Falmer.

Brendtro, L. K., Brokenleg, M., & Van Bockern, S. (1990). *Reclaiming youth at risk: Our hope for the future.* Bloomington, IN: National Education Service.

Brophy, J., & Good, T. L. (1986). Teacher behavior and student achievement. In M. C. Wittrock (Ed.), *Handbook of research on teaching* (3rd ed., pp. 328–375). New York: Macmillan.

Brown, C. E. (1992). Restructuring for a new America. In M. E. Dilworth (Ed.), *Diversity in teacher education: New expectations* (pp. 1–22). San Francisco: Jossey-Bass.

Brown, E. B. (1988). African-American women's quilting: A framework for conceptualizing and teaching African-American women's history. In M. R. Malson, E. Mudimbe-Boyi, J. F. O'Barr, & M. Wyer (Eds.), *Black women in America: Social science perspectives* (pp. 9–18). Chicago: University of Chicago Press.

Bruner, J. S. (1989). *The state of developmental psychology.* Paper presented at the annual conference of the Society for Research in Child Development, Kansas City, MO.

Bullough, R. V., Knowles, J., Jr., & Crow, N. (1992). *Emerging as a teacher.* Baltimore, MD: Routledge.

Burden, P. R. (1990). Teacher development. In W. R. Houston (Ed.), *Handbook of research on teacher education* (pp. 311–328). New York: Macmillan.

Buriel, R. (1983). Teacher–student interactions and their relationship to student achievement: A comparison of Mexican American and Anglo-American children. *Journal of Educational Psychology, 75,* 889–897.

Byram, M. (1988). Foreign language education and cultural studies. *Language, Culture and Curriculum, 1,* 15–31.

Cagan, E. (1978). Individualism, collectivism, and radical educational reform. *Harvard Educational Review, 48*(2), 227–266.

California Association for Bilingual Education. (1991). *Wanted: Over 20,000 bilingual and ELD teachers: A challenge for California's colleges and universities.* Sacramento: Author.

Campos, F. (1983). *Attitudes and expectations of student teachers and cooperating teachers toward students in predominantly Mexican American schools.* Texas University at Austin, Center for Teacher Education.

Cannella, G. S., & Reiff, J. C. (1994). Individual constructivist teacher education: Teachers as empowered learners. *Teacher Education Quarterly, 21*(3), 27–38.

Carr, W., & Kemmis, S. (1986). *Becoming critical: Education, knowledge, and action research.* London: Falmer.

Carrier, J. G. (1983). Masking the social in educational knowledge: The case of learning disabilities. *American Journal of Sociology, 38,* 948–974.

Carter, K. (1990). Teachers' knowledge and learning to teach. In W. R. Houston

(Ed.), *Handbook of research on teacher education* (pp. 291–310). New York: Macmillan.

Carter, R. T., & Goodwin, A. L. (1994). Racial identity and education. In L. Darling-Hammond (Ed.), *Review of research in education* (Vol. 20, pp. 291–336). Washington, DC: American Educational Research Association.

Casey, K. (1993). *I answer with my life: Life histories of women teachers working for social change.* New York: Routledge.

Cazden, C. (1988). *Classroom discourse.* Portsmouth, NH: Heinemann.

Center for Economic Conversion. (1992). *Sustainable economics: A supplementary curriculum for high school economics courses.* Mountain View, CA: Author.

Center for Education Statistics. (1987). *The condition of education.* Washington, DC: U.S. Government Printing Office.

Cere, R. (1988). A new dimension for international and professional studies: Foreign language intercultural courses (FLICS). *The Canadian Modern Language Review, 44*(2), 316–333.

Chan, K. S., & Rueda, R. (1979). Poverty and culture in education: Separate but equal. *Journal of the Council for Exceptional Children, 45,* 422–428.

Charles, C. M. (1992). *Building classroom discipline: From models to practice.* New York: Longman.

Chin, F. (1991). *Donald Duk.* Minneapolis: Coffee House Press.

Chu, H., & Levy, J. (1988). Multicultural skills for bilingual teachers: Training for competency development. *Journal of the National Association for Bilingual Education, 12,* 153–169.

Church, A. (1982). Sojourner adjustment. *Psychological Bulletin, 91,* 640–672.

Clair, N. (1992). *Beliefs, self-reported practices and professional development needs of three classroom teachers with language minority students.* Unpublished doctoral dissertation, Teachers College, Columbia University, New York.

Clark, C., & Lampert, M. (1986). The study of teacher thinking: Applications for teacher education. *Journal of Teacher Education, 37,* 9–11.

Clark, C. M., & Peterson, P. L. (1986). Teachers' thought processes. In M. C. Wittrock (Ed.), *Handbook of research on teaching* (3rd ed., pp. 255–296). New York: Macmillan.

Cochran-Smith, M. (1989, April). Of questions, not answers: The discourse of student teachers and their school and university mentors. Paper presented at the annual meeting of the American Educational Research Association, San Francisco.

Cocking, R. R., & Mestre, J. P. (Eds.). (1988). *Linguistic and cultural influences on learning mathematics.* Hillsdale, NJ: Erlbaum.

College of Education. (1992). College of Education undergraduate teacher education program: Competency document. Unpublished manuscript, Wichita State University, Wichita, KS.

Collier, M. J., & Thomas, M. (1988). Cultural identity: An interpretive perspective. In Y. Y. Kim & W. B. Gudykunst (Eds.), *Theories in intercultural communication* (pp. 99–120). Newbury Park, CA: Sage.

Comer, J. (1980). *School power.* New York: Macmillan.

Commission on Minority Participation in Education and American Life. (1988). *One third of a nation.* Washington, DC: American Council on Education and the Education Commission of the States.

Commission on Teacher Credentialing. (1992). *Standards of program quality and effectiveness for professional teacher preparation programs for multiple and single subject teaching credentials with a (bilingual) crosscultural, language and academic development (CLAD/BCLAD) emphasis.* Sacramento, CA: Author.

Commission on Teacher Credentialing. (1995). *Standards of program quality and effectiveness for professional preparation programs for the (bilingual) crosscultural, language and academic development (CLAD/BCLAD) specialist credential.* Sacramento, CA: Author.

Cook, D. A., & Helms, J. E. (1988). Visible racial/ethnic group supervisees' satisfaction with cross-cultural supervision as predicted by relationship characteristics. *Journal of Counseling Psychology, 33,* 268–274.

Cooper, A., Beare, P., & Thorman, J. (1990). Preparing teachers for diversity: A comparison of student teaching experiences in Minnesota & South Texas. *Action in Teacher Education, 12*(3), 1–4.

Cornelius, W. (1991). *From sojourners to settlers: The changing profile of Mexican migration to the United States.* San Diego: University of California, Center for U.S.-Mexican Studies.

Cortes, C. E. (1986). The education of language minority students: A contextual interaction model. In Bilingual Education Office (Eds.), *Beyond language: Social and cultural factors in schooling language minority students* (pp. 3–33). Los Angeles: California State University.

Cox, G. O. (1974). *Education for the Black race.* New York: African Heritage Studies.

Cremin, L. (1976). *Public education.* New York: Basic Books.

Cummings, R. L., & Bridges, E. F. (1986). *Multiculturalism and teacher education: The rhetoric and a reality.* (ERIC Document No. ED 269 513)

Cummins, J. (1978). Educational implication of mother tongue maintenance in minority language groups. *Canadian Modern Language Review, 34,* 395–416.

Cummins, J. (1986). Empowering minority students: A framework for intervention. *Harvard Educational Review, 56*(1), 18–36.

Cummins, J. (1989). *Empowering minority students.* Sacramento: California Association for Bilingual Education.

Cushner, K., & Brislin, R. (1986). Bridging gaps: Cross-cultural training in teacher education. *Journal of Teacher Education, 37,* 51–54.

Dantley, M. E. (1990). The ineffectiveness of effective schools leadership: An analysis of the effective schools movement from a critical perspective. *Journal of Negro Education, 59*(4), 585–598.

Darling-Hammond, L., & Goodwin, A. L. (1993). Progress toward professionalism in teaching. In G. Cawelti (Ed.), *Challenges and achievements of American education: 1993 ASCD Yearbook* (pp. 19–52). Alexandria, VA: Association for Supervision and Curriculum Development.

David, K. (1972). Intercultural adjustment and applications of reinforcement theory to problems of "culture shock." *Trends, 4,* 1–64.

Davidson, G., Hansford, B., & Moriarty, B. (1983). Interpersonal apprehension and cultural majority–minority communication. *Australian Psychologist, 18,* 97–105.

Dege, D. B. (1981). *Format and evaluation of the cross-cultural component of a foreign teaching assistant training program.* Paper presented at the annual meeting of the International Communication Association, Minneapolis, MN. (ERIC Document No. ED 207 100)

Delgado-Gaitan, C. (1985). Preparing teachers for inter-ethnic communication. *Equity and Choice, 20,* 53–59, 61–65.

Delgado-Gaitan, C. (1987). Traditions and transition in the learning process of Mexican children: An ethnographic view. In G. Spindler & L. Spindler (Eds.), *Interpretive ethnography of education: At home and abroad* (pp. 333–359). Hillsdale, NJ: Erlbaum.

Delpit, L. D. (1986). Skills and other dilemmas of a progressive African American educator. *Harvard Educational Review, 56*(4), 379–385.

Delpit, L. D. (1988). The silenced dialogue: Power and pedagogy in educating other people's children. *Harvard Educational Review, 58*(3), 280–298.

Delpit, L. D. (1995). *Other people's children: Cultural conflict in the classroom.* New York: The New Press.

Deshler, D. D., & Lenz, B. K. (1989). The strategies instructional approach. *International Journal of Disability Development and Education, 36*(3), 203–224.

Dewey, J. (1916). *Democracy and education.* New York: Macmillan.

Dewey, J. (1959). The school and society. In M. Dworkin (Ed.), *Dewey on education* (pp. 33–90). New York: Teachers College Press.

Díaz, S., Moll, L., & Mehan, H. (1986). Sociocultural resources in instruction: A context-specific approach. In *Beyond language: Social and cultural factors in schooling language minority students* (pp. 187–230). Los Angeles: California State University, Evaluation, Dissemination and Assessment Center.

Diez, M. (1988/90). A thrust from within: Reconceptualizing teacher education at Alverno College. *Peabody Journal of Education, 65*(2), 4–18.

Dill, D. (1987). *What teachers need to know: The knowledge, skills, and values essential to good teaching.* San Francisco: Jossey-Bass.

Dillard, C. B. (1994). "We" are part of the curriculum: The role of autobiography in multicultural teacher education. Paper presented at the annual meeting of the National Association for Multicultural Education, Detroit.

Dillard, C. B., & Ford, T. F. (1992). Remembrances as critical lenses: Lived experiences of multiculturalism. Unpublished manuscript.

Dilworth, M. E. (1990). *Reading between the lines: Teachers and their racial/ethnic cultures* (Teacher Education Monograph No. 11). Washington, DC: ERIC Clearinghouse on Teacher Education and AACTE.

Dilworth, M. E. (Ed.). (1992). *Diversity in teacher education: New expectations.* San Francisco: Jossey-Bass.

Dodge, D. T. (1985). *A classroom teacher's handbook for building English proficiency.* Washington, DC: Office of Bilingual Education and Minority Languages Affairs. (ERIC Document No. ED 275 134)

Donmall, B. G. (1985). Some implications of language awareness work for teacher training (pre-service and in-service). Paper presented at the National Congress on Languages in Education Assembly, York, England. (ERIC Document No. ED 277 243)

Dubin, F. (1985). The use of simulation in courses for language teachers. *System*, *13*, 231–236.

Ducharme, E., & Agne, R. (1989). Professors of education: Uneasy residents of academe. In R. Wisniewski & E. Ducharme (Eds.), *The professors of teaching* (pp. 67–86). Albany: State University of New York Press.

Duran, R. P. (1983). *Hispanics' education and background: Predictors of college success*. New York: The College Board.

Dusek, J. B., & Gail, J. (1983). The bases of teacher expectancies: A meta analysis. *Journal of Educational Psychology*, *75*(3), 327–346.

Eisner, E. W. (1985). *The educational imagination: On the design and evaluation of school programs* (2nd ed.). New York: Macmillan.

Elliot, S. N., & Argulewicz, E. N. (1983). The influence of student ethnicity on teachers' behavior ratings of normal and learning disabled children. *Hispanic Journal of Behavioral Sciences*, *5*, 337–345.

Ellwood, C. (1990). The moral imperative of ethnic studies in urban teacher education programs. In M. Diez (Ed.), *Proceedings of the fourth national forum of the Association of Independent Liberal Arts Colleges for Teacher Education* (pp. 1–6). Milwaukee, WI: Alverno College.

Ellwood, C. (1991, April). Can we really look through our students' eyes? An urban teacher's perspective. Paper presented at the annual meeting of the American Educational Research Association, Chicago.

English, S. L. (1980). Critical incidents workshop for ESL teacher intercultural awareness training. In J. C. Fisher (Ed.), *On TESOL '80—Building bridges: Research and practice in teaching English as a second language* (pp. 159–170). Washington, DC: Georgetown University. (ERIC Document No. ED 208 643)

Erickson, F., & Schultz, J. (1991). Student's experience of the curriculum. In P. W. Jackson (Ed.), *Handbook of research on curriculum* (pp. 465–485). New York: Macmillan.

Estrada, L. J., & Vasquez, M. (1981). Schooling and its social and psychological effects on minorities. In W. E. Sims & B. Bass de Martinez (Eds.), *Perspectives in multicultural education* (pp. 53–74). New York: University Press of America.

Everhart, R. (1983). *Reading, writing and resistance: Adolescence and labor in a junior high school*. Boston: Routledge & Kegan Paul.

Feiman-Nemser, S., & Buchmann, M. (1985). Pitfalls of experience in teacher education. *Teachers College Record*, *87*(1), 53–66.

Feldman, R. S. (1985). Nonverbal behavior, race, and the classroom teacher. *Theory into Practice*, *24*, 45–49.

Fine, M. (1991). *Framing dropouts: Notes on the politics of an urban high school*. Albany: State University of New York Press.

Finkelstein, B. (1984). Education and the retreat from democracy in the U.S., 1979–198?. *Teachers College Record*, *86*(2), 275–282.

Flemming, D. N., & Ankarberg, M. R. (1980). *New Hampshire vocational English as a second language project* (Final Report). Keene, NH: Keene State College. (ERIC Document No. ED 189 333)

Foerster, L. M., & Little Soldier, D. (1981). Applying anthropology to education problems. *Journal of American Indian Education, 20*(3), 1–6.

Foster, M. (1994). Effective Black teachers: A literature review. In E. R. Hollins, J. E. King, & W. C. Hayman (Eds.), *Teaching diverse populations: Formulating a knowledge base* (pp. 225–241). Albany: State University of New York Press.

Foster, M. (1989). It's cooking now: A performance analysis of the speech events of a black teacher in an urban community college. *Language and Society, 18*, 1–29.

Fradd, S. H., Weismantel, M. J., Correa, V. I., & Algozzine, B. (1990). Insuring equity in education: Preparing school personnel for culturally and linguistically divergent at risk students. In A. Barona & E. E. Garcia (Eds.), *Children at risk: Poverty, minority status, and other issues in educational equity* (pp. 237–256). Washington, DC: National Association of School Psychologists.

Freire, P. (1970). *Los campesinos tambien pueden ser autores de sus propios textos de lectura*. Mexico, D.F.: Siglo XXI. (Original Portuguese manuscript published 1968)

Freire, P. (1985). *The politics of education: Culture, power, and liberation* (D. Macedo, Trans.). South Hadley, MA: Bergin & Garvey.

Freire, P. (1986). *Pedagogy of the oppressed.* New York: Continuum. (Original work published 1970)

Fried, J. (1993). Bridging emotion and intellect: Classroom diversity in process. *College Teaching, 41*(4), 123–128.

Fullan, M. (1993). *Change forces probing the depths of educational reform.* New York: Falmer.

Fuller, M. L. (1992). Teacher education programs and increasing minority school populations: An educational mismatch? In C. A. Grant (Ed.), *Research and multicultural education: From the margins to the mainstream* (pp. 184–202). London: Falmer.

Gallagher, P. (1993, April). *Teachers' cultural assumptions: A hidden dimension of school teaching.* Paper presented at the annual meeting of the American Educational Research Association, Atlanta.

Garcia, S. S. (1994). Origins and destinies: A May Day political corrido as symbolic personal legacy. *Journal of Folklore Research, 31*(1 & 2), 127–150.

Garcia, S. S. (1995). The transmutation of a cultural constant: The Mexican political corrido as personal legacy. In J. Porter (Ed.), *Ballads and boundaries: Narrative singing in an intercultural context* (pp. 47–60). Proceedings of the 23rd International Ballad Conference of the Commission for Folk Poetry, June 21–24, 1993. Los Angeles: University of California, Department of Ethnomusicology and Systematic Musicology.

Gardner, H. (1983). *Frames of mind.* New York: Basic Books.

Gardner, H. (1991). *The unschooled mind: How students think and how schools should teach.* New York: Basic Books.

Gaston, J. (1984). *Cultural awareness teaching techniques.* Brattleboro, VT: Pro Lingua Associates.

Gay, G. (1977). Curriculum for multicultural teacher education. In F. H. Klassen & D. M. Gollnick (Eds.), *Pluralism and the American teacher* (pp. 31–62). Washington, DC: AACTE, Ethnic Heritage Center for Teacher Education.

Gay, G. (1983). Multiethnic education: Historical developments and future prospects. *Phi Delta Kappan, 64*(8), 560–563.

Gay, G. (1986). Multicultural teacher education. In J. Banks & J. Lynch (Eds.), *Multicultural education in Western societies* (pp. 154–177). New York: Praeger.

Gay, G. (1994). *At the essence of all learning: Multicultural education.* West Lafayette, IN: Kappa Delta Pi.

Gayles, A. R. (1988). *Major guidelines to be followed in developing a successful bilingual/multicultural teacher education program* (Ethnolinguistic Issues in Education). (ERIC Document No. ED 316 035)

Gibbs, J. T., & Huang, L. N. (1989). A conceptual framework for treating and assessing minority youth. In J. T. Gibbs & L. N. Huang (Eds.), *Children of color* (pp. 1–29). San Francisco: Jossey-Bass.

Gibson, M. (1988). *Accommodation without assimilation: Sikh immigrants in an American high school.* Ithaca, NY: Cornell University Press.

Gibson, M., & Ogbu, J. (1991). *Minority status and schooling: A comparative study of immigrant and involuntary minorities.* New York: Garland.

Giroux, H. A. (1988a). *Schooling and the struggle for public life.* Minneapolis: University of Minnesota Press.

Giroux, H. A. (1988b). *Teachers as intellectuals.* South Hadley, MA: Bergin & Garvey.

Giroux, H. A., & McLaren, P. (1986). Teacher education and the politics of engagement: The case for democratic schooling. *Harvard Educational Review, 56*(3), 213–238.

Goffman, E. (1974). *Frame analysis.* Cambridge, MA: Harvard University Press.

Goldsmith, H. H. (1988, April). Does early temperament predict late development? Paper presented at the annual meeting of the American Psychological Association, Atlanta.

Gollnick, D. M. (1977). Multicultural education: The challenge for teacher education. *ERIC Clearinghouse on Teacher Education, 28*(3), 57–59.

Gollnick, D. M. (1992a). Multicultural education: Policies and practices in teacher education. In C. A. Grant (Ed.), *Research and multicultural education: From the margins to the mainstream* (pp. 218–239). London: Falmer.

Gollnick, D. M. (1992b). Understanding the dynamics of race, class and gender. In M. Dilworth (Ed.), *Diversity in teacher education* (pp. 63–78). Washington, DC: American Association of Colleges of Teacher Education.

Gollnick, D. M. (1995). National and state initiatives for multicultural education. In J. A. Banks & C. M. Banks (Eds.), *Handbook of research on multicultural education* (pp. 44–64). New York: Macmillan.

Gollnick, D. M., Osayande, K. I. M., & Levy, J. (1980). *Multicultural teacher education: Case studies of thirteen programs* (Vol. 2). Washington, DC: AACTE.

Gomez, M. L. (1993). Prospective teachers' perspectives on teaching diverse children: A review with implications for teacher education and practice. *Journal of Negro Education, 64*(4), 459–474.

Gomez, M. L. (1996). Teacher education reform and prospective teachers' perspectives on teaching other people's children. In K. Zeichner, S. Melnick, & M. L. Gomez (Eds.), *Currents of reform in preservice teacher education* (pp. 109–133). New York: Teachers College Press.

Gomez, M. L., & Tabachnick, B. R. (1991, April). Preparing preservice teachers to teach diverse learners. Paper presented at the annual meeting of the American Educational Research Association, Chicago.

Gonzalez, R. D. (1990). When minority becomes majority: The changing face of English classrooms. *English Journal, 79*(1), 16–23.

Good, T., & Brophy, J. (1984). *Looking in classrooms* (3rd ed.). New York: Harper & Row.

Goodlad, J. I. (1990a). Common schools for the commonweal. In J. Goodlad & P. Keating (Eds.), *Access to knowledge: An agenda for our nation's schools.* New York: The College Board.

Goodlad, J. I. (1990b). *Teachers for our nation's schools.* San Francisco: Jossey-Bass.

Goodlad, J. I. (1991). Why we need a complete redesign of teacher education. *Educational Leadership, 49,* 4–10.

Goodlad, J. I., Soder, R., & Sirotnik, K. A. (1990a). *The moral dimensions of teaching.* San Francisco: Jossey-Bass.

Goodlad, J. I., Soder, R., & Sirotnik, K. A. (Eds.). (1990b). *Places where teachers are taught.* San Francisco: Jossey-Bass.

Goodman, K. S., Smith, E. B., Meredith, R., & Goodman, Y. (1988). *Language and thinking in schools.* New York: Richard C. Owen.

Goodwin, A. L. (January, 1990). *Fostering diversity in the teaching profession through multicultural field experiences.* Tampa, FL: AACTE, National Symposium on Diversity.

Goodwin, A. L. (1991). Problems, process, and promise: Reflections on a collaborative approach to the minority teacher shortage. *Journal of Teacher Education, 42*(1), 28–36.

Goodwin, A. L. (1993). *Multicultural teacher education: Listening to preservice teachers' stories.* Paper presented at the annual meeting of the American Association of Colleges of Teacher Education, San Diego.

Goodwin, A. L. (1994). Making the transition from self to other: What do preservice teachers really think about multicultural education? *Journal of Teacher Education, 45*(2), 119–130.

Gordon, E. W., Miller, F., & Rollock, D. (1990). Coping with communicentric bias in knowledge production in the social sciences. *Educational Researcher, 19*(3), 14–19.

Gould, S. J. (1981). *The mismeasure of man.* New York: Norton.

Grant, C. A. (1977). Education that is multicultural and P/CBTE: Discussion and recommendations for teacher education. In F. H. Klassen & D. M. Gollnick (Eds.), *Pluralism and the American teacher* (pp. 63–80). Washington, DC: AACTE, Ethnic Heritage Center for Teacher Education.

Grant, C. A. (1981). Education that is multicultural and teacher preparation: An examination from the perspective of preservice students. *Journal of Educational Research, 75*(2), 95–101.

Grant, C. A. (1993). The multicultural preparation of U.S. teachers: Some hard truths. In G. Verma (Ed.), *Inequality and teacher education* (pp. 41–57). London: Falmer.

Grant, C. A., & Koskela, R. A. (1986). Education that is multicultural and the relationship between preservice campus learning and field experiences. *Journal of Educational Research, 79,* 197–203.

Grant, C. A., & Secada, W. G. (1990). Preparing teachers for diversity. In W. R. Houston (Ed.), *Handbook of research on teacher education* (pp. 403–422). New York: Macmillan.

Grant, C. A., & Sleeter, C. E. (1989). *Turning on learning: Five approaches for multicultural teaching plans for race, class, gender, and disability.* Columbus, OH: Merrill.

Green, C. (1993, April 28). English use dwindling in American households. *The Sacramento Bee,* pp. A1, A20.

Greene, M. (1984). "Excellence," meanings, and multiplicity. *Teachers College Record, 86*(1), 283–297.

Greene, M. (1986). In search of a critical pedagogy. *Harvard Educational Review, 56*(4), 427–441.

Greene, M. (1988). *The dialectic of freedom.* New York: Teachers College Press.

Greene, M. (1993). The passions of pluralism: Multiculturalism and the expanding community. *Educational Researcher, 22,* 13–18.

Greenfield, P. M., & Cocking, R. R. (1994). *Cross-cultural roots of minority child development.* Hillsdale, NJ: Erlbaum.

Grove, C. L., & Torbiorn, I. (1985). A new conceptualization of intercultural adjustment and the goals of training. *International Journal of Intercultural Relations, 9,* 205–233.

Grubis, S. (1985). Teaching in the Alaskan village: The challenge. *The Rural Educator, 7,* 17–20.

Gullahorn, J. T., & Gullahorn, J. E. (1963). An extension of the U-curve hypothesis. *Journal of Social Sciences, 14,* 33–47.

Haberman, M. (1987). *Recruiting and selecting teachers for urban schools.* New York: ERIC Clearinghouse on Urban Education, Institute for Urban and Minority Education.

Haberman, M. (1991a). Can cultural awareness be taught in teacher education programs? *Teaching Education, 4*(1), 25–31.

Haberman, M. (1991b). The rationale for training adults as teachers. In C. E. Sleeter (Ed.), *Empowerment through multicultural education* (pp. 275–286). Albany: State University of New York Press.

Haberman, M., & Post, L. (1992). Does direct experience change education students' perceptions of low-income minority children? *Midwestern Educational Researcher, 5*(2), 29–31.

Hagerty, G. J., & Abramson, M. (1987). Impediments for implementing national policy change for mildly handicapped students. *Exceptional Children, 53,* 315–323.

Hale-Benson, J. E. (1988). *Black children: Their roots, culture, and learning styles* (rev. ed.). Baltimore, MD: Johns Hopkins University Press.

Hall, E. T. (1973). *The silent language.* New York: Anchor.

Hall, S. (1991). Ethnicity, identity and difference. *Radical America, 23*(4), 9–20.

Hansen, J. T., & Hansen-Krening, N. (1988). Difficult appointments abroad. *ADE Bulletin, 88,* 71–79.

Harrison, R., & Hopkins, R. (1967). The design of cross-cultural training: An alternative to the university model. *Journal of Applied Behavioral Science, 3,* 341–360.

Hatch, E. (1983). *Culture and morality: The relativity of values in anthropology.* New York: Columbia University Press.

Heath, S. B. (1983). *Ways with words: Language, life, and work in communities and classrooms.* New York: Cambridge University Press.

Heath, S. B. (1986). Sociocultural contexts of language development. In Bilingual Education Office (Eds.), *Beyond language: Social and cultural factors in schooling language minority students* (pp. 143–186). Los Angeles: California State University.

Heath, S. B., & Mangiola, L. (1991). *Children of promise: Literate activity in linguistically and culturally diverse classrooms.* Washington, DC: NEA.

Helms, J. E. (Ed.). (1990). *Black and white racial identity: Theory, research, and practice.* Westport, CT: Greenwood.

Helms, J. E. (1992). Why is there no study of cultural equivalence in standardized cognitive ability testing? *American Psychologist, 47*(9), 1083–1101.

Henington, M. (1981). Effect of intensive multicultural, non-sexist instruction on secondary student teachers. *Educational Research Quarterly, 6*(1), 65–75.

Hiatt, D. S. (1981). The law and minorities in the United States from 1620 to 1980. In W. E. Sims & B. Bass de Martinez (Eds.), *Perspectives in multicultural education* (pp. 17–52). New York: University Press of America.

Hidalgo, N. M., McDowell, C. L., & Siddle, E. V. (Eds.). (1990). *Facing racism in education.* Cambridge, MA: Harvard Educational Review.

Highwater, J. (1981). *The primal mind.* New York: New American Library.

Hill, L. (1977). *Learning thru discussion.* Los Angeles: Author.

Hirsch, E. D. (1987). *Cultural literacy: What every American needs to know.* Boston: Houghton Mifflin.

Hixson, J. (1992). Multicultural issues in teacher education: Meeting the challenge of student diversity. In C. A. Grant (Ed.), *Toward education that is multicultural: Proceedings of the first annual meeting of the National Association for Multicultural Education* (pp. 139–147). Morristown, NJ: Silver Burdett.

Hodgkinson, H. L. (1990). *The demographics of the American Indians: One percent of the people; fifty percent of the diversity.* Washington, DC: Institute for Educational Leadership.

Hoffer Gosselin, C. (1978). Voices of the past in Claude Simon's La Bataille de Pharsale. In J. P. Plottel & H. Charney (Eds.), *Intertextuality: New perspectives in criticism* (pp. 23–33). New York: New York Literary Forum.

Hollins, E. R. (1982a). Beyond multicultural education. *Negro Educational Review, 33,* 140–145.

Hollins, E. R. (1982b). The Marva Collins story revisited. *Journal of Teacher Education, 33*(1), 37–40.

Hollins, E. R. (1990a, April). A re-examination of what works for inner city black children. Paper presented at the annual meeting of the American Educational Research Association, Boston.

Hollins, E. R. (1990b). Debunking the myth of a monolithic white American culture; or moving toward cultural inclusion. *American Behavioral Scientist, 34*(2), 201–209.

Hollins, E. R. (1991). Professional development for teachers of "at-risk" students (Resources in Education). (ERIC Document No. ED 325 475)

Hollins, E. R. (1993). Assessing teacher competence for diverse populations. *Theory into Practice, 33*, 93–99.

Hollins, E. R. (1995). Revealing the deep meaning of culture in school learning. *Action in Teacher Education, 27*(1), 70–79.

Hollins, E. R. (1996). *Culture in school learning: Revealing the deep meaning*. Mahwah, NJ: Erlbaum.

Hollins, E. R., King, J. E., & Hayman, W. C. (1994). *Teaching diverse populations: Formulating a knowledge base*. Albany: State University of New York Press.

Hollins, E. R., & Spencer, K. (1991). Restructuring schools for cultural inclusion: Changing the schooling process for African American youngsters. *Journal of Education, 172*, 89–100.

Holmes Group. (1990). *Tomorrow's schools: Principles for the design of professional development schools*. East Lansing, MI: Author.

Homans, G. C. (1974). *Social behavior: Its elementary forms*. New York: Harcourt Brace Jovanovich.

hooks, b. (1989). *Talking back: Thinking feminist, thinking black*. Boston: South End.

hooks, b. (1994). *Teaching to transgress: Education as the practice of freedom*. New York: Routledge.

Houston, D. E. (1973). CUTE: A training program for inner-city teachers. *Journal of Teacher Education, 24*(4), 302–303.

Howell, W. S. (1981). Ethics of intercultural communication. Paper presented at the annual meeting of the Speech Communication Association, Anaheim, CA. (ERIC Document No. ED 209 689)

Huber, T. (1991). The revised social distance scale. Unpublished manuscript, Wichita State University, Wichita, KS.

Huber, T. (1992). Culturally responsible pedagogy: The "wisdom" of multicultural education. In C. A. Grant (Ed.), *Toward education that is multicultural: Proceedings of the first annual meeting of the National Association for Multicultural Education* (pp. 28–35). Morristown, NJ: Silver Burdett.

Huber, T., & Kline, F. (1993). Attitudes toward diversity: Can teacher education programs really make a difference? *Teacher Educator, 29*, 15–23.

Huber, T., & Pewewardy, C. (1990). Maximizing learning for all students: A review of the literature on learning modalities, cognitive styles, and approaches to meeting the needs of diverse learners. Washington, DC: U.S. Department of Education. (ERIC Document No. ED 324 289)

Huber-Bowen, T. (1993). *Teaching in the diverse classroom: Learner-centered activities that work*. Bloomington, IN: National Education Service.

Huddy, S. L. (1991). *A report on teacher supply: Enrollments in professional preparation programs at California institutions of higher education, 1989–90.* Sacramento, CA: Commission on Teacher Credentialing.

Hymes, D. (1981). Ethnographic monitoring. In H. T. Trueba, C. Cazden, V. John, & D. Hymes (Eds.), *Culture and the bilingual classroom: Studies in classroom ethnography* (pp. 370–394). Rowley, MA: Newbury House.

Iazetto, D., & Russell, S. (1994). Community field experiences in the urban education program. In K. Zeichner & S. Melnick (Eds.), *The role of community field experiences in preparing teachers for cultural diversity* (pp. 10–16). East Lansing, MI: National Center for Research on Teacher Learning.

Idol, L. (1993). *Special educator's consultation handbook* (2nd ed.). Austin, TX: ProEd.

Irvine, J. J. (1990). *Black students and school failure: Policies, practices, and prescriptions.* Westport, CT: Greenwood.

Irvine, J. J. (1991). Culturally responsive and responsible pedagogy: The inclusion of culture, research, and reflection in the knowledge base of teacher education. Paper presented at the annual meeting of the American Association of Colleges of Teacher Education, Atlanta.

Irvine, J. J. (1992). Making teacher education culturally responsive. In M. E. Dilworth (Ed.), *Diversity in teacher education: New expectations* (pp. 79–92). San Francisco: Jossey-Bass.

Jackson, G., & Cosca, C. (1974). The inequality of educational opportunity in the Southwest: An observational study of ethnically mixed classrooms. *American Educational Research Journal, 11,* 219–229.

James, J., & Farmer, R. (Eds.). (1993). *Spirit, space, and survival: African American women in (White) academe.* New York: Routledge.

James, R. L. (1980). The multicultural teacher education standard: Challenge and opportunity. *Viewpoints in Teaching and Learning, 56,* 18–25.

Jencks, C. (1988). Deadly neighbors: How the underclass has been misunderstood. *The New Republic, 6,* 23–31.

Jenkins, M. M. (1990). Teaching the new majority: Guidelines for cross-cultural communication between students and faculty. *Feminist Teacher, 5,* 8–14.

Johnson, D. W., Johnson, R. T., & Smith, K. A. (1991). *Active learning: Cooperation in the college classroom.* Edina, MN: Interaction Book Co.

Johnson, S. D., Jr. (1983). *The cross-cultural counseling specialization at Teachers College, Columbia University.* Paper presented at the annual convention of the American Psychological Association, Anaheim, CA. (ERIC Document No. ED 241 860)

Jordan, J. (1992). *Technical difficulties.* New York: Vintage Books.

Kagan, D. (1992). Professional growth among preservice and beginning teachers. *Review of Educational Research, 62*(2), 129–169.

Kagitcibasi, C., & Berry, J. W. (1989). Cross-cultural psychology: Current research and trends. *Annual Review of Psychology, 40,* 493–531.

Kanowith, V. (1980). *Teacher attitudes and the Spanish bilingual program.* (ERIC Document No. ED 190 713)

Karenga, M. (1993). *Introduction to Black Studies.* Los Angeles: University of Sankore Press.

Kilminster, R. (1979). *Praxis and method: A sociological dialogue with Lukács, Gramsci, and the early Frankfurt School.* London: Routledge & Kegan Paul.

Kim, Y. Y. (1988). On theorizing intercultural communication. In Y. Y. Kim & W. B. Gudykunst (Eds.), *Theories in intercultural communication* (pp. 11–21). Newbury Park, CA: Sage.

Kimball, G. H. (1981). *Evaluation of 1980–81 bilingual Title VII program: Oklahoma City public schools.* (ERIC Document No. ED 217 113)

Kincheloe, J., & Stanley, G. (1983). Teaching on a rural reservation: An authentic learning experience. *Momentum, 14,* 18–19.

King, J. E. (1991). Dysconscious racism: Ideology, identity, and the miseducation of teachers. *Journal of Negro Education, 60*(2), 133–146.

King, J. E. (1992). Diaspora literacy and consciousness in the struggle against miseducation in the Black community. *Journal of Negro Education, 61*(3), 317–340.

King, J. E. (1994). The purpose of schooling for African American children: Including cultural knowledge. In E. R. Hollins, J. E. King, & W. C. Hayman (Eds.), *Teaching diverse populations: Formulating a knowledge base* (pp. 25–43). Albany: State University of New York Press.

King, J. E. (1995). Culture-centered knowledge: Black studies, curriculum transformation, and social action. In J. A. Banks & C. M. Banks (Eds.), *Handbook of research on multicultural education* (pp. 265–290). New York: Macmillan.

King, J. E., & Ladson-Billings, G. (1990). The teacher education challenge in elite university settings: Developing critical perspectives for teaching in a democratic and multicultural society. *European Journal of Intercultural Studies, 1*(2), 15–30.

Klassen, F. H., & Gollnick, D. M. (Eds.). (1977). *Pluralism and the American teacher.* Washington, DC: AACTE, Ethnic Heritage Center for Teacher Education.

Klassen, F. H., Gollnick, D. M., & Osayande, K. I. M. (1980). *Multicultural teacher education: Guidelines for implementation* (Vol. 4). Washington, DC: AACTE.

Kleifgen, J. A. (1988). Learning from student teachers' cross-cultural communicative failures. *Anthropology and Education Quarterly, 19,* 218–234.

Kleinfeld, J. (1989). *Teaching taboo-topics: The special virtues of the case method.* Fairbanks: College of Rural Alaska.

Kleinfeld, J., McDiarmid, G. W., Grubis, S., & Parrett, W. (1983). Doing research on effective cross-cultural teaching: The teacher tale. *Peabody Journal of Education, 61*(1), 86–108.

Kleinfeld, J., & Noordhoff, K. (1988). *Teachers for Rural Alaska (TRA) program: Part A. Project portrayal/Part B. Program assessment report/Part C. Practice profile.* Washington, DC: Office of Educational Research and Improvement. (ERIC Document No. ED 306 055)

Knight, E. M. (1981). *The case for teacher training in nonbiased, cross-cultural assessment.* Paper presented at the Council for Exceptional Children Conference on the Exceptional Bilingual Child, New Orleans. (ERIC Document No. ED 209 829)

Kohler-Riessman, C. (1994). *Narrative analysis.* Newbury Park, CA: Sage.

Kozol, J. (1975). *The night is dark and I am far from home.* Toronto: Bantam.

Kozol, J. (1981). *On being a teacher.* New York: Continuum.

Kozol, J. (1991). *Savage inequalities: Children in America's schools*. New York: Harper Perennial.

Krall, F. R. (1988). From the inside out: Personal history as educational research. *Educational Theory, 38*, 467–479.

Kramsch, C. J. (1981). *Culture and constructs: Communicating attitudes and values in the foreign language classroom*. Paper presented at the annual meeting of the American Council on the Teaching of Foreign Languages, Denver. (ERIC Document No. ED 213 251)

Krashen, S. (1991). *Bilingual education: A focus on current research* (Occasional Papers in Bilingual Education No. 3). Washington, DC: National Clearinghouse for Bilingual Education.

Krashen, S., & Biber, D. (1988). *On course: Bilingual education's success in California*. Sacramento: California Association for Bilingual Education.

Kushner, K., & Brislin, R. (1986). Bridging gaps: Cross-cultural training in teacher education. *Journal of Teacher Education, 37*(6), 51–54.

LA & NYC have largest LEP #s. (1995, April). *LMRI News, 4*, 2–3.

Laboratory of Comparative Human Cognition. (1986). Contributions of cross-cultural research to educational practice. *Educational Psychologist, 41*, 1049–1058.

Ladson-Billings, G. (1990). Like lightning in a bottle: Attempting to capture the pedagogical excellence of successful teachers of Black students. *The International Journal of Qualitative Studies in Education, 3*(4), 335–344.

Ladson-Billings, G. (1994). *The dreamkeepers: Successful teachers of African American children*. San Francisco: Jossey-Bass.

Ladson-Billings, G. (1995). Multicultural teacher education: Research, practice, and policy. In J. A. Banks & C. M. Banks (Eds.), *Handbook of research on multicultural education* (pp. 747–759). New York: Macmillan.

Lake, R. (1990, September). An Indian father's plea. *Teacher Magazine*, pp. 131–134.

Lambert, J. W. (1989). Accepting others' values in the classroom: An important difference. *Clearing House, 62*, 273–274.

Lampert, M., & Clark, C. (1990). Expert knowledge and expert thinking: A response to Floden and Klinzing. *Educational Researcher, 19*(5), 21–23, 42.

Landis, D., & Brislin, R. W. (Eds.). (1983). *Handbook of intercultural training* (Vol. I–III). New York: Pergamon.

Lane, S. (1980). *"But it's English, isn't it?" Teaching English as a second language and/or developmental English—Same methods?* Paper presented at the annual convention of the New York State English to Speakers of Other Languages and Bilingual Educators Association, New York. (ERIC Document No. ED 213 261)

Laosa, L. M. (1977). Inequality in the classroom: Observational research on teacher–student interactions. *Aztlan: International Journal of Chicano Studies Research, 8*, 51–67.

Larkin, J., & Sleeter, C. (Eds.). (1995). *Developing multicultural teacher education curricula*. Albany: State University of New York Press.

Laughlin, M. A. (1980). *An examination of state requirements for multicultural/human relations competencies in elementary and secondary teacher education*. Paper presented at the Annual Midwest Regional Conference of the National Association of Interdisciplinary Ethnic Studies, Ames, IA. (ERIC Document No. ED 202 975)

Law, S. G., & Lane, D. S., Jr. (1987). Multicultural acceptance by teacher education students: A survey of attitudes toward 32 ethnic and national groups and a comparison with 60 years of data. *Journal of Instructional Psychology, 14*(1), 3–9.

LeCompte, M. D. (1985). Defining the difference: Cultural subgroups within the educational mainstream. *The Urban Review, 17,* 111–127.

Lerner, R. M., & Hultsch, D. F. (1983). *Human development: A life-span perspective.* New York: McGraw-Hill.

Lerner, R. M., & Ryff, C. D. (1978). Implementation of the life-span view of human development: The sample case of attachment. In P. B. Baltes (Ed.), *Life-span development and behavior* (Vol. 1, pp. 1–44). New York: Academic Press.

Lerner, R. M., & Spanier, G. B. (Eds.). (1978). *Child influences on marital and family interaction: A life-span perspective.* New York: Academic Press.

Levin, B. K. (1986). *Education of children of undocumented immigrants: Teacher and parent perceptions and expectations.* Unpublished doctoral dissertation, University of Colorado, Boulder.

Levine, L., & Pignatelli, F. (1994, April). *Imagining change through ethnographic inquiry.* Paper presented at the annual meeting of the American Educational Research Association, New Orleans.

Lieberman, D., Kosokoff, S., & Kosokoff, J. (1989). *Do it my way: What's common about common sense? An intercultural communication teaching approach.* Paper presented at the annual meeting of the Western Speech Communication Association, Spokane, WA. (ERIC Document No. ED 304 730)

Limon, J. E. (1994). *Dancing with the devil: Society and cultural poetics in Mexican-American south Texas.* Madison: University of Wisconsin Press.

Lindholm, K. J. (1990). Bilingual immersion education: Educational equity for language-minority students. In A. Barona & E. E. Garcia (Eds.), *Children at risk: Poverty, minority status, and other issues in educational equity.* Washington, DC: National Association for School Psychologists.

Lipka, J. (1991). Toward a culturally based pedagogy: A case study of one Yup'ik Eskimo teacher. *Anthropology and Education Quarterly, 22,* 203–223.

Liston, D., & Zeichner, K. (1991). *Teacher education and the social conditions of schooling.* New York: Routledge.

Lomotey, K. (Ed.). (1990). *Going to school: The African-American experience.* Albany: State University of New York Press.

Lopez, S., Jr. (1981). *The adaptation of culturally different children to the culture of the school and bilingual/bicultural education.* Unpublished doctoral dissertation, University of Michigan, Ann Arbor.

Lorde, A. (1984). *Sister outsider.* Freedom, CA: Crossing Press.

Luke, C., & Gore, J. (1992). *Feminism and critical pedagogy.* New York: Routledge.

Macías, J. (1984). *A study of the Papago early childhood Head Start program.* Unpublished doctoral dissertation, Stanford University, Stanford.

MacLeod, J. (1992). Bridging street and school. *Journal of Negro Education, 60,* 260–275.

Mahan, J. M. (1982). Native Americans as teacher trainers: Anatomy and outcomes of a cultural immersion project. *Journal of Educational Equity and Leadership, 2*(2), 100–110.

Mahan, J. M. (1984). *Cultural immersion for inservice teachers: A model and some outcomes.* Paper presented at the annual meeting of the Association for Supervision and Curriculum Development, New York. (ERIC Document No. ED 254 923)

Mahan, J. M. (1993). *Native Americans as non-traditional, usually unrecognized, influential teacher educators.* Paper presented at the annual meeting of the Association of Teacher Educators, Los Angeles.

Mahan, J. M., Fortney, M., & Garcia, J. (1983). Linking the community to teacher education: Toward a more analytical approach. *Action in Teacher Education, 5*(1–2), 1–10.

Mathews, J. (1988). *Escalante: The best teacher in America.* New York: Henry Holt.

Mayne, D. H. (1980). *Recommendations from teachers in small rural high schools for modification of the teacher training program of the University of Alaska: A survey.* Juneau: University of Alaska. (ERIC Document No. ED 211 458)

Mazon, M. R. (1977). Community, home, cultural awareness and language training: A design for teacher training in multicultural education. In F. H. Klassen & D. M. Gollnick (Eds.), *Pluralism and the American teacher* (pp. 205–215). Washington, DC: AACTE, Ethnic Heritage Center for Teacher Education.

McCaffrey, J. A. (1986). Independent effectiveness: A reconsideration of cross-cultural orientation and training. *International Journal of Intercultural Relations, 10,* 159–178.

McCarthy, C. (1993). After the canon: Knowledge and ideological representation in the multicultural discourse on curriculum reform. In C. McCarthy & W. Crichlow (Eds.), *Race, identity, and representation in education* (pp. 289–305). New York: Routledge.

McCormick, T. (1990). Collaboration works: Preparing teachers for urban realities. *Contemporary Education, 61*(3), 129–134.

McDiarmid, G. W., & Price, J. (1990). *Prospective teachers' views of diverse learners: A study of participants in the ABCD project* (Research Report 90-6). East Lansing: National Center for Research on Teacher Learning.

McGroarty, M. (1988). Issues in design and evaluation of cross-cultural workshops for ESL teachers and administrators. *The Canadian Modern Language Review, 44,* 295–335.

McIntosh, P. (1989, July/August). White privilege: Unpacking the invisible knapsack. *Peace and Freedom,* pp. 10–12.

McKenzie, P., & Ross, S. (1989). *Working with students from diverse cultural backgrounds in basic courses of speech.* Paper presented at the annual meeting of the Eastern Communication Association, Ocean City, MD. (ERIC Document No. ED 305 699)

McLaren, P. (1989). *Life in schools.* New York: Longman.

Mead, G. H. (1934). *Mind, self, and society.* Chicago: University of Chicago Press.

Meier, T. (1989, April). *Effective teaching practices for differing learner characteristics.* Paper presented at the annual meeting of the American Educational Research Association, San Francisco.

Meier, T., & Nelson-Barber, S. (1989). Bold new standards and tired old assumptions: Issues of equity and diversity in teacher assessment. Unpublished manuscript.

Miles, M. B., & Huberman, A. M. (1984). *Qualitative data analysis.* Beverly Hills, CA: Sage.

Miller, M. D. (1988). *Reflections on reentry after teaching in China.* New York: Center for the Study of Intercultural Learning. (ERIC Document No. ED 306 174)

Mills, J. (1984). Addressing the separate but equal predicament in teacher preparation. *Journal of Teacher Education, 35,* 18–23.

Modiano, N. (1977). *La educación indígena en Los Altos de Chiapas.* Mexico, D.F.: Secretaría de Educación Pública.

Moll, L. (1993). Introduction. *Vygotsky and education: Sociohistorical psychology* (pp. 1–30). New York: Cambridge University Press.

Montecinos, C. (1996). Multicultural teacher education for a culturally diverse teaching force. In R. Martin (Ed.), *Practicing what we preach: Confronting diversity in teacher education* (pp. 97–116). Albany: State University of New York Press.

Morris, L., Sather, G., & Schull, S. (Eds.). (1978). *Exacting learning styles from social/cultural diversity: Studies of five American minority groups.* Southwest Teacher Corps Network.

Morrison, T. (1992). *Playing in the dark: Whiteness in the literary imagination.* Cambridge, MA: Harvard University Press.

Murrell, P. C. (1990). Making uncommon sense: Critical revisioning of professional knowledge about diverse cultural perspectives in teacher education. In M. Diez (Ed.), *Proceedings of the fourth national forum of the Association of Independent Liberal Arts Colleges for Teacher Education* (pp. 47–54). Milwaukee, WI: Alverno College.

Murrell, P. C. (1991). Cultural politics in teacher education: What is missing in the preparation of "minority" teachers? In M. Foster (Ed.), *Readings on equal education: Qualitative investigations into school and schooling* (pp. 205–225). New York: AMS Press.

Murrell, P. C. (1993). Afrocentric immersion: Academic and personal development of African American males in public schools. In T. Perry & J. Fraser (Eds.), *Freedom's plow: Teaching in the multicultural classroom* (pp. 231–259). Boston: Routledge.

Murrell, P. C. (1994). In search of responsive teaching for African American males: An investigation of students' experience of middle school mathematics curriculum. *Journal of Negro Education, 63,* 536–551.

Nachmanovich, S. (1990). *Free play: Improvisation in life and art.* Los Angeles: J. P. Tarcher.

National Assessment of Educational Progress. (1985). *The reading report card.* Princeton, NJ: Educational Testing Service.

National Center for Education Statistics. (1989). *Digest of education statistics.* Washington, DC: U.S. Government Printing Office.

National Commission on Excellence in Education. (1983). *A nation at risk: The imperative for educational reform.* Washington, DC: U.S. Department of Education.

National Council for Accreditation of Teacher Education. (1990). *Standards, procedures, and policies for the accreditation of professional education units.* Washington, DC: Author.

National Council for Accreditation of Teacher Education. (1993). *Proposed refinement of NCATE's standards for the accreditation of professional education units.*

Nelson-Barber, S., & Meier, T. (1990, Spring). Multicultural context: A key factor in teaching. *Academic Connections*, 1–9. Princeton, NJ: College Entrance Examination Board.

Nies, J. (1977). *Seven women.* New York: Penguin.

Nieto, S. (1992). *Affirming diversity: The sociopolitical context of multicultural education.* New York: Longman.

Noddings, N. (1988, December 7). Schools face "crisis in caring." *Education Week*, p. 32.

Noddings, N. (1992). *The challenge to care in schools.* New York: Teachers College Press.

Noordhoff, K., & Kleinfeld, J. (1993). Preparing teachers for multicultural classrooms. *Teaching & Teacher Education, 9*(1), 27–40.

Oakes, J. (1990). *Lost talent: The underparticipation of women, minorities, and disabled persons in science.* Santa Monica, CA: Rand.

Office of Bilingual Education and Minority Languages Affairs. (1991). *The condition of bilingual education in the nation.* Washington, DC: Author.

Ogbu, J. U. (1987). Variability in minority school performance: A problem in search of an explanation. *Anthropology and Education Quarterly, 18*, 312–334.

Olneck, M. R. (1990). The recurring dream: Symbolism and ideology in intercultural and multicultural education. *American Journal of Education, 98*, 147–174.

Olsen, L. (1988). *Crossing the schoolhouse border: Immigrant students and the California public schools.* San Francisco: California Tomorrow.

Ongtooguk, P. (1994). Community field experiences in the teachers for Alaska program. In K. Zeichner & S. Melnick (Eds.), *The role of community field experiences in preparing teachers for cultural diversity* (pp. 16–20). East Lansing, MI: National Center for Research on Teacher Learning.

Ornstein, A. (1982). The education of the disadvantaged: A 20-year review. *Educational Researcher, 24*, 197–211.

Orr, E. (1987). *Twice as less.* New York: Norton.

Osborne, B. (1989). Cultural congruence, ethnicity and fused biculturalism: Zuni and Torres Strait. *Journal of American Indian Education, 28*, 7–20.

Paine, L. (1989). *Orientation towards diversity: What do prospective teachers bring?* (Research Report 89–9). East Lansing, MI: National Center for Research on Teacher Learning.

Paley, V. G. (1979). *White teacher.* Cambridge, MA: Harvard University Press.

Pallas, A., Natriello, G., & McDill, E. (1989). The changing nature of the disadvantaged population. *Educational Researcher, 18*(5), 16–22.

Pang, D. B. (1981). *Developing interculturally skilled counselors: Process and productivity of the project.* Paper presented at the annual meeting of the Western Psychological Association, Los Angeles. (ERIC Document No. ED 214 044)

Pang, V. O. (1988). Ethnic prejudice: Still alive and hurtful. *Harvard Educational Review, 58*(3), 375–379.

Pang, V. O. (1994). Why do we need this class? Multicultural education for teachers. *Phi Delta Kappan, 76,* 289–292.

Parsons, T. (1965). *Ethnic cleavage in the California schools.* Unpublished doctoral dissertation, Stanford University, Stanford.

Passow, A. H. (1991). Urban schools a second (?) or third (?) time around: Priorities for curricular and instructional reform. *Education and Urban Society, 23*(3), 243–255.

Paulson, C. B. (1980). *English as a second language: What research says to the teacher.* Washington, DC: NEA. (ERIC Document No. ED 205 010)

Pedersen, P. B. (1984). Levels of intercultural communication using the rehearsal demonstration model. *Journal of Non-White Concerns, 12,* 57–68.

Pepper, S. C. (1942). *World hypotheses.* Berkeley: University of California Press.

Phillips, D. Z. (1984). The devil's disguises: Philosophy of religion, "objectivity" and "cultural divergence." In S. C. Brown (Ed.), *Objectivity and cultural divergence* (pp. 61–78). Cambridge: Cambridge University Press.

Phillips, S. (1983). *The invisible culture: Communities in classroom and community on the Warm Springs Indian Reservation.* New York: Longman.

Plomin, R. (1989). Environment and genes: Determinants of behavior. *American Psychologist, 44,* 105–111.

Portes, A., & Rumbaut, R. (1990). *Immigrant America: A portrait.* Berkeley: University of California Press.

Quintanar-Sarellana, R. (1990). *Teachers' perceptions of the language and culture of linguistic minority students.* Unpublished doctoral dissertation, Stanford University, Stanford.

Quintanar-Sarellana, R. (1992). *Cultural diversity and gender issues in education.* Paper presented at the Issues of Equity and Diversity for Women and Girls Conference, Oakland, CA.

Ramsey, P. G. (1987). *Teaching and learning in a diverse world.* New York: Teachers College Press.

Ramsey, P. G., Vold, E. B., & Williams, L. R. (1989). *Multicultural education: A source book.* New York: Garland.

Raschka, C. (1992). *Charlie Parker played be bop.* New York: Orchard Books.

Ravitch, D. (1990). Multiculturalism, yes, particularism, no. *Chronicle of Higher Education, 37,* 8.

Ravitch, D. (1991/92). A culture in common. *Educational Leader, 49*(4), 8–11.

Research About Teacher Education Project. (1990). *RATE IV; teaching teachers: Facts and figures.* Washington, DC: AACTE.

Reusswig, J. M. (1981). *Immersion: A method in staff development?* Paper presented at the annual meeting of the American Association of School Administrators, Atlanta. (ERIC Document No. ED 204 850)

Reutter, E. E., Jr. (1985). *The law of education* (3rd ed.). Mineola, NY: Foundation Press.

Reyes, M., & Halcon, J. (1988). Racism in academia: The old wolf revisited. *Harvard Educational Review, 58*(3), 299–314.

Reynolds, M. C. (1989). *Knowledge base for the beginning teacher.* Elmsford, NY: Pergamon Press.

Rhinesmith, S. (1975). *Bringing home the world: A management guide for community leaders of international programs.* New York: AMACOM.

Richert, A. E. (1992). Voice and power in teaching and learning to teach. In L. Valli (Ed.), *Reflective teacher education cases and critique* (pp. 187–197). Albany: State University of New York Press.

Ricoeur, P. (1992). *Oneself as another* (K. Blamey, Trans.). Chicago: University of Chicago Press.

Riegel, K. F. (1976). The dialectics of human development. *American Psychologist, 31,* 689–700.

Rist, R. (1970). Student social class and teacher expectations. *Harvard Educational Review, 40*(3), 411–451.

Rivers, W. M. (1988). Curriculum, student objectives, and the training of foreign language teachers. *Babel, 23,* 4–10.

Robarcheck, C. A. (1992). Native Americans meet the new Americans and vice versa: Postmodernism, multiculturalism, and cultural diversity. Unpublished manuscript, Wichita State University, Wichita, KS.

Rodríguez, A. M. (1980). *Empirically defining competencies for effective bilingual teachers.* (ERIC Document No. ED 224 662)

Ross, D., Johnson, M., & Smith, W. (1991, April). *Helping preservice teachers confront issues related to educational equity: Assessing revisions in coursework and fieldwork.* Paper presented at the annual meeting of the American Educational Research Association, Chicago.

Rothenberg, S. (1988). *Racism and sexism.* New York: St. Martin's Press.

Rozema, H. J. (1982). *The interplay between racism and sexism: Using assertiveness training techniques to reduce racism.* Paper presented at the annual meeting of the International Communication Association, Boston. (ERIC Document No. ED 218 695)

Ryan, R. M., & Robinson, K. S. (1990). *Enhancing pre-service teachers' contextual understandings about their learners.* Paper presented at the annual meeting of the American Association of Colleges of Teacher Education, Chicago. (ERIC Document No. ED 319 707)

Santrock, J. W., & Yussen, S. R. (1992). *Child development* (5th ed.). Dubuque, IA: Wm. C. Brown.

Sarbaugh, L. E. (1988). A taxonomic approach to intercultural communication. In Y. Y. Kim & W. B. Gudykunst (Eds.), *Theories in intercultural communication* (pp. 22–40). Newbury Park, CA: Sage.

Scheurich, J. J. (1993). Toward a white discourse on white racism. *Educational Researcher, 22,* 5–10.

Schlesinger, A. M. (1992). *The disuniting of America: Reflections on a multicultural society.* New York: Norton.

Seelye, H. N. (1993). *Teaching culture: Strategies for intercultural communication* (3rd ed.). Lincolnwood, IL: National Textbook Company.

Shade, B. J. R. (Ed.). (1982). *Culture, style, and the educative process.* Springfield, IL: Charles C. Thomas.

Sharp, R., & Green, A. (1975). *Education and social control: A study in progressive primary education.* London: Routledge & Kegan Paul.

Shepard, L. A. (1987). The new push for excellence: Widening the schism between regular and special education. *Exceptional Children, 53,* 327–329.

Shepard, L. A., & Smith, M. L. (Eds.). (1989). *Flunking grades: Research and policies on retention.* New York: Falmer.

Shor, I. (1986). Equality is excellence: Transforming teacher education and the learning process. *Harvard Educational Review, 56*(4), 406–426.

Shor, I., & Freire, P. (1987). *A pedagogy for liberation.* South Hadley, MA: Bergin & Garvey.

Shulman, J. (1992, April). *Tender feelings, hidden thoughts: Confronting bias, innocence, and racism through case discussions.* Paper presented at the annual meeting of the American Educational Research Association, San Francisco.

Shulman, J., & Mesa-Bains, A. (1990). *Teaching diverse students: Cases & commentaries.* San Francisco: Far West Laboratory for Educational Research & Development.

Siegel, H. (1988). *Educating reason: Rationality, critical thinking and education.* New York: Routledge & Kegan Paul.

Simpson, R. J., & Galbo, J. J. (1986). Interaction and learning: Theorizing on the art of teaching. *Interchange, 17,* 37–51.

Sims, W. E. (1981). Humanizing education for culturally different and exceptional children. In W. E. Sims & B. Bass de Martinez (Eds.), *Perspectives in multicultural education* (pp. 1–16). New York: University Press of America.

Sims, W. E. (1983). Preparing teachers for multicultural classrooms. *Momentum, 14,* 42–44.

Sing, B. (Ed.). (1989). *Asian Pacific Americans.* Los Angeles: National Conference of Christians and Jews.

Singer, E. A. (1988). *What is cultural congruence and why are they saying such terrible things about it?* East Lansing: Michigan State University, Institute for Research on Teaching. (ERIC Document No. ED 292 914)

Sirotnik, K. A. (1990). Society, schooling, teaching, and preparing to teach. In J. I. Goodlad, R. Soder, & K. A. Sirotnik (Eds.), *The moral dimensions of teaching* (pp. 296–327). San Francisco: Jossey Bass.

Skrtic, T. M. (1992). The special education paradox: Equity as the way to excellence. In T. Hehir & T. Latus (Eds.), *Special education at the century's end: Evolution of theory and practice since 1970* (Reprint Series No. 23, pp. 203–275). Cambridge, MA: Harvard Educational Review.

Slavin, R. (1989/90). Research on cooperative learning: Consensus and controversy. *Educational Leadership, 47*(4), 52–54.

Sleeter, C. E. (1989). Doing multicultural education across the grade levels and subject areas: A case study of Wisconsin. *Teaching and Teacher Education, 5*(3), 189–203.

Sleeter, C. E. (Ed.). (1991). *Empowerment through multicultural education.* Albany: State University of New York Press.

Sleeter, C. E. (1992). *Keepers of the American dream: A study of staff development and multicultural education.* London: Falmer.

Sleeter, C. E. (1994). White racism. *Multicultural Education, 39,* 5–8.

Sleeter, C. E., & Grant, C. A. (1987). An analysis of multicultural education in the United States. *Harvard Educational Review, 57*(4), 421–444.

Smith, G. P. (1991). *Toward defining a culturally responsible pedagogy for teacher education: The knowledge base for educating the teachers of minority and culturally diverse students.* Paper presented at the annual meeting of the American Association of Colleges of Teacher Education, Atlanta.

Sotomayor, F. (1974). *For the children: Improving education for Mexican Americans.* U.S. Commission on Civil Rights. Washington, DC: U.S. Government Printing Office.

Sparks-Langer, G. M. (1992). In the eye of the beholder: Cognitive, critical, and narrative approaches to teacher reflection. In L. Valli (Ed.), *Reflective teacher education cases and critique* (pp. 147–160). Albany: State University of New York Press.

Spindler, G. D. (1974). *Education and cultural process: Toward an anthropology of education.* New York: Holt, Rinehart & Winston.

Spindler, G. D. (Ed.). (1982). *Doing the ethnography of schooling: Educational anthropology in action.* New York: Holt, Rinehart & Winston.

Spindler, G. D., & Spindler, L. (Eds.). (1987). *Interpretive ethnography of education at home and abroad.* Hillsdale, NJ: Erlbaum.

Starosta, W. J. (1990). Thinking through intercultural training assumptions: In the aftermath. *International Journal of Intercultural Relations, 14,* 1–6.

Stocking, G. W., Jr. (1968). *Race, culture, and evolution: Essays in the history of anthropology.* New York: Free Press.

Study Commission on Undergraduate Education and the Education of Teachers. (1976). *Teacher education in the U.S.: The responsibility gap.* Lincoln: University of Nebraska Press.

Tafoya, T. (1981). *What you say after hello: Pre-service orientation for native programs.* (ERIC Document No. ED 207 734)

Tatum, B. D. (1992). Talking about race, learning about racism: The application of racial identity theory in the classroom. *Harvard Educational Review, 62*(1), 1–24.

Taylor, O. L. (1987). *Cross-cultural communication: An essential dimension of effective education.* Washington, DC: Mid-Atlantic Center for Race Equity. (ERIC Document No. ED 293 786)

Teitelbaum, H., & Hiller, R. J. (1977). Bilingual education: The legal mandate. *Harvard Educational Review, 47*(2), 138–170.

Tharp, R., & Gallimore, R. (1989). *Rousing minds to life: Teaching learning and schooling in a social context.* New York: Cambridge University Press.

Thiagarajan, S. (1988). Performance technology in multicultural environments:

Making sense out of contradictory conceptualizations. *Performance and Instruction, 27,* 14–16.

Thibaut, J. W., & Kelley, H. H. (1959). *The social psychology of groups.* New York: Wiley.

Thomas, A., & Chess, S. (1987). Commentary. In A. H. Buss, R. Plomin, M. K. Rothbart, A. Thomas, A. Chess, R. R. Hinde, & R. P. McCall (Eds.), Roundtable: What is temperament? Four approaches. *Child Development, 58,* 505–529.

Today's numbers, tomorrow's nation: Demographics awesome challenge for schools. (1986, May 14). *Education Week,* pp. 14–37.

Torney-Purta, J. (1986). A model for using intercultural counseling insights and skills to enhance teachers' intercultural competence. In R. J. Samuda & A. Wolfgang (Eds.), *Intercultural counseling and assessment: Global perspectives* (pp. 383–394). Lewistown, NY: C. J. Hogrefe.

Torres, M. (1983). *Participatory democracy and bilingual education: The case of San Jose, California.* Unpublished doctoral dissertation, Stanford University, Stanford.

Triandis, H. C. (1990). Theoretical concepts that are applicable to the analysis of ethnocentrism. In R. W. Brislin (Ed.), *Applied cross-cultural psychology* (pp. 34–65). Newbury Park, CA: Sage.

Trueba, H. (1989). *Raising silent voices: Educating linguistic minorities for the 21st century.* New York: Harper & Row.

Tung, R. L. (1981). Selection and training of personnel for overseas assignments. *Columbia Journal of World Business, 16,* 68–78.

Turnbull, H. R. (1993). *Free appropriate public education: The law and children with disabilities* (4th ed.). Denver: Love.

Tyack, D. B. (1974). *The one best system: A history of American urban education.* Cambridge, MA: Harvard University Press.

Urbanski, A. (1988). The Rochester contract: A status report. *Educational Leadership, 46*(3), 48–52.

U.S. Commission on Civil Rights. (1971–74). *Mexican American educational study.* Washington, DC: U.S. Government Printing Office.

Vallence, E. (1977). Hiding the hidden curriculum: An interpretation of the language of justification in nineteenth-century educational reform. In A. Bellack & H. Kliebard (Eds.), *Curriculum and evaluation* (pp. 590–607). Berkeley, CA: McCutchan.

Vasquez, O. A., Pease-Alvarez, L., & Shannon, S. M. (1994). *Pushing boundaries: Language and culture in a Mexican community.* New York: Cambridge University Press.

Villegas, A. M. (1993, April). *Restructuring teacher education for diversity: The innovative curriculum.* Paper presented at the annual meeting of the American Educational Research Association, Atlanta.

Villegas, A. M., Clewell, B. C., Anderson, B. T., Goertz, M., Joy, M. F., Bruschi, B. A., & Irvine, J. J. (1995). *Teaching for diversity: Models for expanding the supply of minority teachers.* Princeton, NJ: Educational Testing Service.

Wallace, G. (1980). Training for international development. A summary of faculty and foreign student interviews. Washington, DC: Department of State, USAID. (ERIC Document No. ED 206 428)

Wang, J. C. (1984). *Entering the mainstream: A report of the East Coast Asian American Education Conference.* Washington, DC: Conference Proceedings. (ERIC Document No. ED 253 607)

Washington, V. (1981). Impact of antiracism/multicultural training on elementary teachers' attitudes and classroom behavior. *Elementary School Journal, 81*(3), 186–192.

Weiler, K. (1988). *Women teaching for change.* South Hadley, MA: Bergin & Garvey.

Wendt, J. R. (1984). DIE: A way to improve communication. *Communication Education, 13,* 397–401.

West, C. (1993). *Race matters.* Boston: Beacon.

Williams, S. (1991). Classroom use of African American language: Educational tool or social weapon? In C. E. Sleeter (Ed.), *Empowerment through multicultural education* (pp. 199–216). Albany: State University of New York Press.

Willison, S. (1994). Community field experiences in the American Indian Project. In K. Zeichner & S. Melnick (Eds.), *The role of community field experiences in preparing teachers for cultural diversity* (pp. 6–10). East Lansing, MI: National Center for Research on Teacher Learning.

Wilson, A. (1983). Cross-cultural experiential learning for teachers. *Theory into Practice, 21,* 184–191.

Wise, A. E. (1993, June). Draft of the "Proposed refinement of NCATE's professional accreditation standards." [Memo].

Wolf-Wasserman, M., & Hutchinson, L. (1978). *Teaching human dignity: Social change lessons for everyteacher.* Minneapolis: Education Exploration Center.

Wong, L., & Valadez, C. (1986). Teaching bilingual learners. In M. C. Wittrock (Ed.), *Handbook of research on teaching* (3rd ed., pp. 648–685). New York: Macmillan.

Work Group. (1993). *A report on specially designed academic instruction in English (SDAIE).* Sacramento: Commission on Teacher Credentialing and California Department of Education.

Wynter, S. (1992). Re-thinking aesthetics: Notes toward a deciphering practice. In M. Cham (Ed.), *Ex-iles: Essays on Caribbean cinema* (pp. 237–279). Trenton, NJ: Africa World Press.

Wynter, S. (1995). 1942: A new world view. In V. L. Hyatt & R. Nettleford (Eds.), *Race, discourse, and the origin of the Americas* (pp. 5–57). Washington, DC: Smithsonian Institution Press.

Yao, E. L. (1985, April). *Implementation of multicultural education in Texas public schools.* Paper presented at the annual meeting of the American Educational Research Association, Chicago. (ERIC Document No. 264 995)

York, D. E. (1993). *Cross-cultural training and the culturally diverse urban school: Evidence from an ethnographic case study.* Unpublished manuscript.

Yzaguirre, R. (1981). Bilingual education: The key to equal opportunity. *Agenda: A Journal of Hispanic Issues, 11,* 2–3.

Zeichner, K. M. (1983). Alternative paradigms of teacher education. *Journal of Teacher Education, 34,* 3–9.

Zeichner, K. M. (1992). *Educating teachers for cultural diversity.* National Center for Research on Teacher Learning, East Lansing.

Zeichner, K. M. (1993). *Educating teachers for cultural diversity* (Special Report). East Lansing, MI: National Center for Research on Teacher Learning.

Zeichner, K. M. (1995). Preparing teachers for cross-cultural teaching. In W. Hawley & A. Jackson (Eds.), *Toward a common destiny: Race and ethnic relations in American schools* (pp. 397–419). San Francisco: Jossey-Bass.

Zeichner, K., & Gore, J. (1990). Teacher socialization. In W. R. Houston (Ed.), *Handbook of research on teacher education* (pp. 329–348). New York: Macmillan.

Zeichner, K., & Hoeft, K. (1996). Teacher socialization for cultural diversity. In J. Sikula (Ed.), *Handbook of research on teacher education* (2nd ed., pp. 525–547). New York: Macmillan.

Zeichner, K., & Melnick, S. (Eds.). (1994). *The role of community field experiences in preparing teachers for cultural diversity.* East Lansing, MI: National Center for Research on Teacher Learning.

Ziegler, S. (1980). Measuring inter-ethnic attitudes in a multi-ethnic context. *Canadian Ethnic Studies, 12*(3), 45–55.

Zimpher, N., & Ashburn, E. (1992). Countering parochialism among teacher candidates. In M. E. Dilworth (Ed.), *Diversity in teacher education: New expectations* (pp. 40–62). San Francisco: Jossey-Bass.

Zinn, H. (1980). *A people's history of the United States.* New York: Harper & Row.

About the Editors and the Contributors

Mary Gresham Anderson is Assistant Professor of Special Education at the University of Maryland, College Park.

Linda Bakken is Associate Professor at Wichita State University in the Department of Administration, Counseling, Education and School Psychology.

Marianne Benson-Seare, James Gordon, Sharon Grether, Bryan Hunt, Diana LeBaron, Angela Parkin, Tara Stauffer, Pamela Larsen, and Terri Taylor were enrolled in the credential program at the University of Utah.

Anne Bouie is Director of Project Interface in Oakland, California.

Robert E. Carlson is a Consultant in Examinations and Research with the California Commission on Teacher Credentialing.

Frances L. Clark is Assistant Professor in the Department of Curriculum and Instruction at Wichita State University.

Nedra A. Crow is Associate Dean for Professional Education in the Graduate School of Education at the University of Utah.

Mary E. Diez is Professor of Education and Dean of the School of Education at Alverno College in Milwaukee, Wisconsin.

Cynthia B. Dillard is Associate Dean for Diversity and Outreach and Assistant Professor in the Department of Educational Theory and Practice at Ohio State University, Columbus.

Sara S. Garcia is Director of Teacher Education and Assistant Professor in the Division of Counseling Psychology and Education at Santa Clara University.

A. Lin Goodwin is Associate Professor of Education at Teachers College, Columbia University, New York.

Warren C. Hayman is Coordinator of the Johns Hopkins/Dunbar High School Health Professions Program at Johns Hopkins University.

Etta R. Hollins is Chairperson of the Department of Teaching and Learning and Professor of Education at Washington State University, Pullman.

Tonya Huber is Associate Professor in the Department of Curriculum and Instruction at Wichita State University.

Joyce E. King is Associate Vice Chancellor for Academic Affairs and Diversity Programs and Professor of Education at the University of New Orleans.

Frank M. Kline is Assistant Professor in the Department of Curriculum and Instruction at Wichita State University.

Victor Martuza is Director of the Center for Intercultural Teacher Education and Associate Professor of Educational Studies at the University of Delaware.

Susan L. Melnick is Associate Professor and Assistant Chairperson in the Department of Teacher Education at Michigan State University and senior researcher in the National Center for Research on Teaching and Learning at Michigan State University.

Peter Murrell, Jr. is Associate Professor of Psychology and Education at Wheelock College.

Valerie Ooka Pang is a Professor in the School of Teacher Education at San Diego State University.

Della Peretti is the Academic Coordinator of the Developmental Teacher Education Program at the University of California, Berkeley.

Rosalinda Quintanar-Sarellana is Assistant Professor of Education at San Jose State University, California.

Richard Statler is Assistant Professor of Education at the University of Utah.

Priscilla H. Walton is a Consultant in Programs and Research with the California Commission on Teacher Credentialing.

Christine Wahlquist is Assistant Professor of Education at the University of Utah.

Darlene Eleanor York is Associate Professor at Emory University, Atlanta.

Kenneth M. Zeichner is Hoefs-Bascom Professor of Teacher Education at the University of Wisconsin, Madison.

Index

AACTE (American Association of Colleges of Teacher Education), xv–xvi, 5, 12, 21
Ability-based instruction, 116–127
  assessment in, 119–120
  components of, 116–119
  praxis in, 120–127
Abramson, M., 130
Academic counseling, in Project Interface, 216
Accreditation, 5–6, 21, 26, 225–226. *See also* National Council for Accreditation of Teacher Education (NCATE)
Acculturation, 131, 134
Adair, A. V., 134
Adamopoulos, J., 79
Adams, D. W., 97, 104
Adler, M. J., 86
Adler, N., 76
African Americans
  after-school program for middle school students. *See* Project Interface
  Black Power movement, 131
  Black Studies programs, 156–169
  enculturation of, 97
  as ineducable, 7
After-school programs. *See* Project Interface
Agne, R., 23
Ahlquist, R., 29, 44
Alatorre Alva, S., 130
Albert, R. D., 79
Algozzine, B., 130
Allameh, J., 79
Allington, R. L., 8
American Association of Colleges of Teacher Education (AACTE), xv–xvi, 5, 12, 21
American Council on Education, 11

American Educational Research Association, 68
American Indian Reservation Student Teaching Project (University of Indiana), 2, 27, 29–32, 36
Anderson, B. T., 23
Anderson, J. G., 45
Anderson, Mary Gresham, 2–3, 53–70
Ankarberg, M. R., 82
Anyon, J., 87, 105, 161–163
Apple, M. W., 42, 86, 87
Aptheker, B., 93
Argulewicz, E. N., 45, 47
Armstrong, T., 132
Ashburn, E., 26
Asian Americans, 131
Assessment, 73
  in ability-based instruction, 119–120
  in CLAD/BCLAD systems, 233
  in culturally responsible pedagogy, 132–133, 143–144
Associated Colleges of the Midwest, 2, 30, 31, 34, 35, 37
Association of Teacher Educators (ATE), 35
Attitudes, in multicultural teacher education, 10, 41–42, 46–52
Au, K. H., 105
Authenticity
  of assessment, 119–120
  of voice, 91–92
Awards, in Project Interface, 217
Awareness model, 80

Baca, J. D., 45, 47
Baca de McNichols, P., 45, 49
Baines, A., 83
Baker, G. C., 10
Bakken, Linda, 111–112, 129–145